Irresistible Forces

Other titles in the Diálogos series available from the University of New Mexico Press:

Independence in Spanish America: Civil Wars, Revolutions, and Underdevelopment (revised edition)
—Jay Kinsbruner

Heroes on Horseback: A Life and Times of the Last Gaucho Caudillos
—John Charles Chasteen

The Life and Death of Carolina Maria de Jesus
—Robert M. Levine and José Carlos Sebe Bom Meihy

¡Que vivan los tamales! Food and the Making of Mexican Identity
—Jeffrey M. Pilcher

The Faces of Honor: Sex, Shame, and Violence in Colonial Latin America
—Edited by Lyman L. Johnson and Sonya Lipsett-Rivera

The Century of U.S. Capitalism in Latin America—Thomas F. O'Brien

Tangled Destinies: Latin America and the United States
—Don Coerver and Linda Hall

Everyday Life and Politics in Nineteenth Century Mexico: Men, Women, and War
—Mark Wasserman

Lives of the Bigamists: Marriage, Family, and Community in Colonial Mexico
—Richard Boyer

Andean Worlds: Indigenous History, Culture, and Consciousness Under Spanish Rule, 1532–1825
—Kenneth J. Andrien

The Mexican Revolution, 1910–1940—Michael J. Gonzales

Quito 1599: City and Colony in Transition—Kris Lane

A Pest in the Land: New World Epidemics in a Global Perspective
—Suzanne Austin Alchon

The Silver King: The Remarkable Life of the Count of Regla in Colonial Mexico
—Edith Boorstein Couturier

National Rhythms, African Roots: The Deep History of Latin American Popular Dance
—John Charles Chasteen

The Great Festivals of Colonial Mexico City: Performing Power and Identity
—Linda A. Curcio-Nagy

The Souls of Purgatory: The Spiritual Diary of a Seventeenth-Century Afro-Peruvian Mystic, Ursula de Jesús
—Nancy E. van Deusen

Dutra's World: Wealth and Family in Nineteenth-Century Rio de Janeiro
—Zephyr L. Frank

Death, Dismemberment, and Memory: Body Politics in Latin America
—Edited by Lyman L. Johnson

Plaza of Sacrifices: Gender, Power, and Terror in 1968 Mexico
—Elaine Carey

Women in the Crucible of Conquest: The Gendered Genesis of Spanish American Society, 1500–1600
—Karen Vieira Powers

Beyond Black and Red: African-Native Relations in Colonial Latin America
—Edited by Matthew Restall

Mexico OtherWise: Modern Mexico in the Eyes of Foreign Observers
—Edited and translated by Jürgen Buchenau

Local Religion in Colonial Mexico
—Edited by Martin Austin Nesvig

Malintzin's Choices: An Indian Woman in the Conquest of Mexico
—Camilla Townsend

From Slavery to Freedom in Brazil: Bahia, 1835–1900
—Dale Torston Graden

Slaves, Subjects, and Subversives: Blacks in Colonial Latin America
—Edited by Jane G. Landers and Barry M. Robinson

Private Passions and Public Sins: Men and Women in Seventeenth-Century Lima
—María Emma Mannarelli

Making the Americas: The United States and Latin America from the Age of Revolutions to the Era of Globalization
—Thomas F. O'Brien

Remembering a Massacre in El Salvador: The Insurrection of 1932, Roque Dalton, and the Politics of Historical Memory
—Héctor Lindo-Fuentes, Erik Ching, and Rafael A. Lara-Martínez

Raising an Empire: Children in Early Modern Iberia and Colonial Latin America
—Ondina E. González and Bianca Premo

Christians, Blasphemers, and Witches: Afro-Mexican Rituals in the Seventeenth Century
—Joan Cameron Bristol

Art and Architecture of Viceregal Latin America, 1521–1821
—Kelly Donahue-Wallace

Rethinking Jewish-Latin Americans
—Edited by Jeffrey Lesser and Raanan Rein

True Stories of Crime in Modern Mexico
—Edited by Robert Buffington and Pablo Piccato

Aftershocks: Earthquakes and Popular Politics in Latin America
—Edited by Jürgen Buchenau and Lyman L. Johnson

Black Mexico: Race and Society from Colonial to Modern Times
—Edited by Ben Vinson III and Mathew Restall

The War for Mexico's West: Indians and Spaniards in New Galicia, 1524–1550
—Ida Altman

"Damned Notions of Liberty": Slavery, Culture, and Power in Colonial Mexico, 1640–1769
—Frank Proctor

SERIES ADVISORY EDITOR:
LYMAN L. JOHNSON,
UNIVERSITY OF NORTH CAROLINA AT CHARLOTTE

Irresistible Forces

Latin American Migration to the United States and Its Effects on the South

GREGORY B. WEEKS

JOHN R. WEEKS

University of New Mexico Press ✣ Albuquerque

 Published 2009
Printed in the United States of America
15 14 13 12 11 10 1 2 3 4 5 6

LIBRARY OF CONGRESS CATALOGING-IN-PUBLICATION DATA

Weeks, Gregory Bart.
Irresistible forces : Latin American migration to the United States and its effects on the South /
Gregory B. Weeks, John R. Weeks.
p. cm. — (Diálogos)
Includes bibliographical references and index.
ISBN 978-0-8263-4918-7 (pbk. : alk. paper)
1. Latin Americans—Southern States.
2. Hispanic Americans—Southern States.
3. Latin America—Emigration and immigration—Social aspects.
4. Southern States—Emigration and immigration—Social aspects.
5. Immigrants—Southern States—Social conditions.
I. Weeks, John Robert, 1944–
II. Title.
F220.S75W44 2010
304.8´8075—dc22
2010014707

DESIGN AND LAYOUT

Composed in 10/13.5 Janson Text Lt Std
Display type is Bernhard Modern Std

Contents

Acknowledgments

This book began as two professors, father and son (a demographer and political scientist, respectively) coincidentally were working on the topic of immigration from very different perspectives. Discussions about how politics and demography intersect led to a very rewarding experience of research collaboration and coauthorship.

Gregory Weeks would like to thank the UNC Charlotte Urban Institute for a grant in 2006 that facilitated the initial data collection and analysis. Wendy Sause provided tremendous help with collecting data. The College of Liberal Arts and Sciences at UNC Charlotte provided a semester off to finish the writing. Finally, many thanks to Amy Weeks, who was not only supportive of the book project but also geocoded birth data and made the map in chapter six. John Weeks would like to thank Deanna Weeks for her unusually good insight and wordsmithing that have improved the book's readability, and also Greg for doing most of the heavy-lifting on this project.

Both authors are indebted to Lyman Johnson for his guidance through the process and very useful suggestions.

CHAPTER ONE

The Power of Migration

AFTER MONTHS OF ANALYSTS DEBATING WHETHER OR NOT TO USE the word "recession," in September 2008, stock markets across the world crashed, and the United States economy suffered a serious shock. Billions of dollars of wealth evaporated, homeowners were forced into foreclosure across the country, and the rate of unemployment rose to levels not experienced in decades. New buzzwords became common currency overnight, with one of the biggest being "credit crunch." At a very basic level, it was suddenly harder to get money to do anything.

It would seem logical to assume that, as a result, Latin American immigrants—at least the several million here without legal documentation—would start making their way back to their home country, maybe even in very large numbers. Once the economic boom was over, they would pack up and leave because there would be no more reason to stay. Developers were no longer building at the same rate and thus not hiring every day, wealthier Americans began cutting back on services they used to pay others to do, and no one seemed to know how far away the light at the end of the tunnel might be. In fact, the problem of undocumented immigration might almost take care of itself. The phrase "self-deportation" came into vogue as reporters began scouring the country to find people who might be leaving, and as headlines grew more and more lurid.

It all makes perfect sense except for one problem: the argument is wrong. Most migrants are, in fact, choosing to stay. Where is the flaw in the logic? As we will show, conventional wisdom about immigration too often fails to take demography and politics into account. The ebb and flow of migration is subject to many more influences than a simple economic model would suggest. The age structure of a country, for example, tells us a surprising amount about why people move, and the politics of both sending and receiving countries will tell us a lot about how they will be received.

To be sure, some people are returning permanently to Mexico, Guatemala, El Salvador, Colombia, or wherever they originally came from. Even in the best of times not all migrants stay, but there is no mass exodus. At the same time, the flow of people coming to the United States certainly hasn't reversed, it hasn't even stopped, but it has slowed down.

The Migration Slowdown

In February 2009, the president of the board of Mexico's National Statistics, Geography and Information Institute (INEGI) noted, "There is declining tendency of people going abroad, but we have not detected, up to now, any increase in people returning to the country."[1] That conclusion is consistent with a report by the Migration Policy Institute in January 2009.[2]

As we will explain in the pages that follow, the decrease in the number of immigrants coming to the United States comes as no surprise, since the crash in the United States has accelerated forces that were already in motion. For years the labor market was wide open and in need of workers because the United States was not producing enough working-aged people through natural increase. As we will see, that labor market open window has slowly been closing as children of immigrants—born in the United States and thus U.S. citizens—have been filling in the younger age cohorts and, at the same time, helping to anchor their families in the country.

We have to remember that migrating to the United States is hard, no matter what talents you have or what your family situation might be. So people do not make the decision lightly. To enter legally, you must fill out reams of paperwork and jump through many bureaucratic hoops. As you wait, you also hope that the numerical limit is not reached before your name comes up. If it is, then that's it for the rest of the year, and you will just have to wait and reapply.

If you do not possess many skills beyond willingness to work hard for long hours, your chances are even slimmer because so few legal slots are open to you. Your only real avenue is therefore the illegal one, which is very risky and hazardous, not to mention expensive. The journey could include arrest (on the U.S. side of the border), robbery or rape (especially on the Mexican side of the border), or even death (after crossing the border into the United States). Would-be migrants know how hard it can be, so they do not set off unless they believe they have a very good chance to get a job when they arrive. A combination of factors—demographic, economic, and political—are increasingly reducing that likelihood.

Staying in the United States

In the context of recession, there is an important and quite simple economic reason why migrants already in the United States would decide not to go back to their country of origin. The economic crisis is global, rippling outward from the United States, and reaching every corner of the world. A quick phone call home is enough to let everyone know that there are no jobs to go back to in the country of origin, so migrant workers don't leave but rather "buckle down"[3] and do whatever they can to wait out the recession and hope for the best. Since the prospects of new jobs appearing or old jobs returning are better in the United States than they are back home, undocumented migrants gamble that they have less to lose by staying than by returning home. This is especially true in the post-9/11 era, when increased border enforcement has increased the risk and cost of getting back into the United States once you leave.

Incentives for people not to leave the United States are strong. By late 2008, Lander Mondragon was finding it more and more difficult to obtain construction work in Alabama, to the point that sometimes paying bills was hard. But he had no intention of going back to Mexico: "I ain't got nothing to go to in Mexico. This is my hometown now."[4] Carmina Manuel was so intent on remaining in the United States despite the recession that when her husband mentioned the possibility of returning, "I told him if he left, he was going by himself."[5] Thousands, even millions, of Hispanic immigrants are grappling with the same dilemma. There are many factors in play, and a bad economy is only one of them.

In the words of day laborer Antonio García, "All we can do is have faith that there will be more jobs again."[6] So he keeps making his way back to the hiring area in Tucson. Many are willing to be as flexible as possible, even if it means taking more dangerous work, just to make sure they do not have to leave the United States.[7]

Signs of this began appearing in late 2008, when it became clear that fewer Mexicans were going home for the holidays. In Ciudad Juárez, transit officer Salvador Macía Medina waited to help cars make their way through the city to the south after crossing the border from El Paso, but fewer cars were coming than in previous years.[8] Given tight budgets, more Mexicans decided that an extra vacation was too much. That is part of the overall ripple effect. Less money made in the United States means less money sent home and fewer goods brought home in person. With less money coming in, the Mexican economy takes a hit, which makes economic prospects there even worse.

Like the rest of the population, Latinos in the United States are feeling the pinch. A Pew Hispanic Report in January 2009 found that 36 percent of Latino homeowners are worried that their home might go into foreclosure.[9] Further, 84 percent of foreign-born Latinos believe their economic situation to be "fair" or "poor." Yet, despite these grim perceptions, people are choosing to stay and wait it out.

To understand why they persevere, we must understand what happens once someone moves to the United States. We have ideas and images of what immigrants are like, especially if they are in the country illegally, but very often these images are outdated or just plain mistaken. The popular conception of a newly arrived migrant is of a young male who came alone. It's entirely possible that he has a family, but they did not make the trek with him. He is working and wiring or sending money home; his work is temporary and seasonal; and he quite possibly moves all over the country, especially following the agricultural harvests.

In this scenario, there is nothing much tethering him to his host country, and he could return to his family if the economy soured and bide his time until the jobs became plentiful again, and initiate the same cycle. Many others in his community would be doing the same.

But this is not an accurate depiction of the typical migrant experience. True, they are young, and many are men, but they are not only young men. Migrants are putting down roots, getting married, and having children. Children born in the United States are automatically citizens no matter what the status of their parents, and are popularly known as "anchor babies." These sons and daughters attend local schools and are fully bilingual. They are fluent in Spanish, but English is the currency of the country, so outside the home they tend not to speak Spanish as much.

The longer the family lives here, the less contact they have with their home country, and the less they are likely to move. Those children, incidentally, will no doubt put up a huge fuss if the topic is raised. They may have visited the "home country"—Dominican Republic, or Ecuador, or Mexico—but the key word is "visit." In his novel *The Brief Wondrous Life of Oscar Wao*, Pulitzer Prize–winning author Junot Díaz describes it this way: "Every summer Santo Domingo slaps the Diaspora engine into reverse, yanks back as many of its expelled children as it can."[10] The children (like his main character) often view it with some ambivalence, something to do because their parents wish it.

Many undocumented immigrants have lived in the United States for many years. In Cicero, Illinois, "Sal" lost his job at a factory and glumly decided how to proceed—a plan that would not include a return to Mexico. "We can't move back to Mexico. I don't even know anyone there."[11] This is not the sort of statement Americans expect. The same is true of Odilio Perez, an undocumented immigrant who moved to Atlanta in the 1990s, "This country says it doesn't want us, but when there's a job to be done, it needs us."[12]

Strange as it might seem, there are thousands upon thousands of people in the United States illegally who feel more American than anything else, although their citizenship may not reflect that feeling. They have seen economic ups and downs, and would prefer to ride them out in their adopted country.

A final point about the lack of return migration is that no condition is permanent. If the U.S. economy plummets further, perhaps more immigrants will decide that returning to and hunkering down in their country of origin is preferable to doing so in the United States. No one knows if or when that tipping point might be reached. However, history tells us that people often very much want to stay and will do so if at all possible for as long as possible.

The Power of Migrant Connections

A central concern of this book is to examine a new and little-studied phenomenon: the Latino in the U.S. South. In 1990, when scarcely 1 percent of the population in the South was Hispanic, you would have been hard pressed to find anyone who knew what a taco truck was. Two decades later, they were in the news, slapped in front of city council members as their constituents cried out for reform of ordinances, noise laws, and littering. Similar issues spread throughout Southern cities and towns, even rural areas. Southerners ask, exactly who are these newcomers? Where did they come from? What are they doing here? And, of course, the most pressing question of all: What do we do about them?

We will get to all those questions, but the last one will receive special attention. If there is one constant about U.S. immigration policy, it is that long-term consequences are generally different from what was originally expected. In some cases, policies have had the exact opposite effect of what they were intended to accomplish. Many people believe, sometimes very fervently, that what they deem undesirable can be legislated away. Pass the right laws, then enforce them, and what we don't like will vanish. Policymakers at all levels of government have heard this message and dutifully passed laws. Sometimes the laws have worked as intended, other times they functioned in an unexpected way, and in too many instances they were unenforceable and therefore ignored.

Take the example of Georgia, which in 2006 passed a law ordering all governments within the state to use the federal government's E-Verify system to determine whether prospective employees were in the country legally. Three years later, at which point we could reasonably assume that Georgians believed the law had been enforced for a long time, a spokesman for the state's Department of Labor tossed a bucket of cold water on that assumption: "As far as any enforcement responsibilities under the law, we don't have any."[13] When asked who could determine whether anyone at all was complying with the law, he was similarly unambiguous: "There is no central agency that has the authority to do that."

United States immigration policy is littered with these types of situations, where economic and demographic realities collide with policy preferences. In recent years, there is even confusion about who should be enforcing what. Is immigration the responsibility of a county commissioner or the U.S. Congress? Or, more accurately, if Congress refuses to do anything, do local folks have the ability to take up the legislative slack? The jumble of laws that has emerged poses a serious obstacle to any coherent solution to migration. For a variety of reasons, some laws are doomed to failure, especially when they are enacted without a good understanding of why things are happening as they are.

It is common, for example, for undocumented immigrants to be called "criminals" who have engaged in "unlawful activity" because they have entered the country without authorization. But, in fact, this is not a criminal but rather a civil offense—the same level of seriousness as a minor traffic violation. And why have these immigrants broken the law to get here? Because the demand for immigrants in the United States exceeds the limits allowed by legal migration, which arises directly from the fact that the legal migration system favors relatives of current legal residents, whether or not they are workers, whereas the economy is looking specifically for workers. This problem can't be solved by trying to shut the doors to undocumented immigrants because the economy has, until very recently, wanted those immigrants, and those immigrants wanted the work. It was a nice fit—a set of irresistible forces.

Chain Migration

When people move, their destination is rarely randomly selected. People do not put a map on the wall, close their eyes, and then move to wherever their finger happens to land. Instead, they use the information available to determine where they will likely find both the best job prospects and the support of a community. That information sharing is often part of the phenomenon of chain migration, especially when it involves moving to a new country, such as Latin Americans migrating to the United States.

Chain migration is the process whereby pioneer migrants establish themselves in a particular part of a new country and then help others from their country of origin to follow them—pulling them up the chain, so to speak. Chain migration thus reduces the risk for subsequent migrants since the earlier arrivals have already scoped out the situation and laid the groundwork.[14] Because the people being helped are most likely to be relatives, chain migration is often a process of family reunification. Elaine Lacy describes the situation of Griselda López Negrete, a teenager in Aiken, South Carolina, whose grandfather came from Mexico to Aiken "in the early 1980s to work grooming horses and, following an age-old migratory pattern, he sent for family members and friends. Eventually over half of his home village of San Juan Palmira emigrated to the United States, most of them to the Aiken area."[15]

The classic scenario is thus one in which a person comes to the United States (or to any other country), obtains citizenship or legal long-term residency, then works to bring other family members into the country. In the United States, political acceptance of the idea that families of migrants should have a chance to follow them dates back at least to the 1920s. However, immigration reforms pushed by President Lyndon Johnson (1963–1969) dramatically increased the number of legal migrants to the United States. Family reunification of that much larger pool of legal migrants has now become the most important reason for the rapid growth of the immigrant population. Immediate family members are not included in national immigration quotas. At the same time, family members are not automatically granted legal entry to the United States. There is a lot of paperwork and many hurdles to get over before this can be accomplished, and the processing can take years to complete. This is the source of the complaint that there is a long line of people waiting to enter the country legally, and so it is not fair that others are "allowed" to enter without documentation, essentially circumventing the long line. Most of those who are in line are family members of earlier legal migrants (mainly from Mexico and the Philippines).

Immigration laws since 1965 have left family unification provisions largely unchanged, which is why the issue is so often injected into debates about immigration policy. It is noteworthy that during the presidential campaign in 2008, then-candidate Barack Obama repeatedly mentioned his support for continuation of family unification. He reiterated it after taking office, noting in a 2009 interview that "people want to reunify families and they don't want to wait 10 years."[16] This suggests that the Obama administration has not questioned the importance of family reunification and that, if anything, it wants to speed up the process whereby family members obtain visas to move to the United States. That will, of course, increase the volume of legal migration during the time that the backlog is being cleared.

As we've discussed, the decision to migrate is not made lightly, but having some connection to the destination outweighs at least some of the risks. An individual knows full well how difficult the transition will be, but also feels confident that he or she will have assistance when they arrive.

Coming to the South

How, then, did Latinos begin coming to the South, as opposed to other parts of the United States? The short answer is economic development. Beginning in the 1980s, small numbers of migrant agricultural workers arrived in the area, but they alone are not responsible for the very large growth that came a decade or so later. Digging a little deeper, we can see that very specific events in the 1990s created a spark that brought the first large group of migrants into the region. Before long, it was evident that the southeast was quite prosperous and was therefore a worthy destination. The two largest metropolitan areas in the South are Atlanta and Charlotte, and they perfectly illustrate how the first link in the chain can be formed.

The 1990s was a decade of banking expansion in Charlotte. A flurry of mergers began in the 1970s that would culminate in Bank of America, having been purchased by NationsBank, moving its headquarters to Charlotte in 1998. One of the first concrete signs of growth was the construction of the NationsBank Corporate Center, which opened in 1992 (and was later renamed the Bank of America Corporate Center). At 60 stories and 871 feet tall, at the time it was the largest building in the southeast, and as of 2009 was still the 24th tallest building in the United States. Of course, it took years to build and required intensive labor. Some of the subcontractors, with experience building in Texas, recruited from the Mexican population there.[17]

It's not hard to picture how the process unfolded from there. The workers sent word back to places like Guanajuato (a state in central Mexico), which then became the major sending state to Charlotte. This was no random occurrence, but rather the rational consequence of economic growth in a specific part of the United States. Of course, immigrants were arriving in other new and different parts of the country, as well, from the plains of Nebraska to New England mill towns. But those areas were not seeing the same explosion of economic activity as the South. For years, the South's economic potential had few rivals.

The skyscraper was not the culmination of growth, but only the onset. Capital flowed into Charlotte, and the downtown skyline was becoming dotted with new construction. White-collar employees moved in and looked to the suburbs for homes and apartments. Their children needed schools, which were built at a prodigious pace. They also needed all the accoutrements of modern suburban life, including supermarkets, restaurants, coffee shops, shopping malls, gas stations, and office buildings. Developers fell over themselves to oblige, and everywhere there was work to be found. It certainly didn't hurt that the weather was pleasant year round. The South was a good place to be.

Atlanta became a Latino destination around the same time as Charlotte, with its economic expansion beginning with sports rather than banking. In 1987, public officials in Atlanta began lobbying the International Olympic Committee to bring the games there in 1996. In 1990, it won by a tight vote, and for the next six years was a true beehive of economic activity, which included the construction of Olympic Village, Olympic Stadium, and Centennial Olympic Park. Atlanta also beefed up its transportation system. It even got its own NationsBank building in 1992 (also eventually becoming the Bank of America). The newly arrived Atlantans desired the same sorts of development as Charlotteans, and they were willing to pay for it. Among the newly arrived to Georgia was Serafico Jaimes, who moved to Atkinson County in 1991 to pick peppers and cut tobacco.[18] He had heard that the quality of life in Georgia was much better than in border states. There were good jobs, good schools, more open spaces than in the traditional immigrant destinations, and in general it was much better for families. Eventually he made enough money to open his own video store. He has no plans to leave.

Like Charlotte, Atlanta needed a lot of manual labor in a relatively short period of time, and the economic effect moved outward like a spider web. For example, Buford Highway, which leads out of Atlanta, was a dying stretch of strip malls until it was reborn with immigrant businesses. Inexpensive rent combined with a steady stream of traffic gave it an allure to entrepreneurs.[19] Latino workers flocked to the area looking for construction jobs. The Atlanta branch of the Latin American Association is on Buford Highway. "La Buford" even has housing patterns that reflect the country a migrant came from, or even the specific Mexican state. Those from Jalisco form a cluster, with another grouping of migrants from Nuevo León, Guerrero, Michoacán, and Oaxaca.[20]

The first locations for migration to the South were therefore urban. However, as migrants moved to the area, they also found plenty of work to be had in rural areas, especially in agriculture and poultry processing.

They heard about a wide variety of jobs in smaller cities. From those first encounters in the early 1990s, the entire southeast became known as a good place to come. The overall message was like a big neon sign: you will have contacts, and you will find a job. The effect was hypergrowth.

So, into the twenty-first century, Hispanic communities could be found in virtually every nook and cranny of the Southern landscape. Take the example of Diana, an undocumented Peruvian immigrant,[21] whose son had moved to Carthage, Mississippi, to work in a poultry processing plant. She came for five months, then returned to Peru. Given the lack of work back home, however, she decided to migrate again and stay indefinitely. Since she had made some contacts there, she returned to Mississippi. Once there, she learned about casino jobs in Biloxi, where there was a small Peruvian community. Fellow migrants helped her get an apartment and a job. Then Hurricane Katrina hit the gulf coast, and in the aftermath there was a huge demand for construction workers. Employers put out the word: if you know someone, tell them about the jobs. This led to a new influx of Peruvians into Mississippi.

Then there is the Pelayo family from Mexico.[22] They lived in Seattle selling tacos, then heard from a friend that North Alabama had a large Latino population but not too many businesses. Seeing the opportunity, they moved to Huntsville to open a taco truck. They were soon successful enough to buy a second, then build a permanent garage for them.

The notion that natives of Peru or Mexico would settle in the deepest south would likely have been deemed impossible not too long ago. These days, it is a common occurrence. As we will discuss in future chapters, an important consequence of both family reunification and community building is that immigrants often stay. Though certainly many people will come and go, overall they are becoming established, and soon the second-generation Peruvian immigrants will feel much closer to Mississippi, just as second-generation Mexicans will feel more at home in Alabama, growing up with a Southern, rather than a Spanish, accent.

The Book's Structure

Chapter Two discusses the relevance of political demography for the study of migration and its policy consequences. Very few current works consider demography and politics in tandem, which limits our ability to understand immigration's complexities.

Chapter Three provides a historical background to migration from Latin America to the United States, tracing both the policy and demographic changes that have taken place over time. It will conclude in 1996, when the last major immigration legislation (the Illegal Immigrant Reform and Immigrant Responsibility Act) was enacted. It provides the context necessary for understanding why immigration policies were enacted, why they succeeded and failed, and why migrants started moving to the U.S. South.

Chapter Four lays out our political demographic framework, focusing on the demographic fit between the United States and Latin America. Demographic structures of different countries, especially those in close proximity, play a large role in determining whether people will migrate. Since demography is always changing, the decision to migrate, as well as the political reaction in the receiving country, will also change. The chapter further explains the interplay between demography and public policy.

Chapter Five analyzes the Latin American reaction. An essential—but too often neglected—aspect of the immigration debate is the role of Latin American governments. This chapter will examine the policy responses in Latin America, focusing on why governments have recently begun reconnecting with emigrants in the United States, and the ways in which they do so. It is increasingly clear that this factor must be incorporated into an overall understanding of Latin American migration.

Chapter Six details the dynamics of Latino immigration to the southeastern United States, which is a relatively new and less explored migration pattern, especially for political scientists and demographers. Of particular analytic interest are the social and political ramifications of Latino immigration, which condition the particular public policy responses we see.

Chapter Seven concludes the book by discussing the current and future changes occurring in the U.S. South, and the different political ramifications that will likely accompany them. It also explores the myths that persist about Latino immigration and highlights the empirical fallacies within them to analyze policy consequences.

CHAPTER TWO

Irresistible Forces at Work

ALONG WITH COTTON, TOBACCO IS THE CROP THAT HAS TRADItionally defined Southern agriculture. The tobacco plantation was a central part of traditional Southern culture and remains an important—albeit declining—economic engine for the region.[1] Picking tobacco is back breaking and often induces nausea. This is especially true when it is wet, as concentrated nicotine water droplets seep into the worker's skin. That is compounded by the brutal heat and humidity characteristic of summers in North Carolina and Virginia, where the labor was first relegated to slaves, and then to the poor, whether white or African American. As the twentieth century drew to a close, tobacco growers were finding it increasingly difficult to recruit enough workers. The reasons for the labor shortage are a matter of continuing debate: Do U.S. citizens simply not want jobs like these? Are the wages too low? Does mechanization play a part? Are there too few young workers available locally, especially because of the low birth rate that now prevails in the country?

Farmers have turned to the United States government's H-2A visa program, which allows a limited number of temporary agricultural workers, popularly known as "guest workers."[2] Men like Mario Elias Gervacio, the foreman of a group of migrant workers in Gibsonville, North Carolina, sometimes come for four to six months at a time, working twelve-hour days at over $8 an hour.[3] In a good week, Mario could send as much as $500 home to his family in Mexico, and along with the other men in his crew, he volunteered to work half days on Sundays to earn more money. The work was tiring but regular, and paid much better than what he could make back home. As a result, the H-2A slots fill up very quickly. Given the relatively small number of these temporary visas being granted, as we will discuss later in the book, many of the workers who pick crops, clean homes, landscape yards, and do construction are in the country without the benefit of a guest worker visa.

This book seeks to understand how and why Mario and hundreds of thousands of other migrants from Latin America have arrived not only in the United States, but more specifically in the South, both legally and illegally.[4] The migration of Latin Americans, though a highly visible, politicized, and controversial phenomenon, is also very poorly understood by the U.S. public, even by most policy makers.[5] This is especially true in the southeastern region of the United States, where such migration is very recent, and where, outside of south Florida, Spanish is rarely heard. Only since 1970 has the U.S. Census asked questions about Hispanic origin on the decennial census forms, and in that year less than 1 percent of the population of the South was Hispanic. Yet now, from the back country to the bayou, from small towns to major cities, it is clear that the "New South" is taking on a Latino flavor.[6]

Defining the South

The South has numerous definitions, but a history of slavery and a concentration of blacks in the population are key elements in deciding whether to include a state as part of the South.[7] Counting West Virginia as separate from Virginia, sixteen states were slave states at the time of the Civil War. Eleven of those states seceded from the Union: Alabama, Arkansas, Florida, Georgia, Louisiana, Mississippi, North Carolina, South Carolina, Tennessee, Texas, and Virginia. Of these eleven states, the two with the lowest percentage of blacks over time are Texas and Florida. In Texas, the eastern part of the state has a fairly high percentage of black residents, but the western portion of the state is heavily Hispanic. In Florida, the northern part of the state has a fairly high percentage of black residents, but the southern portion is heavily Hispanic. For our purposes, we are interested in what might be called the "previously non-Hispanic" South, which would thus exclude Texas and Florida. Since we are simultaneously concerned with those states generally deemed as belonging in the South, we define the South as those states that seceded from the Union in the Civil War, except Texas and Florida. Thus, when we speak of the "South" or the "Southern states," we are referring to the following states: Alabama, Arkansas, Georgia, Louisiana, Mississippi, North Carolina, South Carolina, Tennessee, and Virginia.

The central argument of this book is that only through an analytic combination of politics and demography can the dynamics of migration (and the reactions to it) be fully grasped. This political demographic approach will demonstrate that irresistible forces are at work changing the face, quite literally, of the South—changes that are broader than often realized. People in Latin America are not only moving to the traditional "gateways" in the United States (that is, the border states of California, Arizona, New Mexico, Texas, and Florida); they are also arriving in new areas of the country. Furthermore, these new migrants are not only from Mexico, but are from all over Latin America.

We will also explore the fact that this migration is a direct but unintended consequence of immigration policies in the United States, combined with policies of other countries in the Americas, that push people in some directions and pull them in others. Policies often have effects that their supporters neither anticipated nor wanted, such as prompting migrants to stay in the country rather than leave.

Political Demography

We thus address the question of what drives migration north to the United States by placing that migration flow within a political demographic framework. Our approach is a macro-level one in that we are trying to understand the patterns of migration in the context of the interaction between demographic changes and political changes taking place simultaneously in countries of origin (focusing on Latin American origins), and the country of destination (focusing on the United States).

For thousands of years, philosophers and politicians alike have argued that governments should influence demographic trends. Population growth, the argument goes, should be controlled for the best interests of the country (or perhaps even of the world). For example, it has often been maintained that demography affects economic growth and, perhaps, even the rise and fall of great powers.[8] As long ago as 340 B.C., Aristotle was arguing that the city-state should limit the number of children its citizens could have to ensure that the population did not outstrip resources.[9] However, the most famous proponent of this argument was Thomas Robert Malthus, who wrote in 1798, "Nature has scattered the seeds of life abroad with the most profuse and liberal hand; but has been comparatively sparing in the room and the nourishment necessary to rear them."[10] Misery would result unless population pressures were eased, whether by the lower classes having fewer children or by higher mortality rates (such as those found during wartime).

A more recent and widely debated example of this perspective is that of neo-Malthusian Paul Ehrlich, whose book *The Population Bomb* (1968) summed up the dilemma as "too many people . . . too little food . . . a dying planet." He warned of a "death rate solution," whereby "ways to raise the death rate—war, famine, pestilence—find us."[11] According to this view, citizens of the world must work together to conserve resources and thereby avoid disaster. At the extremes, a Malthusian view can prompt state-sanctioned population control. In recent years, for example, China has come under intense criticism for its one-child policy, which (with some exceptions) punished those who had more than one child, a policy remarkably reminiscent of Aristotle, and an inherently Malthusian approach to keeping population growth within the bounds of societal resources.[12] China's population growth did slow, but parents preferred having a boy, which led to infanticide and gender imbalance. Legislating population is simpler in theory than in practice.

Other prominent historical figures believed demography affected democracy itself. Plato argued that "the number of hearth-fires established by our present division must remain forever unchanged," or else the delicate balance of society, based on a careful mathematical calculation of the division of duties, would be overturned.[13] Centuries later, in letters to James Madison, Thomas Jefferson used his own calculations of generations (now proved inaccurate) to assert a nineteen-year limitation on debt and other important government actions, to give new generations the ability to make fresh decisions.[14]

Much less attention has been paid to the impact that demography can have as an independent influence on political decisions. Works on this topic focus primarily on the ways in which population growth sparks a need for more resources, which in turn leads to armed aggression and territorial expansion. For example, "youth bulges" may contribute to invasion (often of neighboring countries) in search of new resources to serve their growing populations. We have witnessed this often in sub-Saharan Africa; it was instrumental as well in the lengthy conflict in the 1980s between Iraq and Iran that led ultimately to the First Gulf War in 1992.[15] In line with Malthus, this reasoning views demography almost entirely in terms of the relationship between overpopulation (usually defined as too many people for available resources) and resource depletion. Sociologist Charles Westoff, for example, notes that the "remarkable thing about the immigration debates and discussion in the United States is the absence of any reference to immigration's effect on population size and growth."[16] His contention, like Malthus's, is that the impact on finite resources should be central to the debate.

But political demography logically extends beyond simple consumption of resources. What of analyses that consider changing demographic trends within and between countries, with the attendant political effects? There has been what Wiener and Teitelbaum refer to as a "deficit of attention" to political demography.[17] Political scientists consider other variables (globalization, economic policies, ideology, nationalism among them) as more important than demography, whereas demographers rarely incorporate political arguments into their work. What we seek to do is bring demography back into political analysis—and vice versa—while fully recognizing that other factors are also present and contributing to migratory patterns and to policymaking. Political demography is a central analytical tool because, although migration is obviously an inherently demographic process, it is readily facilitated and constrained by political processes, both direct and indirect. Furthermore, migration does not occur in a demographic vacuum, but is itself a consequence of changing patterns of mortality and fertility in both sending and receiving areas. Those changes typically elicit a political response because communities are forced to adjust to them, and this rarely happens in a quiet, automatic way.

We begin with the assumption that people prefer to remain in place, and because staying in place is the usual and expected human behavior, migration must be explained. Few people choose to embark on lengthy, difficult, and even life-threatening journeys on a whim. It is much more desirable to remain in one's country of birth, surrounded by the familiar and comforting. This is not a trivial assumption, because it permits us to ignore the vast majority of people in the world who do not migrate. Even if we accept the results of the Mexican Migration Project, suggesting that it has become a rite of passage in many Mexican villages for young men to spend time working in the United States, there is a presumption that these young men go north with the view of returning home.[18] As we discuss later, it may be U.S. policy, more than the intentions of migrants, that increasingly encourages many of them to stay in the United States.

If we accept that staying home is the norm, we can then assume that people (individuals and/or households more generally) are most likely to move only when they cannot achieve their goals or even survive in their current location. At some point, individuals come to the conclusion that migration—though arduous—is the only means of fulfilling their goals. Although the explanations for this are often expressed in economic terms, we recall Kingsley Davis's theory of demographic change and response, which emphasizes the kind of everyday decisions that produce demographic behavior.[19] Davis argued that the people's response to population growth is determined by the means available to them. Families grow larger in the context of the demographic transition that is almost always associated with a drop in the death rates (especially at the youngest ages) before the birth rate goes down. The first reaction that households likely have to a greater number of surviving children is to work harder—the adults take on more work if they can, and the children are put to work. But if the local economy is not capable of absorbing new workers, or if there is not enough work available even to expand the work of those already in the labor force, then people must start thinking about the alternatives, the most obvious one of which may be migration. This is the "push," but of course people will only respond by moving if there is someplace reasonable to go—somewhere that is "pulling" them.

This approach underscores the fact that the underlying reason for economic distress in many areas of the world, including much of Latin America, is an increase in population that cannot be sustained by the local economy. If there are more people of working age (commonly defined as

15 to 64) than there are jobs, pressure to find employment elsewhere will build. The greater the disparity, the greater the pressure. We will return to this theme later because it is a core element in our perspective.

If local conditions cannot meet the needs of all members of a community (the push), the decision to move is typically bound up with the choice of where to move (the pull). Information about alternatives is a key to this decision-making, and this is where some of the conceptual elements of international migration come into play. Network theory and chain migration theory suggest that the more people a person knows in a given potential destination, the more likely it is that the migrant will move.[20] Over time migrants choose their new home based on where family members or friends have already gone. A person may decide to move, but acting on that decision may depend critically upon information gleaned from a network about a specific destination location.

The options of where to move are bound to be influenced by the availability of opportunities at given destinations. When would-be migrants perceive greater opportunities, it is more likely they will move. In the American South, for example, the turn of the twenty-first century was marked by widespread economic growth and low unemployment, suggesting the existence of job opportunities just waiting to be discovered. Of course, this would change with the 2008 crash, but the rapid influx had already occurred by then. The opportunities will themselves be simultaneously influenced by demography (especially the "fit" that will help create economic opportunities) and politics (how easy it is to get to a place, and how easy it is to stay there). Thus the direction of flows and the resulting stock of immigrants are closely tied to government policy, encompassing laws, and the enforcement of those laws. Put another way, we cannot understand migration between countries without understanding the way in which politics interacts with demography.

The Political Context

In the United States, the public is bombarded from all sides on the issue of migration. Politicians talk of "losing control" (as President Ronald Reagan once put it) over the border as a result of the influx of immigrants. Coast Guard patrols have increased along the many miles of U.S. coastline. Parts of the U.S.-Mexico border are being fenced and militarized. Meanwhile, private citizens in U.S. border states organize vigilante groups to track undocumented immigrants who, they argue, commit crimes in the United States and are generally a drain on state resources. It is important to point out that these things are not happening along the similarly lengthy border that the United States shares with Canada, even though Canada is fourth on the list of countries whose citizens are detained by the U.S. Border Patrol. The most likely explanation for the difference is the well-known phenomenon of xenophobia, the fear of strangers. Humans are highly suspicious of those who look different, act differently, speak a different language, or are in some way not "one of us."

Even legal immigration is often decried as a sure way to cheat U.S. citizens out of jobs because of the lower wages often accepted by new immigrants.[21] All of this is captured in newspapers, radio, television, and the internet, and brought into U.S. homes on a daily basis. The late Harvard political scientist Samuel Huntington rather famously asserted that the United States faces the possibility of losing its very identity as a result of so much immigration.[22] In short, immigration is widely viewed as scary, dangerous, and regrettable.

Simultaneously, of course, advocates for immigrants and immigration are equally passionate in their arguments. Advocacy groups counseling against restricting immigration into the United States argue that legal immigrants constitute the backbone of the U.S. economy and deserve better treatment. Most European countries, along with Japan, worry about depopulation as a result of low birth rates, but immigrants to the United States have kept birth rates above replacement level, sheltering the country from the threat of depopulation, and providing an answer to the question of who will be paying the future taxes to support retirees. Since many recent immigrants are undocumented, their advocates call for greater rights to be granted illegal immigrants, such as allowing them to obtain driver's licenses and have an eventual path to citizenship.[23]

Although different groups favoring immigration have very different agendas (focusing on a specific country, or on legal versus illegal immigrant status), their overall message is that Latin American immigration into the United States is a natural, inevitable process that should be embraced, not rejected. Furthermore, as many remind us, the United States has always been a nation of immigrants, an image enshrined in Emma Lazarus's poem "The New Colossus" at the pedestal of the Statue of Liberty: "Give me your tired, your poor / Your huddled masses yearning to be free / The wretched refuse of your teeming shore / Send these, the homeless, tempest-tossed to me." The sentiment of the majority of Americans toward immigrants, however, could perhaps best be expressed as "not too tired, not too poor, and not too many."

Regardless of which side one embraces, all believe that much is at stake. It is no wonder, then, that the issue raises so many hackles. The fact is that the United States is already the largest recipient of immigrants in the world. (Canada, for its part, receives more immigrants *per capita* than nearly any other country.) North America is the world's most popular migrant destination, and that fact has huge consequences for the future. Data from the U.S. Census Bureau's American Community Survey show 38 million foreign-born people living in the United States as of 2007, of whom more than half (20 million) are from Latin America. Among those, more than half (12 million) are from Mexico.

Since the Census Bureau's survey methods include all known household addresses and never ask about a person's legal status in the country, it is assumed that undocumented immigrants are proportionately included in the Census and survey figures. By subtracting estimates of the legal immigrant population from the total count of foreign-born people, it is thus possible to derive estimates of the undocumented immigrant population in the United States, as first elaborated by Warren and Passel in their now classic approach to "counting the uncountable" in the 1980 census.[24] Using this methodology, the Pew Hispanic Center has calculated that in 2008, there were 11.9 undocumented immigrants, representing 30 percent of all foreign-born persons.[25] The Department of Homeland Security uses similar methods to obtain similar results.[26]

Most of the undocumented immigrants have arrived since 1990, and most are from Latin America. Indeed, 9.6 million of the 11.9 million unauthorized immigrants (81 percent) are from Latin America, and 7 million of those are estimated to be from Mexico. These numbers suggest that more than half (56 percent) of foreign-born Mexicans in the United States are undocumented immigrants, whereas slightly less than half of immigrants from elsewhere in Latin America are undocumented.

Since recent migrants tend to be undocumented, it follows that areas that have absorbed a lot of new immigrants, such as the Southern states, are experiencing a disproportionate increase in the undocumented population that will, in turn, bring along a train of political issues and consequences. For example, the 2007 American Community Survey showed

630,000 foreign-born people in North Carolina, of whom 376,000 (60 percent) were from Latin America.[27] At the same time, the Department of Homeland Security's estimates of the undocumented immigrant population in North Carolina as of 2007 is 380,000.[28] This suggests that 60 percent of the foreign-born population in North Carolina is undocumented. If we further assume that North Carolina mirrors the nation, for which 83 percent of the undocumented immigrants are from Latin America, then we would conclude that 315,000 of North Carolina's 376,000 Latin American immigrants—84 percent—were undocumented as of 2007. Keep in mind that most of these individuals are adults—indeed, mainly young adults—and many of them are building families in the United States, and their U.S.-born children are U.S. citizens, thereby increasing the likelihood that the parents will prefer to stay in the United States. This helps to explain why there were 1,086,000 Hispanics in North Carolina. The foreign-born (legal and unauthorized) account for scarcely more than one-third of North Carolina's Latino population. The U.S.-born children of immigrants from this and previous generations account for the rest.

The United States accepts more immigrants (legal and otherwise) than any other country in the world, and at the same time Mexico sends more migrants to other places (mainly, but not exclusively, the United States) than any other country in the world. The symmetry here is obvious. The 2000 census in the United States found that Hispanics (including the foreign-born and their U.S.-born descendents) constituted 12.6 percent of the population—more than African Americans—and the Census Bureau projects that the percentage will increase to 20.1 in 2030 and to 24.4 in 2050.[29] In several U.S. states Hispanics are now a significant minority of the population overall, and in every state bordering Mexico births to Hispanic mothers now represent the majority of all babies born.

Between 2000 and 2005, the states with the most rapid increase in the number of Latin American immigrants were, in descending order, South Carolina, Alabama, and Tennessee, whereas Georgia, Kentucky, and North Carolina were also among the top fifteen states for growth in Latin American population.[30] Significantly, California had a very slow increase in new Latin Americans, whereas Washington, D.C.—home to a fairly substantial Central American immigrant population—actually experienced a decline in that number. Since Southern states have a disproportionate share of Central American immigrants who are not from Mexico, it may be that the decline in Washington, D.C., represents an exodus to nearby Southern states. These changes carry with them the potential for significant impacts on virtually every aspect of U.S. life. There is indeed much at stake.

In short, the issue of Latin American migration must be addressed because it is an integral part of America's future, but at the same time it should not be reduced to a caricature. The phenomenon has very clear push and pull factors that influence who migrates, why they move, where they go, how they are received in the host country, and ultimately, whether they return to their place of origin. The roots lie deep within complementary demographic changes taking place in the Americas, tempered and conditioned by U.S. as well as Latin American policy responses to these changes.

Although U.S. policy will receive much of the attention in this book, it is also necessary to understand how migration plays out within Latin America itself, and how at times it has generated considerable debate. Large numbers of people move from country to country within Latin America, or migrate internally within any given Latin American country, often from rural areas to cities, and these movements have tremendous political, economic, and social consequences. Most importantly, they prompt political decisions that seek to influence migratory patterns. Latin American governments are acutely aware of the demographic realities their societies face, as well as the importance of the money being sent home by their compatriots abroad. As a consequence, they work to enact policies that will best serve their own country's needs. The face of Latin America is itself being changed by migration into, out of, and within the region. The United States may be becoming more Latino, but at the same time Latin America is becoming more American as a result of the interaction between immigrants to the U.S. and their family members back home, and more generally as a result of the increased awareness of Latin America on the part of U.S. businesses, occasioned especially by the presence of millions of migrants. Both U.S. and Latin American policies have responded to these internal demographic and related economic shifts.

Politics and Demographics

A central thesis of this book is, as mentioned above, that migration is best understood by examining demographics and politics together. Migration is one of the three basic demographic processes—the other two being mortality and fertility—but unlike deaths and births, which are natural events, there is nothing biological about migration. People choose to move (even if the choice is sometimes move or die), but in the modern world of nation-states, the choices of whether and where to move are constrained by government policies that either encourage, or more typically, discourage migration.

The migration of more than a handful of people from a given place is almost never a reaction to personal or family circumstances, but to events in that locale that may originate in demography (such as an excess of births over deaths, leading to more people than can be supported by the local economy) or in politics (such as political revolution and/or violence that forces people to flee for their lives). Thus, policies can be a reason for moving—a push factor—or they may limit migration even when people are motivated for other reasons to try and move. The United States sets limits on the number of people that can enter the country legally, and then sets barriers to slow the entrance of people who are not authorized to migrate. Mexico does the same thing with its southern border, trying to slow the movement of Central Americans into Mexico.

Political demography also recognizes that population movements can, in and of themselves, become political issues. Population growth created by death rates that decline more quickly than birth rates is the opening salvo of the demographic transition. However, the demographic transition is now known to constitute a series of transitions in human society that are set into motion by the widespread decline in the death rate.[31] Since the beginning of the twentieth century, a drop in mortality has always preceded a drop in the birth rate, and this is the direct cause of worldwide population growth—from about 1.5 billion at the beginning of the twentieth century to 6.5 billion early in the twenty-first century, with a projected 9 billion by the middle of the century.[32]

In 1900, the population of Latin America was 75 million, almost identical to the 76 million enumerated in the U.S. census that year. Death rates and birth rates dropped faster in the United States than in Latin America for most of the first half of the twentieth century, and by 1950, Latin America had pulled only a bit ahead of the United States, 167 million compared to 152 million. But the end of World War II brought significant declines in the death rate throughout Latin America, without appreciable drops in the birth rate. As a result, the population of Latin America shot past that of the United States, reaching 323 million in 1975 (a doubling in only 25 years), compared with only 219 million in the United States. By 2000, Latin America held nearly twice as many people, 521 million, as the United States, 288 million.

Almost everything happening in the world is connected in some way to the worldwide increase in the number of human beings, but this is especially the case when some places are growing at very different rates than others. In particular, the richest countries have birth rates that are low—sometimes even lower than the death rate; whereas in the rest of the world, birth rates still exceed death rates (even if they are coming down), and the populations continue to be young and ever more numerous.

When the world's population began to grow in earnest early in the twentieth century, humans were largely concentrated in rural areas and were engaged principally in agricultural activities. But population growth both depends upon and creates a demand for increased agricultural output that can only be accomplished by mechanization. Humans cannot work as much as larger animals such as horses and oxen, which in turn are inferior to tractors and other mechanical devices. Machines thus replace people. Population growth almost automatically creates a larger rural population than the economy can handle. This leads to migration, as people leave rural communities to find work elsewhere: first in other rural areas (the early part of the migration transition) where the population isn't growing so quickly (think of the takeover of the Americas by European colonizers, or of the movement of Brazilians to the rain forest); then to urban areas where, in fact, wages are almost always higher than in rural areas (leading to the urban transition, the follow-on to the migration transition). For example, over time Mexico City transformed into a massive, sprawling city, ringed with the slums occupied by those arriving from a countryside that could no longer support them.

The shift of people from rural to urban places and the shift to higher levels of international migration that results from increasing population growth in rural areas is the migration transition, whereas the shift over time from a largely rural population to a largely urban population is the urban transition. The flow of migrants out of rural places does not take place immediately after the death rate goes down, however, because the migration transition is also dependent upon an age transition. Throughout human history—across time and space—migrants have been and continue to be disproportionately young adults. This is the time when people are moving into the labor force, getting married, and starting their own families. It is only when the young adult population begins to grow that the pressures build within a community to figure out how these young people are to be employed and housed, and it is at this time in life that people think of migration as a strategic option. The young are also the best physically equipped to deal with the rigors of migration. This change in the number of young adults in a community is part of the age transition, the shift from a predominantly younger to a predominantly older population as a society moves through the demographic transition. The age transition is typically not smooth, however; it is often characterized early on by a youth bulge produced by the effect of declining death rates among children prior to a major drop in the birth rate.

In general we can say that any population with a high proportion of young adults now, relative to the number in the past, is likely building a reservoir of migrants. The places to which they go will also depend at least partly on the age structure of potential host communities. Those areas with an aging population—produced by a declining fertility rate—may well have vacancies in the labor force that can be filled by the excess number of young people growing up in places that have not yet experienced a long-term decline in fertility. This is the South-to-North migration in a nutshell. The same dynamic holds for the movement of people from the Middle East and Africa to Europe.

World systems theorists, such as Immanuel Wallerstein and Saskia Sassen, tend to locate the cause of the South-to-North migration in the structural changes that occur as firms in the developed nations disrupt local economies in developing nations in the course of globalization.[33] We argue—in a complementary, not contradictory way—that the underlying source of globalization, and thus of the migration associated with it, is population growth. Globalization is, in large part, a response to the mismatch in rates of growth in the labor force between the rich and poor nations.

Slow population growth in the rich countries makes it harder for companies to find cheap labor and thus to manufacture the cheaper goods that people want to buy from stores like Wal-Mart. On the other hand, rapid population growth in poorer nations, especially in the young adult age range, creates large pools of low-wage labor that can be exploited by multinational companies to produce those cheaper goods, which enables them to expand their markets. Of course, those markets are also expanding because of population growth in developing countries. Thus, it is our view that even if the proximate cause of migration between countries is consistent with world systems theory—the forces of globalization disrupt local economies and create dependencies that force migrants to leave local areas to seek employment elsewhere—the underlying distal cause of this migration is actually the population growth that made a place attractive to multinational forces in the first place.

Overall, then, population growth generated by an excess of births over deaths leads to situations in which local communities may not be able to offer young people the kind of employment they need to get on with life, unless there is a dedicated program of local economic development, such as it was hoped NAFTA would generate in Mexico (more on this later). The lack of local jobs creates direct pressures for migration and has the potential to lead to political instability, which can also eventually force people out of an area. Demography is, after all, destiny—but a destiny conditioned by policy.

The Policy Consequences of Demography

Demography has a direct and significant impact on politics and policies of all kinds. As demographic factors change, so do public perceptions of migration and, in turn, so do the policy responses made by government officials. For example, in a richer economy, vacancies in the labor force will compel businesses to pressure policy makers to relax immigration restrictions to allow a new flow of foreign workers. In turn, if the sociodemographic characteristics of those immigrants (race/ethnicity, religion, language, educational levels, and so forth) attract attention (which is typically negative) in the receiving country, public pressure can mount to turn off the immigration spigot. United States immigration policy has routinely had to contend with the competing, yet interlocking, pressures of the economy and society. In Europe, this contradiction is sometimes referred to as the "Polish plumber" problem: people in Western Europe like the good job that Polish plumbers do in their houses, but are not so sure that they want the eastern European immigrants in their community.[34] The contributions that immigrants make to the local economy are appreciated, but the presence of the immigrants themselves is less appreciated.

Obviously, the other side of the coin is represented by a country with an excess of workers—especially young workers—who are competing for a limited number of jobs in the local economy. Government policy in such situations may be to make sure that immigration is restricted, even as it encourages outmigration (emigration). Mexico guards its southern border with Guatemala from encroachment by undocumented immigrants (albeit not too successfully), while trying to protect the safety of Mexican citizens attempting to cross into the United States without authorization.

Public outcry and policy responses are especially accentuated when dealing with illegal immigrants. Is it a crime to move? Not exactly; it is a misdemeanor to be in the United States without government authorization. (There have been unsuccessful legislative efforts to make it a felony.) The penalty is deportation, not jail, but it is nonetheless a penalty. Furthermore, we routinely put the label of "legal immigrant" on those people who migrate with proper authorization, so the public is naturally inclined to call anyone else an "illegal immigrant." The problem arises when the labor pool in the sending country is very large relative to the number of entry visas made available in the host country, or if the process of legalization is too difficult and/or expensive. Under these conditions, which currently prevail in the relationship between the United States and Latin American countries, people decide that if they cannot get in through the front door, they'll try the back door. The number of different strategies employed is nearly endless, limited only by human ingenuity, and many are also extremely dangerous.

The Dangers of Illegal Immigration: The Yuma 14

In May 2001, twenty-six Mexican men paid coyotes (professional human smugglers) to bring them into the United States through the so-called Devil's Highway desert region of Arizona. As the border region in more populated areas to the west became more difficult, they sought a more desolate and less patrolled area to cross. Unfamiliar with the terrain, the coyotes got lost, and the group wandered without direction in temperatures that topped 100 degrees during the day and stayed in the 90s at night.

Increasingly desperate, in vain they sought shade in twisted mesquite trees and water in cactus, becoming more and more disoriented.

After two days, the two coyotes claimed they would go alone to find help, and asked for money to buy water, a common occurrence when such trips go bad. They left and were later found miles away. The rest of the group remained behind, waiting for rescue. Four days after the group entered the United States, a Border Patrol agent found several of the men, and a large operation was launched to rescue all of them. Fourteen, including one coyote, died. As a member of the Yuma sector of the Border Patrol put it, "It's in the middle of nowhere there." Dead less than nine weeks, the bodies were mummy-like, as if they had been dead for months.

In his book, Luis Alberto Urrea recounts the testimony of a survivor, and notes that it reads like poetry:

We were in the trees, trying to hide from the sun.
And they would yell to me, there's a guy dead over here.
And there's a guy dead over here . . .
I don't know why I survived.
Maybe it's a miracle.
Some of them just died of desperation.
Some of them went insane.
Some of them lost their minds.
You could hear them screaming.
Some fell all alone.[35]

SOURCE: Dell'orto 2001.

Furthermore, it is no longer sufficient to analyze only those policies made at the federal level in the United States. Courts have consistently ruled that immigration is the sole provenance of the federal government, but particularly in the absence of decisive federal action, state and local governments are far more active than ever before. This has entailed debates about declaring English the official language of cities and counties, pushing local law enforcement to check the immigration status of anyone arrested, reducing the number of individuals who may live in a single home (on the assumption that Latino immigrants will live together in greater numbers to save money), and passing laws to deny illegal immigrants access to any local services. A few communities, most notably San Francisco, have responded in the other direction by declaring themselves to be sanctuaries where undocumented immigrants can be assured of *not* being arrested.

In the South, the local context is especially important because the phenomenon is so new. Traditionally, local governments grappled with the racial divide between whites and African Americans, but not since the days of slavery have they dealt with the rapid growth of a population that not only looks different, but also speaks a different language. These debates are still in their early stages, so it is critical to analyze how local leaders deal with the issue. Chapter Six will address this in detail.

Also important is an understanding of the context of political decisions made at the local, state, and federal levels. To what degree do they have empirical grounding, or are they responding to conventional wisdom, which is often misleading? For example, it is often argued that the poorest Latin Americans migrate, that they are more likely to use social services than legal residents and citizens, or that they refuse to assimilate. None of these assertions is accurate, as we discuss later, but how much do such assumptions filter into policymaking?

Migration spawns myriad unintended consequences that can generate unexpected policy responses in sending countries. For example, Mexicans represent the largest single group of foreign-born people living in the United States, and they represent the largest group of immigrants flowing into the country on an annual basis, legally and otherwise. If we look at the numbers from the perspective of the sending countries, however, as shown in Table 2.1, we can see that Mexico is not the top country in terms of the percentage of its population that is living in the United States. More than 30 Guyanans are living in the United States for every 100 at home, compared with about 11 Mexicans. The difference, however, is that Guyana is a former British Colony (British Guiana) where the major language is English. It is in South America, but it is not exactly part of Latin America. In fact, as shown in Table 2.1, of the five Latin American countries whose expatriates in the United States represent 19 percent or more of the home country population, all are smaller, English-language nations—Barbados, Jamaica, Trinidad and Tobago, Belize, and Guyana. If we focus on Spanish-speaking countries, we can see that Mexico is second only to El Salvador in the foreign-born population in the United States as a percentage of the home country.

Policy makers in Mexico and Central American countries have discovered that migrants to the United States and Canada not only provide a demographic safety valve for a country with a rapidly growing population, they also send back money that keeps the economy afloat in the countries they have left. Recent estimates of remittances from the United States to Latin American countries are listed in Table 2.1 and Figure 2.1 displays them per foreign-born person living in the United States. Once again we can see that, although Mexico may have the greatest absolute volume of "migra-dollars" heading its way, immigrants from several other countries, especially those in South America, are actually sending more home on a per-person basis.

In response to this realization, Latin American political leaders are increasingly trying to engage their fellow citizens living in the United States, exhorting them to continue sending money home (and attempting to facilitate the process), increasing consular services, allowing them to vote from abroad, and even seeking their vote. Latin American political leaders have discovered a vested interest in ensuring that their citizens who live in wealthier countries do not forget about their homelands. That is even more imperative in the context of the recession, since many sources of capital literally disappeared overnight.

Increasingly it is also recognized that migrants move back and forth from the United States to their home countries. Many, in fact, have no desire to relocate permanently, but are only trying to save enough money to retire comfortably at home. Many migrants find only seasonal or other temporary work and may return home regularly to visit friends and family. From a policy perspective, this creates a dilemma for the elected officials in the United States. Opening the border too widely may be detrimental, but closing it too tight also tends to trap migrants, especially those in the country illegally, who will likely decide not to return home because it will be more difficult to come back in the future.[36] This is perhaps the single most important reason for the recent rise in the undocumented population in the United States. A related problem is that most illegal immigrants from Latin America are workers—thus constituting an important part of the U.S. economy—whereas most legal immigrants are not chosen on that basis; rather, they are family members of earlier migrants who have now become U.S. citizens. This results from policy decisions that have had huge consequences across the whole pattern of migration to the United States.

Table 2.1. The Stock and Flow of Migrants from Latin American into the United States

Latin American and Caribbean Countries	Major language	Number of people born in country who were residing in U.S. in 2007	Foreign-born from this country as a percent of all Latin American immigrants	Foreign-born in U.S. as a percent of total U.S. population
Caribbean				
Barbados	English	55,693	0.27	0.02
Cuba	Spanish	983,454	4.82	0.33
Dominican Republic	Spanish	755,539	3.70	0.25
Haiti	French	530,897	2.60	0.18
Jamaica	English	597,940	2.93	0.20
Trinidad and Tobago	English	225,528	1.11	0.07
Other Caribbean		237,953	1.17	0.08
Central America				
Mexico	Spanish	11,738,537	57.51	3.89
Belize	English	57,813	0.28	0.02
Costa Rica	Spanish	85,605	0.42	0.03
El Salvador	Spanish	1,104,390	5.41	0.37
Guatemala	Spanish	700,567	3.43	0.23
Honduras	Spanish	430,504	2.11	0.14
Nicaragua	Spanish	230,902	1.13	0.08
Panama	Spanish	102,158	0.50	0.03
South America				
Argentina	Spanish	172,736	0.85	0.06
Bolivia	Spanish	70,219	0.34	0.02
Brazil	Portug	338,853	1.66	0.11
Chile	Spanish	85,057	0.42	0.03
Colombia	Spanish	604,527	2.96	0.20
Ecuador	Spanish	406,907	1.99	0.13
Guyana	English	242,667	1.19	0.08
Peru	Spanish	401,129	1.97	0.13
Uruguay	Spanish	50,578	0.25	0.02
Venezuela	Spanish	155,492	0.76	0.05
Other South America		44,031	0.22	0.01
Total		**20,409,676**		**6.77**

SOURCES: Foreign-born population and country population data are from the U.S. Census Bureau (factfinder.census.gov); immigration data are from the U.S. Citizenship and Immigration Services (http://www.dhs.gov/ximgtn/statistics/); remittance data are from the Inter-American Development Bank (www.iadb.org).

Population of country of origin as of 2007	Foreign-born in U.S. as a percent of total population in country of origin	Legal Permanent Residents admitted to the U.S. in 2007	Deportable Aliens arrested by Border Patrol in 2007	Remittances from U.S. to country of origin in 2007 (US$ millions)	Remittances per foreign-born living in U.S. (US$)
280,946	19.82	689	28	—	—
11,394,043	8.63	29,104	4,932	—	—
9,365,818	8.07	28,024	2,118	3,120	4,130
8,706,497	6.10	30,405	1,004	1,830	3,447
2,782,221	21.49	19,375	804	1,975	3,303
1,056,608	21.34	6,829	210	125	554
2,413,867	9.86	3,691	155	—	—
108,700,891	10.80	148,640	854,261	23,979	2,043
294,610	19.62	1,073	113	105	1,816
4,137,374	2.07	2,540	377	560	6,542
6,948,073	15.89	21,127	19,699	3,695	3,346
12,728,111	5.50	17,908	23,907	4,128	5,892
7,483,763	5.75	7,646	28,263	2,561	5,949
5,680,208	4.07	3,716	2,118	990	4,288
3,258,329	3.14	1,916	112	320	3,132
40,048,816	0.43	5,645	227	920	5,326
9,119,152	0.77	2,590	189	1,050	14,953
193,918,575	0.17	14,295	2,902	7,075	20,879
16,303,851	0.52	2,274	135	850	9,993
44,379,598	1.36	33,187	1,893	4,520	7,477
13,755,680	2.96	12,248	1,771	3,085	7,582
769,095	31.55	5,726	156	424	1,747
28,809,303	1.39	17,699	944	2,900	7,230
3,460,607	1.46	1,418	109	125	2,471
26,023,528	0.60	10,692	314	330	2,122
5,911,795	0.74	751	32	815	18,510
567,731,359	**3.59**	**429,208**	**946,773**	**65,482**	**3,208**

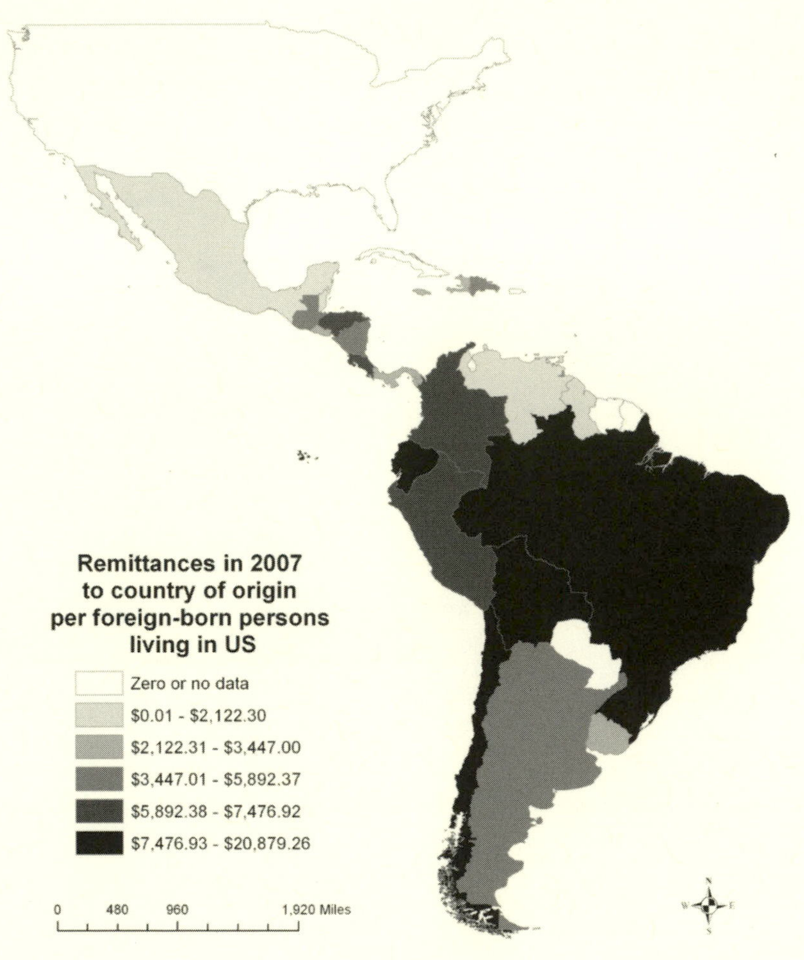

FIGURE 2.1

Remittances per foreign-born person living in the United States, 2007

SOURCE: Data from Table 2.1

The United States and Immigration Today

Currently, U.S. laws covering immigration and the status of immigrants constitute a complex web of state and federal regulations, spiced with periodic court decisions and lawsuits that result in an ever-shifting and difficult-to-understand set of rules. Given demographic changes over time, government responses have also varied, so that immigration policy as a whole has lurched from more open to more closed and back again, reflecting short-term political exigencies rather than a coherent vision of long-term goals.

One point that will become clear throughout the book is that neither the Democratic nor Republican party responds to migration as an easily recognizable bloc. There are rifts within and between parties depending on the Latin American country involved, the personal background of the elected official, the district he or she represents, and their overall philosophy of the desirability of immigration. The politics of immigration is messy by any standard. No one should not be too surprised, then, to learn that U.S. immigration policies have sometimes changed drastically and often appear incoherent. Members of Congress and the President face a variety of demands that often conflict. Currently, many businesses across the country seek Latin American labor because it is cheap and/or because it is too difficult to fill the jobs with anyone else. Sometimes the work is both grueling and gruesome—such as the poultry industry, where workers have to perform jobs unimaginable to most of us—but there are many other types of jobs as well in the construction, hospital, and restaurant industries, and in housekeeping, and other relatively low-skilled areas. The businesses employing these people wield their influence with elected officials to keep the flow of labor coming, and can make a powerful economic argument that politicians do not want to ignore. Migrant advocacy groups add their voices, arguing that restricting immigration only forces people to take a more dangerous route to enter illegally.

Migrants and their children have in fact softened the blow of the impending Social Security shortfalls as baby boomers begin to retire in large numbers. The birth rate among non-Hispanic whites in the United States (and Canada, as well) is below replacement level. This means that the group traditionally accounting for the vast majority of people in the United States has not been producing enough children to pay the Social Security benefits already promised to the baby boomers and other older

Americans. Migrant workers, and the children they are having, have at least delayed any crisis by contributing their taxes to the Social Security system. The irony is that the demographic group least tolerant of migrants is currently the group benefiting from their presence in the country.

However, another economic argument is that, especially when the U.S. economy turns sour (as happened in 2008), migrants *will* be taking scarce jobs, so the number of such migrants should be carefully controlled and limited. Over the course of the twentieth century, there have been clear cyclical patterns to periods of migration restrictions, not to mention expulsions. Economic factors go hand in hand with demography. As unemployment rates grow, a potential backlash is always in the background.

After the terrorist attacks of September 11, 2001, the perceived security aspect of immigration became highly salient, since those who hijacked the planes were originally in the United States legally. There have been calls for greater scrutiny of visas, better follow-up on migrants whose visas have expired, and increased border patrols to prevent illegal immigration. Despite intelligence reports that Al Qaeda operatives contemplated using the U.S.-Mexico border to infiltrate the United States, in 2008 the governments of both the United States and Mexico stated that there had been no such activity.[37] Nonetheless, given the sensitivity of the issue, such concerns will likely remain for the foreseeable future.

But even the context of the global "war on terror" can only tell us so much, some immigrants continue to be, by and large, welcomed with open arms. The continued presence of Fidel Castro, a *bête noire* for U.S. policy makers since the Eisenhower administration, means that Cuban immigrants receive preferential treatment not enjoyed by immigrants from any other Latin American country, a topic that will be addressed in more detail in Chapter Three. Few politicians have thus far shown much willingness to risk the ire of the powerful lobbies opposed to changing immigration policy toward Cuba.

Demography, then, must play a central role in any political analysis of Latin American migration, and vice versa. They are bound together tightly and help us to cut through much of the rhetoric, both pro and con (so often argumentative and acerbic), about migration. If we want to get a clear view of the significant changes taking place in the United States, demography is the place to start.

CHAPTER THREE

Huddled Masses on the Move

AT THE TIME OF EUROPEAN DISCOVERY, THE POPULATION OF NORTH America consisted of an estimated three to five million Native Americans,[1] a large percentage of whom were wiped out by diseases brought by the Europeans for which they had no resistance. Since then, North America has essentially been a land of immigrants and settlers. As Europeans disembarked in the east after crossing the Atlantic Ocean, the more arid western part of the land mass became a far-flung and largely ignored corner of the Spanish Empire. Although adventurers of European descent went west in search of their fortunes, for centuries it was sparsely populated, and Spanish was the main European language spoken. Only later—much later—did an English-speaking population take root, in search of potentially untapped riches, land, and minimal government presence.

The southeast was different. British colonizers fought Native Americans and settled permanently in the lush green mountains, piedmont, and coasts. Except in Florida, which remained in Spanish hands until the early nineteenth century, and Louisiana, which had strong French influence, English became the dominant language, political authority was

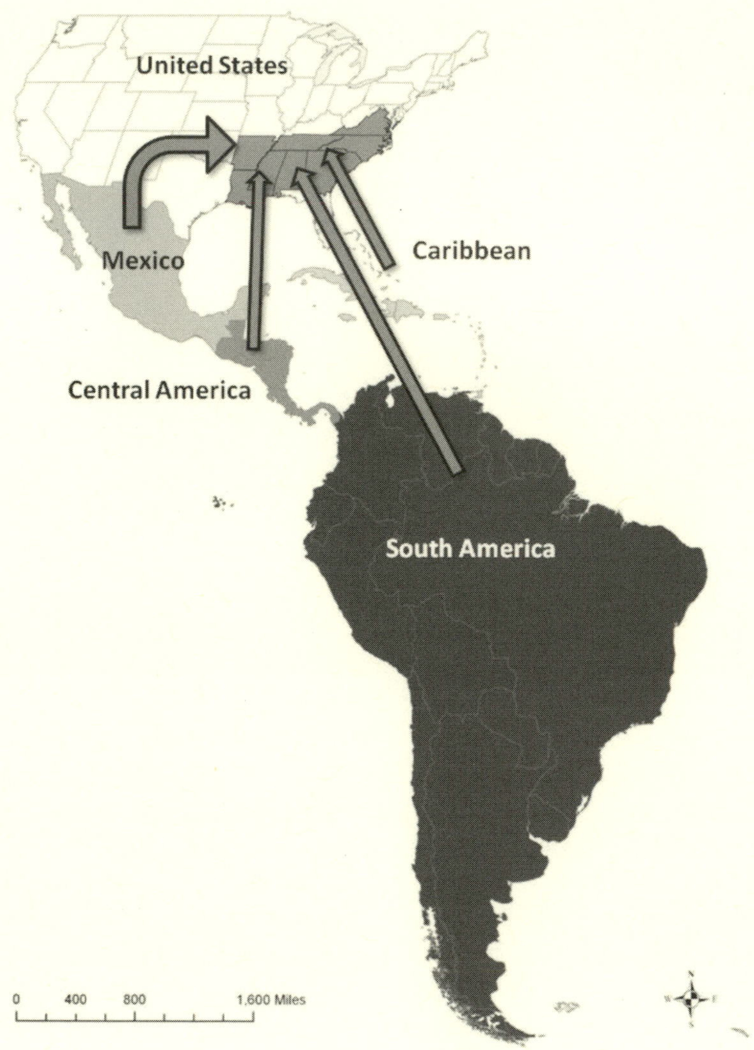

Figure 3.1
The geodemographic regions analyzed in this book

well-established and elitist, and a considerable amount of land was owned by a small slave-holding minority. In short, the west and the southeast had little in common with regard to race, culture, or socioeconomic distribution. In the South, the question of how to address immigration from Latin America was not even close to being on the radar screen. When it was considered at all, immigration was considered as something distant that the west would have to grapple with on its own. Not until the 1990s would Southerners take stock of how things had changed.

In this chapter, we trace the historical trajectories of Latin American migration to the United States until September 11, 2001, which sets the geodemographic context for the current debate over immigration and roughly coincides with the dramatic increase of Latino migrants to the U.S. South. We first address migration from Mexico and Central America, then the Caribbean, and finally South America, with attention to the policy responses in the United States and elsewhere. Finally, we place this migration in the context of the southeastern United States. Figure 3.1 provides a visualization of these regions and migration flows.

Migration and Mexico

In 1519 the Spaniard Hernán Cortés and his soldiers fought their way into what is now Mexico, arriving in Tenochtitlán (the site of Mexico City) and meeting the emperor Moctezuma. As in other parts of the hemisphere colonized by the Spanish and Portuguese, the combination of European men and subjugated indigenous women quickly led to a new racial category, the mestizo (or mix between white and indigenous), which were neither European nor indigenous, but something entirely new and, eventually, Latin American. This was a pattern across all of the new Spanish and Portuguese colonies. The racial composition of what became Latin America was further complicated by the import of African slaves.

When Mexico became independent from Spain in 1821 after over a decade of bloodshed, it was an enormous country, including most of the western half of what is now the United States, although much of that territory was sparsely populated by indigenous peoples not yet subjugated or killed by Europeans. Until the middle of the nineteenth century, there was no appreciable migration from Mexico to the United States, whose territory was concentrated east of the Mississippi River. Only in 1848 would the contemporary border begin to solidify, when the Mexican-American

Table 3.1 Immigration from Latin America and Other Regions to the United States, 1820–2008

Years	Total	Latin America	Asia
1820 to 1829	128,502	7,358	34
1830 to 1839	538,381	20,030	55
1840 to 1849	1,427,337	16,231	121
1850 to 1859	2,814,554	19,974	36,080
1860 to 1869	2,081,261	12,314	54,408
1870 to 1879	2,742,137	20,700	134,128
1880 to 1889	5,248,568	31,961	71,151
1890 to 1899	3,694,294	34,252	61,285
1900 to 1909	8,202,388	154,742	299,836
1910 to 1919	6,347,380	361,824	269,736
1920 to 1929	4,295,510	641,963	126,740
1930 to 1939	699,375	67,591	19,231
1940 to 1949	856,608	142,149	34,532
1950 to 1959	2,499,268	508,127	135,844
1960 to 1969	3,213,749	1,218,373	358,605
1970 to 1979	4,248,203	1,724,050	1,406,544
1980 to 1989	6,244,379	2,538,933	2,391,356
1990 to 1999	9,775,398	4,942,918	2,859,899
2000 to 2008	12,678,612	7,078,522	3,928,522

SOURCES: U.S. Department of Homeland Security 2008b, Table 2, http://www.dhs.gov/ximgtn/statistics/publications/LPR08.shtm; 2000 to 2008 data are augmented by estimates of the undocumented immigrant population from Hoefer, Rytina, and Baker 2008, Table 3.

War culminated in the Treaty of Guadalupe Hidalgo. For $15 million (about $500 million in current prices), the United States took possession of the west, with the Rio Grande becoming its southern border with Mexico, and everything north of the river and west of Texas becoming part of the United States. In a short span of time, Mexico had lost approximately half its land (though only a small percentage of the total Mexican population resided there) and rich natural resources. The Gadsden Purchase of 1853, through which the United States acquired what would become southern Arizona and southern New Mexico, finalized the transfer of land.

NW Europe	SE Europe	Other	% from Latin America
95,945	3,327	21,838	5.7
416,981	5,790	95,525	3.7
1,364,950	4,309	41,726	1.1
2,599,397	20,283	138,820	0.7
1,851,833	25,893	136,813	0.6
2,078,952	172,926	335,431	0.8
3,802,722	835,955	506,779	0.6
1,825,897	1,750,514	22,346	0.9
1,811,556	5,761,013	175,241	1.9
1,112,638	3,872,773	730,409	5.7
1,273,297	1,287,043	966,467	14.9
257,592	186,807	168,154	9.7
362,084	110,440	207,403	16.6
1,008,223	396,750	450,324	20.3
627,297	506,146	503,328	37.9
287,127	538,463	292,019	40.6
339,038	329,828	645,224	40.7
405,922	942,690	623,969	50.6
379,613	935,924	356,031	55.8

Until the twentieth century, however, the U.S.-Mexico border was more of a social construction than a true demarcation line.[2] Movement back and forth was constant and mostly local, border security was minimal, and there was little perception that cross-border interaction was indeed international. In Tijuana, for example, Mexican ranchers often used surveyors from the United States, and registered their land both in Mexico and in San Diego.[3] The Treaty of Guadalupe Hidalgo had created land disputes that lasted decades (some of which persist to the present time). The border existed in law, but in practice life continued as before.

Despite (or maybe because of) the openness of the border, Latin Americans represented only a tiny fraction of immigrants throughout the nineteenth century, as can be seen in Table 3.1. Almost all migrants to the United States during this time were from Europe. As large numbers of poor Irish Catholics and Germans settled in the eastern United States in the mid-nineteenth century, nativism grew—in part tied to Protestant concerns about Catholics, it was a manifestation of the kind of xenophobia that we mentioned in the previous chapter. Toward the end of that century, the U.S. Congress passed a series of measures that Christopher Mitchell refers to as "the crystallization of restrictive laws" aimed at specific immigrants.[4] Between 1875 and 1907, for example, Congress passed laws to exclude immigrants who were prostitutes, had a criminal conviction, suffered from mental illness, were likely to become a "public charge," were contract laborers, epileptics, "vagrants," polygamists (aimed at Mormons), espoused radical beliefs, or were unaccompanied children.[5] As President William McKinley (1897–1901) put it in 1896, Congress should pass legislation "as will secure the United States from invasion by the debased and criminal classes of the Old World."[6]

Such generalized restrictions were not aimed at any particular country (although there was an eye to European socialists), but more targeted laws were also enacted. The first and most prominent was the Chinese Exclusion Act of 1882, which marked the beginning of the end of open immigration. Through the Immigration Act of 1891, Congress established for the first time that immigration was a federal responsibility and created a new office of the Superintendent of Immigration.[7] That would evolve into the Immigration and Naturalization Service (INS) in 1933, which was split up, renamed, and brought into the Department of Homeland Security in 2003 in the aftermath of 9/11.

Immigration Acts in 1921 and 1924 assigned quotas to different countries, with the 1921 law allowing a number of immigrants from each country not to exceed 3 percent of the number of foreign-born from that country residing in the United States according to the 1910 census, with some waivers for family members. By 1924, the country's mood had shifted even more decidedly against immigrants, especially the rapidly increasing number from southern and eastern Europe (see Table 3.1), which reflected a fear of jobs being taken, assaults on American values, and generalized xenophobia.[8] These immigrants were associated in the public mind with radicalism and violence, which made them appear even more dangerous. Thus, the new 1924 law lowered the quota to 2 percent of the 1890 census—a date prior to substantial immigration of southern and eastern Europeans, which would thus allow even fewer to enter. The

Western Hemisphere (except for European colonies) was not assigned quotas because southwestern landowners insisted they needed the labor. The legislation also required, for the first time, that a U.S. consulate issue a visa with a photograph before a person would be allowed to enter the country.

Mexico, then, was not included in the string of restrictions. Mexican labor was in great demand in the west and midwest, areas that, unlike the northeast where so many southern Europeans settled, were wide open and sparsely populated in comparison. Border towns in particular were, as one author puts it, a "demographic sponge."[9] It was, indeed, an era of perfect demographic fit: a clear shortage of young laborers in the United States, and a surplus of young Mexican men looking for work.

Because of debt peonage, abuse by owners of haciendas, and other means of exploitation in Mexico, peasants fled to find places where they were not known and could not be found. Freedom, it was said, awaited those who fled to the north.[10] Simultaneously, the dictatorship of Porfirio Díaz (1876–1911) actively promoted privatization and foreign investment strategies as ways to boost economic development. Since Mexico was overwhelmingly poor and rural, foreign immigrants to Mexico could provide the lacking capital and expertise. Racism played a key role as well, as one hacienda owner explained in 1900: "Indians are a burden which the Mexicans must carry . . . We can not become great by ourselves; in order to produce more, we require the colonizing element."[11] As a result, Díaz welcomed Europeans, especially Spaniards and Germans, who could contribute to a "whitening" that would bring civilization and economic development to the country. For example, the regime passed legislation in 1883 allowing foreigners to own land and subsoil resources, and hired a German-born agent to advertise Mexico at the 1898 World's Fair as a place of "wide-open spaces."[12] Between 1900 and 1910, the number of foreigners counted in the Mexican census doubled, although it remained a small fraction of the total population.[13]

Construction of railroads facilitated the movement of Mexicans from south to north, and then from northern Mexico into the United States. The railroads were one part of a Porfirian strategy to expand capitalist development and to increase Mexico's City's control over the restless northern area. The U.S. railroad system was simultaneously being expanded from north to south, greatly facilitating the meeting of potential employers in the United States and potential workers in Mexico.

By and large, Mexican workers were more acceptable to the U.S. government and to locals in the United States than were people from other places. Not only were they familiar, given their long-standing presence in the southwest, but they were considered "homing pigeons" who would work and then return home, with no risk of attempting to stay permanently.[14] For the most part, this was true. In the 1900–1930 period, between 60,000 and 100,000 Mexicans migrated to the United States, but between 42,000 and 70,000 returned.[15] Assumptions about the seasonal nature of migration permeated contemporary accounts, which refer to "labor" and do not mention "immigration."[16]

Despite federal law prohibiting offers of employment as a lure for immigrants, contractors and company agents could be found all along the border. This included the infamous *engancho* (hook) whereby recruiters would be paid according to how many Mexican laborers they could locate. This became another form of debt peonage, since the costs of bringing the laborer north would be deducted from his or her wages, and company stores would offer them credit.

In general, then, the relative absence of U.S. workers resulted in a heavy reliance on Mexican labor. This was not a function of differential age structures, but simply an overall lack of people needed to perform jobs. Mexicans could be found especially in agriculture, mining, and railroads, but also worked in restaurants, laundries, and other occupations requiring relatively low-skilled, low-wage workers.

As the northward movement of Mexican migrants continued, albeit in relatively small numbers (see Table 3.1), the Mexican government was criticized domestically from all sides. Some believed it should act to protect Mexicans in the United States, since they were often mistreated. Some stressed that grossly inadequate living conditions in Mexico, which was the main impetus of emigration, were the fault of Porfirio Díaz's dictatorship.[17] The leaders of the Mexican Revolution, which would engulf the country after Díaz's ouster in 1911, used the emigration issue as an example of the government's failures. In fact, they also found willing recruits to their revolutionary cause from the large number of migrant workers in northern Mexico, who were already often far from their homes in search of a steady wage.[18] The most important initial leader of the revolution, Francisco Madero, proclaimed that his government would directly address the problem of emigration.[19]

Migrant workers were generally viewed as a threat to Mexican political institutions, not only because they epitomized the government's inability to generate economic development that would ultimately lead to their employment, but also because their political loyalties were shifting and unpredictable. Throughout the revolutionary period, Mexican leaders would try unsuccessfully to convince workers to remain rooted in Mexico and contribute to domestic economic prosperity. Ultimately, however, jobs were more plentiful and wages were better north of the border.

Thus, even Porfirio Díaz's successors and detractors could not halt the flow of workers, which was augmented further by the U.S. jobs vacated by Americans who left to fight in World War I. In addition, the violence associated with the Mexican revolution prompted even more emigration. Between 1911 and 1920, the years of the Mexican Revolution, 219,004 Mexicans officially entered the United States, a 441 percent increase over the previous decade.[20] Many others came unofficially, then returned to Mexico when the revolution was over. We would now call them refugees, but that term wasn't applied at the time.

In 1920 and 1921, the Mexican government was forced to face the issue of migration when thousands of Mexican workers were unceremoniously deported as the U.S. economy went into a recession.[21] President Alvaro Obregón (1920–1924) worked to address their plight (especially by providing small amounts of money, food, and transportation vouchers) through consular officials, and sought to maintain the revolutionary tenets upon which his government was based. But in the wake of war and economic dislocation, Mexico simply lacked the resources to do much, and the loss of remittances also hurt. In 1922, the Mexican government estimated that the average emigrant remitted $300 annually.[22] According to the Consumer Price Index, that would represent just over $3,000 in 2007 dollars—roughly similar to the level now, as shown in Table 2.1 in the previous chapter.

The post–World War I recession had been serious, and while the economy recovered robustly in the 1920s, the crash of the U.S. stock market in 1929 was truly catastrophic for Mexico as the United States. The Mexican government lacked even the meager resources it had in the early 1920s, and could do almost nothing as migrants came back in the early 1930s to an economy that could barely support them.

Into the twentieth century, the U.S. government continued its relaxed policies toward Mexico and rarely enforced even the minimal restrictions on cross-border travel that already existed. When restrictive laws were passed (such as the Immigration Acts of 1903 and 1907), Mexicans were granted exemptions. Until the crash of the U.S. stock market in 1929, Mexicans came and went essentially in response to the demand for their labor. Although many voices called for greater restriction on migration, business interests were well organized and well connected to government. Continued Mexican migration was a priority, and recruiters actively sought out labor.

However, soon after the 1929 crash, U.S. employers laid off Mexican workers in droves, encouraged by the Hoover administration to provide as many jobs as possible to U.S. citizens. As William Doak, Hoover's Secretary of Labor put it, "one way to provide work for unemployed Americans was to oust any alien holding a job and to deport him."[23] The federal government initiated the Mexican Repatriation Program, and cities like Los Angeles decided that the cost of repatriation was cheaper than providing unemployment assistance, so more than 6,000 Mexicans were shipped back over the border.[24] By the mid-1930s, approximately half a million Mexicans had returned to their homeland, either voluntarily or forcibly. Los Angeles County shipped some in boxcars. As one migrant later recounted, authorities told them they would be taken by train to Mexico: "In Mexico you will transfer and we'll take you where you come from, close, not actually there, but to the closest town."[25]

Despite that experience, in 1940 a State Department geographer wrote that "few boundaries anywhere in the world operate with less friction and with greater adaptation to the needs and interests of the peoples concerned than the frontiers of the United States with both Canada and Mexico."[26] Nonetheless, he also added, "If on either side of either boundary a spirit of ill will were engendered or if problems related to the boundary were allowed to go unresolved until personal grievances and local issues became national issues, problems of considerable magnitude might develop."[27]

World II and the Bracero Program

The U.S. declaration of war in December 1941 set into motion powerful demographic and policy shifts with regard to immigration—shifts that continue to reverberate in the twenty-first century. Young men in the United States were being sent to the European and Asian theaters, and although women famously filled some of the labor gap, more workers were needed. Even more importantly, regular labor, rather than unpredictable seasonal spurts, was critical to maintaining a food supply in the midst of war. When World War II started, the draft age in the United States was 21 to 31, but that quickly was expanded to include men aged 18 to 44. Using data from the 1940 census for males aged 15 to 44, we can estimate that there were 32 million men of that age range in the United States. Data from the U.S. Census Bureau show that 16 million Americans (of both sexes, but mainly men) served in the military between 1941 and 1946, with an average service of just less than three years.[28] Thus, we can estimate that at any given time, at least eight million men in from 18 to 44 years old were in the active military and thus not in the civilian labor force. Help was needed.

The United States was in a reasonably favorable demographic situation for a war, which typically benefits from a youth bulge. Although the birth rate had dropped to below replacement levels during the Great Depression of the 1930s, the U.S. age structure was still fairly young, and the age groups of 15 to 19 and 20 to 24 had the highest percentages of any five-year age group in the United States in 1940, as can be seen in Figure 3.2.

In Mexico, meanwhile, the birth rate remained high (averaging more than six children per woman), resulting in 59 percent of the Mexican population under age 25, compared to 43 percent in the United States (see Figure 3.2). Many young workers sought employment, and the growth of Mexican railways and highways made the trip north more feasible. The U.S. government therefore sought what in current parlance is a guest worker or temporary worker program.

The Mexican federal government was largely opposed to the idea. In part, this was the legacy of the revolution: since the revolution was aimed at the common person, the departure of such a person was an indictment of the revolution itself. In 1930, a Mexican government official had written a series of newspaper articles on emigration, calling it "a veritable hemorrhage suffered by the country."[29] In fact, unregulated hiring of Mexicans constituted (and continues to constitute) a violation of Article 123 of the 1917 Mexican Constitution, which grants power over contract labor to the Mexican government and guarantees workers a wide range of rights and privileges.[30] Plus, regardless of demographic realities, Mexican authorities believed emigration would deprive native employers of the labor they required to succeed. Until the Great Depression, the Mexican government had consistently encouraged repatriation, hoping it would spark economic growth. Yet, into

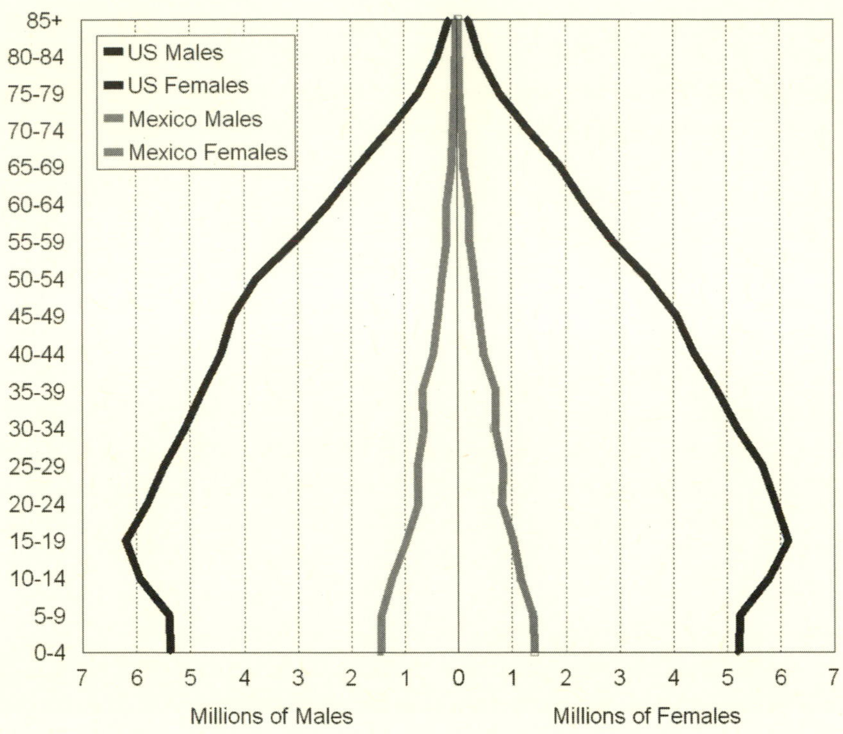

Figure 3.2

Population by age and sex in the United States and Mexico, 1940

SOURCES: United States data from U.S. Census Bureau, Statistical Abstract of the United States 1945 (http://www2.census.gov/prod2/statcomp/documents/1944-02.pdf); Mexico data from Instituto Nacional de Estadística y Geografía 1994, Table 1.6.

this mix went the obvious ambivalence created by the U.S. government's Mexican Repatriation Program and the likely desire on the part of Mexicans and the Mexican government not to experience another round of deportations when Mexican labor was no longer needed in the United States (which indeed happened again in the 1950s, as we note below).

However, under pressure from the U.S. government, and because Mexico was in accord with the United States with regard to the war, the Mexican government relented after receiving a number of assurances about the rights of Mexicans working in the United States.[31] The assurances given to Mexico regarding temporary workers included the following: (1) the need for labor had to be proven by the employer; (2) the worker would not be encouraged to remain in the United States; (3) workers' round trip travel would be guaranteed; (4) racial discrimination would be prohibited; (5) written contracts were necessary; (6) workers would not be subject to military service; (7) housing would be satisfactory; (8) wages would be guaranteed; and (9) money would be deducted for social security, payable in Mexico.[32] Mexican authorities wanted their citizens to work, be treated fairly, but then to return. That sentiment was widely shared on both sides of the border.

What would become known as the Bracero program involved a large number of Mexican agencies jointly determining the number of participants from each Mexican state, coordinating transportation, notifying workers, and handling other logistical matters. On the U.S. side, each individual was inspected, fingerprinted, examined for health problems, then further reviewed by potential employers. This could be a terrifying process. As a character in Eugene Nelson's novel *Bracero* puts it, "There are many fine things about the Estados Unidos—large beautiful cities, good highways, plenty of water, plenty of jobs—but the thing I always remember longest is this agony of waiting to find out if one will be accepted or rejected after all the suffering one has gone through."[33]

Many of these jobs were in agriculture, but other industries related to the war effort were also facing shortages. Over time, the number of participants in the Bracero program increased, and overall approximately 4.6 million contracts were issued.[34] On an annual basis, however, the number was actually fairly small during the war, averaging fewer than 100,000 workers per year between 1942 and 1946.[35] To be sure, it could hardly have been otherwise, because during this time the Mexican population was significantly less than the U.S. population, as can be seen in Figure 3.2. The 32 million U.S. males aged 15 to 44 in 1944 were matched by only 4 million Mexican males of that age. Thus, even 100,000 temporary workers per year consumed more than 2 percent of the entire male Mexican labor force. There could have been little thought at this time that the American labor force might be dramatically affected by Mexican workers, even if there had been an open border policy.

Although the labor shortage created in the United States by World War II was the original motivation for the Bracero program, it was during the postwar boom that the program blossomed, peaking in 1956 when nearly half a million Mexicans entered the United States to work as contract laborers. In the 1950s alone, those workers sent as much as $120 million back to Mexico as remittances.[36]

The Bracero program evolved into an unwieldy creature, with multiple layers of bureaucracy—in some cases corrupt—on both sides, and as a result the postwar years saw an increase in the number of Mexicans entering the United States illegally, rather than trying to navigate the program's obstacles. In 1951, the President's Commission on Migratory Labor reported that illegal crossings constituted "virtually an invasion."[37] Since the end of the war, the steady rise in the number of contract workers under the Bracero program had been matched by a parallel rise in the number of Mexicans apprehended at the border who were trying to find jobs outside of the contract system. This led in 1954 to the crudely named Operation Wetback, which consisted of workplace raids, particularly in Arizona and California, to convince Mexican migrants that they should leave the country.[38] Needless to say, it worked imperfectly, but because of it and perhaps for other reasons as well, the number of apprehensions at the border dropped significantly in the decade following Operation Wetback, whereas the number of Mexicans applying for visas under the Bracero program increased, as did the number of workers in the Bracero program who applied for immigrant visas to remain permanently in the United States.[39]

Congressional opposition to the Bracero program emerged strongly in 1960. Reports of abuses were combined with popular concern that Mexicans were taking jobs from U.S. citizens. Demography helps explain that perception, as we discuss in some detail in the next chapter. Political debate over the program also set a precedent that continues today, with opinions on immigration falling clearly on neither party nor geographic lines. Arizona Senator Barry Goldwater, the conservative Republican presidential nominee in 1964, favored extending the program, as did the liberal Democratic California governor Edmund Brown and the conservative Democratic Arkansas Senator William Fulbright.[40] Others, however, were opposed not for nativist reasons but out of human rights concerns. Mexican American Congressman Henry González (Democrat, Texas), for example, voted to end the program because of widespread reports of abuse, which also led to opposition from César Chávez and the United Farm Workers.

The national debate in the 1960s about ending the Bracero program essentially set the stage for viewpoints that continue to the present, with political opinions on immigration falling unevenly along the different axes of the Democratic and Republican parties. Libertarian and/or pro-business sentiments, most notably in the Republican Party, can prompt pro-immigration sentiment, as migrants provide a ready (and steady) stream of workers at a low cost. Other Republicans, from pro-law (in the case of undocumented workers), pro-English, or pro-security perspectives, consider the large scale of immigration to be a threat. Pro-union activists, especially among Democrats, are often leery of immigration, viewing it as a strategy to obtain cheap labor at the expense of unionized workers. In more recent years, some unions have shifted this position, viewing migrant labor (at least by those in the country legally) as new union recruits in an era when union membership is declining.[41]

In early 1964, outgoing Mexican President Adolfo López Mateos (1958–1964) raised the issue of illegal immigration with outgoing President Lyndon Johnson. He noted that once the Bracero program concluded, the number of illegal crossings would increase because Mexicans would still want work and many U.S. farmers would still seek cheap labor. He further argued that the Mexican government would need to begin a large public works program to accommodate returning workers.[42] His successor, Gustavo Díaz Ordaz (1964–1970), who met with President Johnson later that year, echoed the request for the United States to ensure that workers did not enter the country illegally.

Thus, undocumented immigration was already a well-understood phenomenon, and as both Mexican presidents predicted, the termination of the Bracero program in 1964 accelerated it. Faced with the choice of working illegally or returning to Mexico, where work would likely be scarcer, many people chose to risk the former. Figure 3.3 demonstrates the rapid rise of apprehensions when the Bracero program ended. A decade after the Bracero program, the number of apprehensions had again reached the level that had triggered Operation Wetback, and it has never fallen below that since.

The United States did very little in response to Mexican requests to deal with the problems created by ending the Bracero program, but the Mexican government responded with the Maquiladora program, which was designed specifically to absorb workers who decided to return to Mexico rather than remain in the United States illegally. Given the clear political and social signals coming from the United States, already by 1961 the Mexican government had embarked on plans to promote economic development at the border, thus anticipating repatriation. One early example

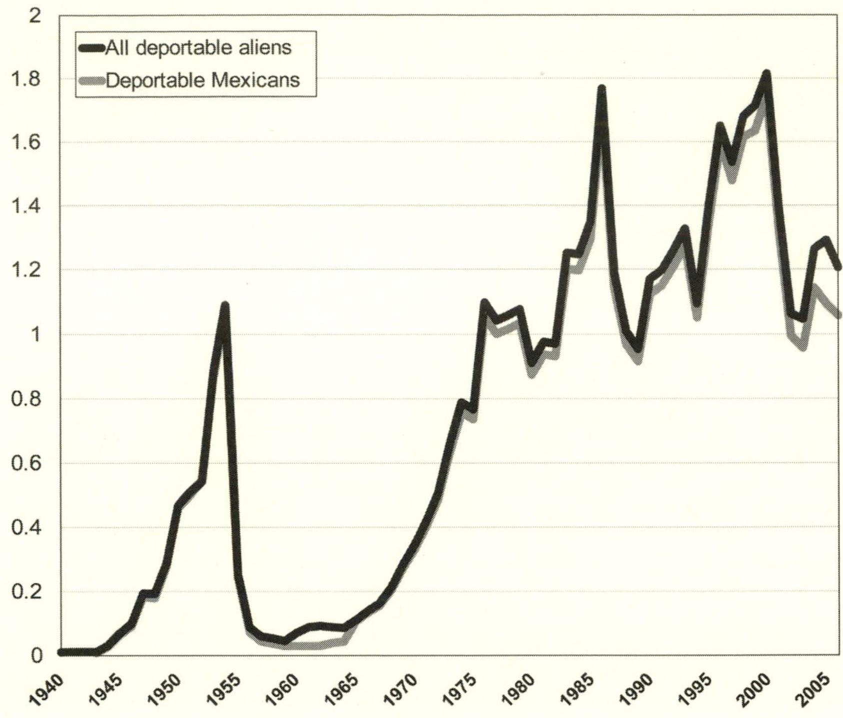

Figure 3.3

Apprehensions of "deportable aliens," 1940–2006

SOURCES: Data on all deportable aliens is from U.S. Department of Homeland Security 2006, Table 34; data on deportable Mexicans for 1943 through 1964 is from Garcia y Griego, Weeks, and Ham-Chande 1990, Table 12.2; data on deportable Mexicans for 1965 through 2006 are from individual Yearbooks of Immigration Statistics (see U.S. DHS).

from that year was Programa Nacional Fronterizo, intended to fund development projects along the U.S.-Mexico border, which would then be a window into Mexico, but it remained underfunded.[43] Nonetheless, combined with the rapid growth of border cities, it sparked greater interest in facilitating export industries. In 1971, the Mexican government established a legal framework, summarized as follows:

> According to the respective Regulations, it is a promotional program granting assistance to investors to establish industrial

> units within a 20 kilometer strip parallel to the international border line or to the coast line. It authorizes tax free importations of raw materials, parts, components, machinery, tooling equipment, and everything else needed for the transformation or processing, assembly and finishing of products to be entirely exported.[44]

The North American Free Trade Agreement (NAFTA), which went into effect in 1994 and was itself a government response to demographic pressures, opened the door even further for U.S. and Canadian investment in Mexico. Maquiladoras would soon become an integral part of northern Mexico's economy.

Reforms in the 1960s

In the United States in the 1960s, public resistance to further immigration, based in part on demographic shifts, led to legal limits being set on the number of Latin Americans who could come to the United States. In 1965, amendments to the Immigration and Nationality Act (which in 1952 had brought all existing immigration laws under one piece of legislation) raised the total number of immigrants who could enter each year from all countries, from 150,000 to 290,000, and eliminated the numerical restrictions (the quota system) established in 1921 that had strictly limited immigration from most non-Western European countries (the vast majority of immigrants thus came from Great Britain, Ireland, and Germany). Under the new legislation, for example, a ceiling for the eastern hemisphere was set at 170,000, and no more than 20,000 could come from any single country. In that era of civil rights activism, the idea was to end the blatant discrimination that existed in the immigration policies. For the western hemisphere, 120,000 could enter with no ceiling on any specific country, and no restrictions on family members of legal immigrants already residing in the United States. We will return later in the book to the ramifications of this family reunification philosophy.

Proponents argued that this package of changes would not have a major impact on the number of people migrating to the United States. For example, during the debate Congressman John Tunney (Democrat, California) said categorically:

> Many fear that the bill will result in a wholesale increase in immigration. This is not true. It is estimated that immigration which has averaged around 360,000 annually in recent years, will not surpass 360,000 under the bill.[45]

When he signed the bill into law, President Lyndon Johnson argued that its impact was mostly symbolic:

> This bill that we sign today is not a revolutionary bill. It does not affect the lives of millions. It will not reshape the structure of our daily lives, or really add importantly to either our wealth or our power.[46]

The assessments by Tunney and Johnson turned out to be incredibly wrong. From that period on, migration from everywhere, but especially from Latin America, increased considerably, as shown in Table 3.1. At the height of the first wave of immigration, in the 1900–1909 decade, more than eight million immigrants were admitted to the United States, but only 2 percent of those were from Latin America. Latin America was still fairly sparsely populated, and Mexicans tended to enter as temporary workers rather than permanent immigrants. The restrictive immigration policies put into place after that, as noted above, cut immigration dramatically, but the period after World War I was one in which Latin Americans "discovered" the United States as a migration destination, partly as a result of aggressive recruitment by U.S. employers. From 1940 to the present, the number of immigrants has risen each decade, and each decade the percentage of those immigrants who are from Latin America has risen. This was already happening when President Johnson signed the 1965 Immigration and Nationality Act, but that legislation propelled it forward, in total contradiction to what Johnson professed would happen. If we include the undocumented immigrants who reside in the United States, we can see that more than half of all people now coming to the United States are from Latin America.

Although the majority of Latin American immigrants to the United States (and to the southern states more specifically) are of Mexican origin, millions more are from other parts of the region. Their reasons for emigrating are similar but, especially in Central America and the Caribbean, include important political factors worth examining.

Politics and Migration in Central America

Throughout most of the nineteenth century, Central America reeled from postindependence political conflict. The early dreams of a unified isthmus (dreams that would never come to fruition but also would never die) were dashed as political elites fought for power. As in Mexico, Central American governments—especially those associated with the Liberal Party, which was more associated with encouraging foreign migration and investment—sought to encourage European immigration as a way to create economic development in the middle to late nineteenth century.[47]

At the beginning of the twentieth century, the total population of all the Central American countries combined was scarcely five million (roughly equivalent to the greater Washington, D.C., metropolitan area today), and no country had as many as one million people, as seen in Table 3.2 and Figure 3.4. Since that time, however—and especially since the end of World War II—the region has exploded in population size, just as Mexico has. This explosion resulted directly from health measures that were aimed at keeping infants and children alive—hospital deliveries, immunizations, vitamins, clean water, and oral rehydration therapy. The 1950 infant death rate in Guatemala was 141 deaths under age one per 1,000 live births, equivalent to the highest rates found today in equatorial Africa. One in every seven children died before reaching her or his first birthday, and life expectancy for females was only 42 years. Today the infant death rate has dropped to 30 per 1,000 and life expectancy has climbed to 74 years. The same story is told throughout Central America and in Mexico.

A drop in the death rate results in population growth because the birth rate takes years to adjust to the lower death rates. In 1950, the average Guatemalan woman had seven children, two of whom would die before age ten. As recently as the mid-1980s, women still averaged six children each, but by then almost all survived to adulthood. Guatemala is Mexico's nearest neighbor to the south and the most populous country of the isthmus. Its population in 1950 was 3.6 times larger than it had been in 1900, and in 2000 was again 3.6 times larger than in 1950, and the United Nations Population Division projects that it will more than double again by 2050 (Table 3.2). Like Mexico, these countries have all been under intense demographic pressure, and some have responded more beneficially for their residents than others.

Table 3.2 Growth of the Central American Countries Since 1900 in Comparison to the United States and Mexico (population in thousands)

Country	1900	1950	2000
Guatemala	885	3,146	11,229
Belize	42	69	245
Honduras	544	1,487	6,196
El Salvador	801	1,951	6,195
Nicaragua	429	1,295	5,108
Costa Rica	310	966	3,929
Panama	263	860	2,950
Total	5,174	11,724	37,852
Mexico	13,607	27,741	99,735
US	76,212	157,813	284,857
US/Central America	14.7	13.5	7.5
US/Mexico	5.6	5.7	2.9
Mexico/Central America	2.6	2.4	2.6

SOURCES: Data for 1900 are from http://www.populstat.info; data for other years are from the U.N. Population Division 2009.

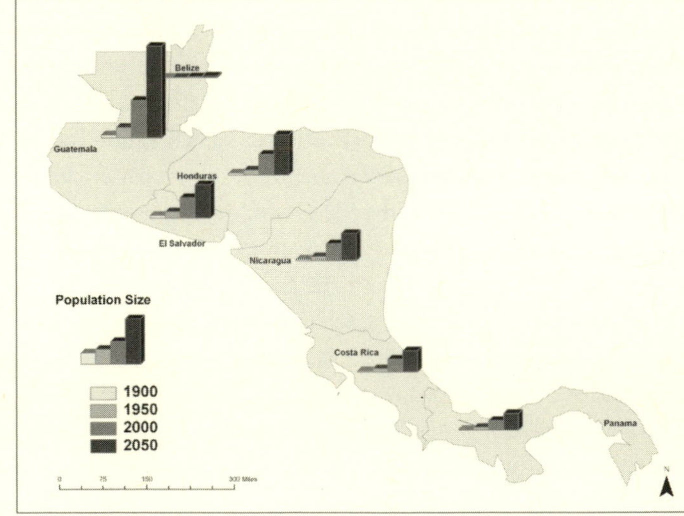

Figure 3.4 Population growth in Central America, 1900–2050

SOURCE: Data from Table 3.2.

2050	1950/1900	2000/1950	2050/2000
27,473	3.55	3.57	2.45
487	1.64	3.55	1.99
12,079	2.73	4.17	1.95
10,040	2.44	3.18	1.62
8,169	3.02	3.94	1.60
6,426	3.12	4.07	1.64
5,093	3.27	3.43	1.73
71,817	2.27	3.23	1.90
132,278	2.04	3.60	1.33
402,415	2.07	1.81	1.41
5.6			
3.0			
1.8			

As we have discussed before, if the demographic pressure from an increase in the number of young adults cannot be met by the creation of new jobs and opportunities for participation in civil society, one option for young people is to migrate, and many have chosen this path. Indeed, increasing numbers of people have been migrating to the United States from each of the Central American countries, as shown in Table 3.3. There was a noticeable increase in the decade of the 1960s, after Lyndon Johnson signed the 1965 Immigration Act, and then another noticeable surge in the 1980s.

Although the increase in immigration is clearly associated with the population increase in Central American countries, demography alone cannot explain the swell of immigrants from El Salvador, Guatemala, and Nicaragua that occurred in the 1980s, though it does add to our understanding about why their native countries have been politically unstable as well as why immigrants from those countries choose to stay in the United States once they arrived. Guatemalans have tended to migrate to Mexico, as well as the United States, since this is clearly an easier journey for them,

Table 3.3 Immigrants Admitted to the United States from Each of the Central American Countries, by decade, 1820–2007

	Belize	Costa Rica	El Salvador
1820 to 1829	0	0	0
1830 to 1839	0	0	0
1840 to 1849	0	0	0
1850 to 1859	0	0	0
1860 to 1869	0	0	0
1870 to 1879	0	0	0
1880 to 1889	0	0	0
1890 to 1899	0	0	0
1900 to 1909	77	0	0
1910 to 1919	40	0	0
1920 to 1929	285	0	0
1930 to 1939	193	431	597
1940 to 1949	433	1,965	4,885
1950 to 1959	1,133	4,044	5,094
1960 to 1969	4,185	17,975	14,405
1970 to 1979	6,747	12,405	29,428
1980 to 1989	14,964	25,017	137,418
1990 to 1999	12,600	17,054	273,017
2000 to 2007	7,496	16,732	212,958
Immigrants in 2000–2007 period as a percent of total national population in 2000	3.1%	0.4%	3.4%

SOURCE: Data from Table 2.1.

but residents of the other Central American countries have been especially buffeted by the history of relations between their own country and the United States.

For the full story, we must begin by examining U.S. foreign policy in the context of the Cold War. In 1979, Marxist guerrillas known as the Sandinistas (named for a Nicaraguan rebel who fought against U.S. occupation in the 1920s) overthrew a U.S.-backed dictator, Anastasio Somoza.

Guatemala	Honduras	Nicaragua	Panama
0	0	0	0
0	0	0	0
0	0	0	0
0	0	0	0
0	0	0	0
0	0	0	0
0	0	0	0
0	0	0	0
0	0	0	0
0	0	0	0
0	0	0	0
423	679	405	1,452
1,303	1,874	4,393	5,282
4,197	5,320	7,812	12,601
14,357	15,078	10,383	22,177
23,837	15,651	10,911	21,395
58,847	39,071	31,102	32,957
126,043	72,880	80,446	28,149
129,320	50,834	62,500	14,536
1.2%	0.8%	1.2%	

The following year, Ronald Reagan won the presidency in a landslide with a foreign policy message that focused on rolling back Communism. Nicaragua would become the first battleground, as President Reagan (1981–1989) immediately signed an executive order to fund a covert force to topple the Sandinista government.

In El Salvador and Guatemala, the U.S. was allied with military-dominated regimes intent not only on combating Marxist rebellion, but also on crushing all signs of incipient dissent. Throughout the 1980s, both countries were in the midst of civil war and awash in U.S. weapons, counterinsurgency training, and billions of dollars in U.S. military aid. The level of violence, which reached every remote rural corner, was staggering. In El Salvador and Guatemala in particular, hundreds of thousands were dead, hundreds of thousands more detained without due process, tortured, raped, or forcibly conscripted into the army.

An entirely rational decision, therefore, was to escape and to make the northward trek. In the case of Nicaragua, spikes in emigration correlated closely to episodes of violence by the Contras, the U.S.-funded group dedicated to overthrowing the Sandinista government.[48] This entailed considerable risk, not only because of the war-torn regions people had to traverse, but because Mexico was struggling to accommodate the refugee flow. For example, when Guatemalan dictator José Efraín Ríos Montt launched a counterinsurgency campaign in 1982, tens of thousands streamed into Chiapas, already the poorest Mexican state.[49]

Fleeing Civil War in El Salvador: Gabriel Serrano

In 1979, Gabriel Serrano was in the eighth grade in the small town of San Julian in El Salvador. Born poor, his family and friends were viewed as potential Communist sympathizers at a time when the country was on the cusp of civil war and in a region deemed central to the Cold War by the United States. In El Salvador, the military-backed government used local National Guard forces to kill alleged "subversives" and forcibly conscript others. The military also wanted informants (called *orejas*, ears) who would point fingers (*poner el dedo*) at suspected revolutionaries. Young Gabriel saw the dead body of his teacher, murdered by the National Guard because an *oreja* had fingered the wrong person.

Later, just short of twenty years old, Gabriel would be stopped at a military checkpoint, which was intended not only to find members of the resistance, but also to recruit young men forcibly into the army. He was let go after a soldier recognized him, but his family feared that the next time, he might not be seen again. Thus, in 1984 he made the decision to go to the United States. His older brother found a coyote to guide him, and he joined a group of forty-eight Salvadorans (including a few women and children) going north. After twenty days, they made it to

Mexicali, where they were told money was running out so they would receive only one meal a day.

Given a sandwich and told to cherish it as the last food until Los Angeles, they set off, even swimming across the New River. With only water (and eventually some unripe cantaloupe) they walked and hid for four days until finally picked up by vans at a highway. They were taken to an apartment and told they could not leave until they had paid more money, but Gabriel managed to escape and seek refuge with some people he knew in Los Angeles. He then made his way to New York City and worked in a restaurant. For the next several years, he improved his English, found better paying jobs, and sent remittances home to El Salvador. His timing was good, as the passage of Immigration Reform and Control Act in 1986 gave him the opportunity to achieve legal status, and in 1995 he became a citizen. Ultimately he formed his own video production company and even pursued a university degree. That goal was interrupted in 2007 when he launched a campaign as mayor of his hometown, San Julián, in El Salvador, and won in 2008.

SOURCE: Gabriel Serrano, interviews with GBW

The flow of Central American migrants became a prominent political issue in the United States, in both the short and long term. They were seeking asylum with claims of persecution. As Gabriel's story shows (see text box, left), the impetus to leave and the passage itself were sometimes literally matters of life and death.

The problem was that the governments of El Salvador and Guatemala were U.S. allies, and the Reagan administration had expended considerable effort to insist they were democratic and upholding basic human rights. Those who fled, therefore, found it very difficult to do so legally. If the U.S. government were to admit the refugees were facing a "well-founded fear of persecution," the key requirement for granting asylum, it would be accepting the basic premise that the governments were repressive. Nicaraguan refugees, meanwhile, did not face the same difficulties, since they were leaving a country run by a government the U.S. had labeled as "Communist," so their emigration served a political purpose.

Meanwhile, Salvadorans and Guatemalans received help from many religious groups in the United States that were highly critical of U.S.

policy toward Central America, an attitude that sparked the ire of the U.S. government. In 1985, eight sanctuary workers were convicted of conspiracy and alien smuggling.[50] In response, activists filed a class action lawsuit against the U.S. government, *American Baptist Churches v. Thornburgh*, which would become known as ABC. It sought an end to prosecutions and to asylum decisions based on foreign policy preferences, and recognition that Salvadorans and Guatemalans deserved safe haven.

Beginning in 1990, the U.S. Congress finally recognized the problem and allowed asylum seekers the option of applying for Temporary Protected Status (TPS). The Justice Department also settled the ABC case out of court, and under the terms allowed Guatemalans and Salvadorans the right to apply for asylum under new rules. Approximately 240,000 were eligible and applied in the 1990s, as is very evident in Table 3.3, though the investigation of cases took years.

With a large backlog and no political incentive to grant asylum, most applications have remained unresolved, leaving tens of thousands of people effectively in limbo. Central American governments—especially El Salvador—have lobbied the U.S. government for continuation of TPS regularly since 1990. It has become a common strategy for Salvadoran presidents to visit the U.S. shortly after inauguration to discuss TPS, even to visit Salvadoran communities in the United States to encourage people to apply for TPS.[51] Thus far, it has remained a permanently temporary solution. People cannot leave the country without permission, they cannot apply for relatives to join them, and their time in the U.S. does not count toward citizenship requirements. For this reason and others, Salvadorans are the third most populous nationality among foreign-born Latin Americans in the United States, as you will recall from Table 2.1.

Demography intertwines with economic and political reasons to explain why Central American immigrants are not returning to their home countries even though the civil wars are over. There are too few employment opportunities, as a growing and youth-heavy population competes for a limited number of jobs. Free market reforms (such as privatizing state-owned industries) and free trade have also contributed to the uncertainty about employment, since the state is less able to shield vulnerable populations from foreign competition. In addition, the creation of social networks offers an additional inducement to stay in the United States.

Since Salvadorans were (and are) less likely to obtain asylum, they tended to become indebted to friends and family to pay the coyote.[52] The risk and expense of going back and forth is another incentive to work, pay off the debt, and remain in the United States.

Susan Coutin has estimated that between 1980 and 1992, more than a million Salvadorans came to the United States,[53] although Table 3.3 does not reflect quite such a high number, perhaps because many entered without inspection and have never received Temporary Protected Status. The total population was roughly 5.3 million. Along with Washington, D.C., Los Angeles was the most common destination, and the young men who arrived immediately faced serious obstacles. They were not well educated, but because of the civil war from which they escaped, many were well versed in weapons, and they immediately faced hostility from already existing gangs in Los Angeles. The most prominent Salvadoran gang to emerge was Mara Salvatrucha, also known as MS-13, which quickly became known for its criminal and extremely violent behavior. Starting in 1996, the U.S. government reacted to this violence by deporting noncitizens convicted of felonies with sentences over a year, and expanding the list of deportable offenses.[54] As increasing numbers of Salvadorans have moved to southern states from California and elsewhere, the gang problem has manifested itself in U.S. southern cities. In fact, the South has a higher fraction of non-Mexican Latin Americans than most of the rest of the United States.

Costa Rica is the Central American exception. This is partly because, at a time when its neighbors had very young and highly unstable populations, it was further along in its demographic transition, with characteristics more in line with the developed world.[55] Today, as in 1950, it has the highest life expectancy in Central America (indeed, slightly higher than the United States), and it has experienced a rapid and sustained fertility decline from nearly 7 children per woman in 1950 to less than 2—below replacement and, in fact, lower than in the United States. Demographically, it now resembles Europe more than Central America. A relatively strong economy and political stability (the military was abolished in 1948, and the country has suffered no coups since) have made it a magnet for neighboring countries, but it has also been able to absorb that labor, thus reducing the pressure to emigrate. Nicaraguans in particular have moved south into Costa Rica, taking jobs such as picking coffee.

Migration and the Caribbean

Caribbean countries have also experienced political upheaval. Cuba is the most famous example, as the revolution that swept Fidel Castro into power in 1959 has affected U.S. immigration policy toward Cubans ever since. Initially, many middle and upper class Cubans emigrated in response to Castro's reforms (which quickly were declared Marxist), with the state taking almost complete political and economic control of the country. By the 1970s, however, emigration was linked more directly to economic factors, which would increase after the Soviet Union eliminated its aid to Cuba in 1990 and 1991. As you will recall from Table 2.1, Cubans constituted the second—albeit a distant second behind Mexico—most populous foreign-born group from Latin America living in the United States.

Demographically, Cuba has become more European than its Caribbean neighbors, except of course Puerto Rico, which is part of the United States. Shortly after the Cuban revolution in 1959, the crude birth rate soared from 27 births per 1,000 population in 1958 to 37 per 1,000 in 1962. Cuban demographer Juan Perez de la Riva explained that after the revolution, rural unemployment disappeared, new opportunities arose in towns, and an exuberant optimism led to a lowering of the age at marriage and an abandonment of family planning.[56] It is probable that the emigration of so many Cubans to the United States did in fact create opportunities for those who stayed behind. Eventually, the birth rate in Cuba reestablished its prerevolutionary decline, facilitated by eased restrictions on abortion and increasing availability of contraceptives.[57] Perhaps not surprisingly,

Table 3.4 Growth of the Caribbean Countries Since 1900 (population in thousands)

Country	1900	1950	2000
Cuba	1,600	5,920	11,142
Haiti	1,294	3,221	8,573
Dominican Republic	600	2,427	8,744
Jamaica	720	1,403	2,589
Puerto Rico	986	2,218	3,834
Total	**5,200**	**15,189**	**34,882**

SOURCE: Data from Table 2.2.

given its established ties to the Soviet Union, Cuba's life expectancy and fertility are similar to Eastern European countries, although its fertility is still not quite as low. Nonetheless, the United Nations Population Division projects Cuba's population to be less in 2050 than in 2000, as shown in Table 3.4 and Figure 3.5.

The flow of Cubans to the United States has been steady, as shown in Table 2.5, and Castro, in fact, has been adept at using the threat of large-scale migration as leverage to extract policy concessions from the U.S. government and to demonstrate that he could unleash what has been termed a "demographic bomb."[58] In 1965, he announced that any Cuban who wished to leave could do so, which rid him of dissidents and demonstrated to the U.S. that he had the power to create a crisis at the U.S. doorstep. To protest the U.S. granting asylum to emigrants who had hijacked boats, and in response to an economic downturn, in 1980 Castro again announced that any Cuban could emigrate, and almost 100,000 people left Cuba in all manner of makeshift watercraft in what would be called the Mariel Boatlift. The administration of Jimmy Carter eventually agreed to negotiate migration policy, and again in 1984, President Ronald Reagan pledged to allow 20,000 Cubans to enter the U.S. annually.

Those agreements, however, were not always honored, especially since the United States government continued to accept Cubans who had committed crimes (such as hijacking) in the course of leaving the island. Castro therefore used the same strategy in 1994 as he had in 1965 and 1980: threaten mass emigration. Rhetoric over the *balseros* (rafters) crisis escalated quickly, and the administration of Bill Clinton decided that responding to Castro's demands was preferable to repeating the experience of the Mariel Boatlift.

2050	1950/1900	2000/1950	2050/2000
9,911	3.70	1.88	0.89
15,275	2.49	2.66	1.78
13,972	4.05	3.60	1.60
2,763	1.95	1.85	1.07
4,422	2.25	1.73	1.15
46,343	**2.92**	**2.30**	**1.33**

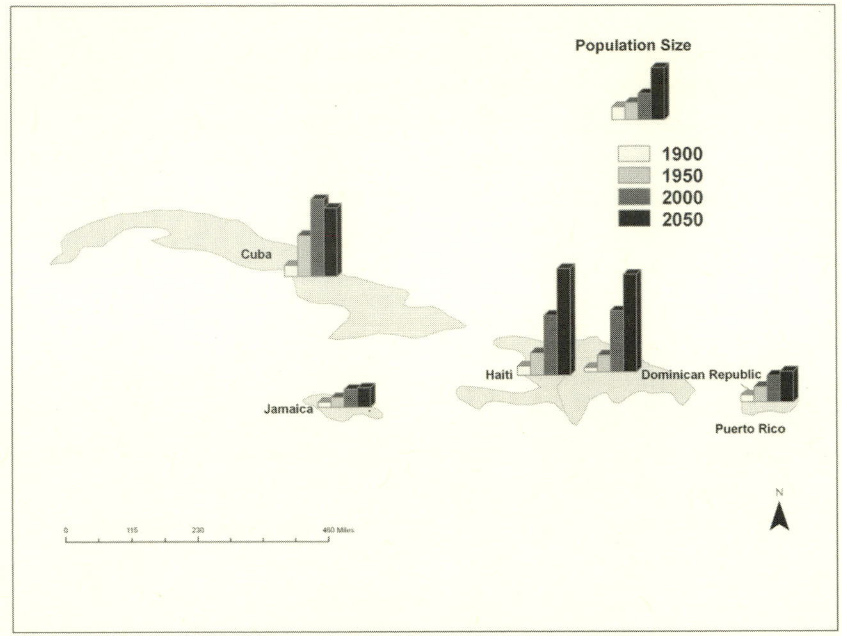

Figure 3.5
Population growth in the Caribbean, 1900–2050

SOURCE: Data from Table 3.4.

Negotiations with the Castro government yielded an agreement that Cuba would deter illegal immigration, and in return the United States would allow a *minimum* of 20,000 Cubans annually and would not allow rafters to enter the country. Soon dubbed the "wet foot, dry foot" policy, it differentiated between Cubans caught at sea (who were returned unless they could prove persecution) and those who reached U.S. land (who were allowed to stay). This contrasts sharply with the case of Haiti, where in 1993 the Clinton administration ordered that Haitians who reached land should be sent first to the U.S. naval base in Guantánamo Bay, Cuba, before being deported back to Haiti, while those caught at sea were sent back immediately.

Haitians began coming to the United States in appreciable numbers after 1957, when François "Papa Doc" Duvalier became president and created his own private militia to maintain power. By the end of the 1970s, between 5,000 and 10,000 Haitians a year were trying to reach the U.S. by boat.[59] Papa Doc was followed by his son, "Baby Doc," who ruled from the time of his father's death in 1971 until he was overthrown in 1986. The fall of the Duvalier dynasty accelerated the number of emigrants, which reached approximately 150,000 during the 1980s and 160,000 during the 1990s, as shown in Table 3.5.

Subsequent governments (most prominently that of Jean-Bertrand Aristide) have all suffered severe instability in a country already the poorest in the western hemisphere, and with a demographic profile more reminiscent of sub-Saharan Africa than of its Latin American neighbors. Haiti

Table 3.5 Immigrants Admitted to the United States from Each of the Caribbean Countries, by decade, 1820–2007

	Cuba	Dominican Republic	Haiti	Jamaica	Other Caribbean
1820 to 1829	0	0	0	0	3,061
1830 to 1839	0	0	0	0	11,792
1840 to 1849	0	0	0	0	11,803
1850 to 1859	0	0	0	0	12,447
1860 to 1869	0	0	0	0	8,751
1870 to 1879	0	0	0	0	14,285
1880 to 1889	0	0	0	0	27,323
1890 to 1899	0	0	0	0	31,480
1900 to 1909	0	0	0	0	100,960
1910 to 1919	0	0	0	0	120,860
1920 to 1929	12,769	0	0	0	70,713
1930 to 1939	10,641	1,026	156	0	6,229
1940 to 1949	25,976	4,802	823	0	14,593
1950 to 1959	73,221	10,219	3,787	7,397	21,037
1960 to 1969	202,030	83,552	28,992	62,218	50,443
1970 to 1979	256,497	139,249	55,166	130,226	127,712
1980 to 1989	132,552	221,552	121,406	193,874	120,725
1990 to 1999	159,037	359,818	177,446	177,143	131,243
2000 to 2007	185,574	210,310	154,311	132,952	91,181

SOURCE: Data from Table 2.2.

has the lowest life expectancy, highest infant death rate, and highest fertility rate of any country in the Americas. The numbers line up very much like countries in West Africa. Interestingly enough, the situation in Haiti is much more severe demographically and economically than it is in the Dominican Republic, with whom Haiti shares its island.

Unlike Cubans, Haitians have not been fleeing an ideological enemy of the United States, and as a result the U.S. response has been different. Asylum is much more difficult to obtain, and the vast majority of Haitians are repatriated, even if they had reached land. Concern about an exodus has prompted the U.S. government (regardless of party) to maintain stricter rules and to treat Haitians as economic, and not political, refugees.

Although the politics of Cuban and Haitian immigration have been high profile in recent years, particularly in south Florida, the issue has been of much less importance in the U.S. South outside of Florida. As a result, immigrants from the Caribbean will play a lesser role in subsequent chapters.

Migration and South America

Given the considerable distances and hazards of travel, until the latter part of the twentieth century relatively few South Americans ventured to the United States. Instead, there was significant internal migration within the subregion and, importantly, immigration from Europe into the "southern cone" (that is, Argentina, Brazil, Chile, and Paraguay, the southernmost countries of South America) during the nineteenth century. Spaniards, Germans, and Italians, in particular, made their way to the "new world" for many of the same reasons cited by those British who flocked to the United States, namely vast areas of arable land and large cities where new business could be created and money could be made. These influences are still indelibly stamped into the culture, architecture, cuisine, and even the military training (particularly the German influence in Chile) of southern cone countries.

Life was, however, harsh in terms of death rates, as was true everywhere in Latin America until the middle of the twentieth century. Arriaga estimated that life expectancy at birth in every South American country at the end of the nineteenth century was less than 30.[60] These were essentially premodern levels of mortality—a virtual "demographic hell."[61] Fertility rates had to be high simply to balance the treacherously high death rate. However, as we mentioned above with regard to Mexico, death rates began to decline in the 1930s, and the two decades after the end of World War II were genuinely miraculous in terms of increased life expectancy. Between 1945 and 1960, Latin Americans added nearly one year of life expectancy every calendar year.[62] Of course, with the still high fertility rates, this translated into rapid population growth, as shown in Table 3.6 and Figure 3.6. Brazil, which has always been South America's most populous country, has contributed disproportionately contributions—compare Table 3.2 and Table 3.6. Whereas in 1950, South America had only about two-thirds the number of people as the United States, by 2000, it had far exceeded the United States, and the gap is projected to be even larger by 2050.

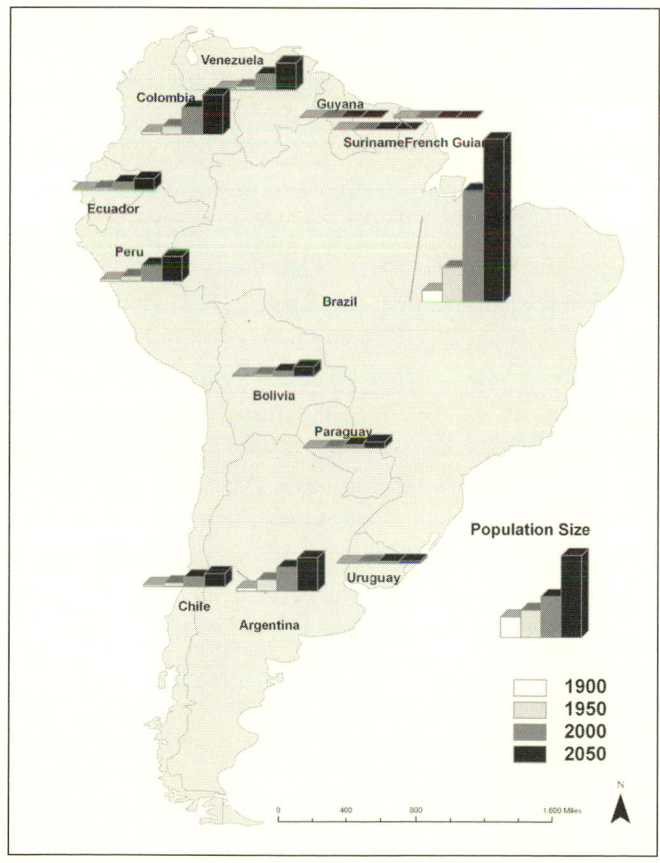

Figure 3.6 Population growth in South America, 1900–2050

Table 3.6 Growth of the South American Countries Since 1900 (population in thousands)

Country	1900	1950	2000
Argentina	4,542	17,150	36,896
Bolivia	1,766	2,714	8,317
Brazil	17,984	53,975	174,161
Chile	3,110	6,082	15,412
Colombia	3,894	12,568	41,683
Ecuador	1,272	3,387	12,306
French Guiana	33	25	165
Guyana	287	423	734
Paraguay	636	1,473	5,349
Peru	3,000	7,632	25,663
Suriname	82	215	436
Uruguay	943	2,239	3,318
Venezuela	2,445	5,094	24,402
Total	**39,994**	**112,977**	**348,842**

SOURCE: Data from Table 2.2.

Rapid population growth eventually translated into the need to find jobs outside South America because governments in the region were not dealing well with the changes taking place. Much of the out-migration was initially to Europe, even Asia, rather than the United States—often back to the countries from which ancestors had originally migrated. The movement of South Americans to the United States became more pronounced in the 1970s and 1980s for political reasons, as people fled repression and violence. A Brazilian coup in 1964 (democracy would not return until 1985) would be followed by military governments throughout the region, the most repressive of which were in Argentina (1966–1973 and 1976–1983), Bolivia (various, 1971–1982), Brazil (1964–1985), Chile (1973–1990), and Uruguay (1973–1985). In others, such as Colombia and Peru, political violence was associated not with military dictatorship but with guerrilla movements and government response to them. Indeed, these two countries have the greatest number of immigrants to the United States from South America, as shown in Table 3.7.

Some emigrants and exiles from these countries remained in Latin

2050	1950/1900	2000/1950	2050/2000
51,382	3.78	2.15	1.39
14,908	1.54	3.06	1.79
254,085	3.00	3.23	1.46
20,655	1.96	2.53	1.34
61,860	3.23	3.32	1.48
17,988	2.66	3.63	1.46
165	0.76	6.60	1.00
477	1.47	1.74	0.65
9,868	2.32	3.63	1.84
39,049	2.54	3.36	1.52
426	2.62	2.03	0.98
3,641	2.37	1.48	1.10
42,049	2.08	4.79	1.72
516,553	**2.82**	**3.09**	**1.48**

America, as Mexico and Venezuela were both stable and largely non-aligned ideologically, and many from the left were accepted into Cuba. Europe, the United States, and Canada, however, were common destinations. Unlike those leaving a country for economic or demographic reasons, political emigrants usually arrived with no intention to stay and with their attention riveted on politics in the country of origin. Because of the coercive circumstances of their departure, they also suffered high rates of depression, divorce, alcoholism, and suicide.[63]

Given the distance and weaker historical ties to the United States (compared with, for example, Mexico, Central America, and the Caribbean), South Americans came to the United States in relatively small numbers, and since the last South American dictatorship (in Chile) came to an end in 1990, the flow of political refugees has been reduced to a trickle (though more Venezuelans have been applying for asylum, following the expansion of socialism and the personal political influence of President Hugo Chávez). The political impact of South American immigrants in the United States has thus not been significant, at either the

Table 3.7 Immigrants Admitted to the United States from Each of the South American Countries, by decade, 1820–2007

	Argentina	Bolivia	Brazil	Chile	Colombia	Ecuador
1820 to 1829	—	—	—	—	—	—
1830 to 1839	—	—	—	—	—	—
1840 to 1849	—	—	—	—	—	—
1850 to 1859	—	—	—	—	—	—
1860 to 1869	—	—	—	—	—	—
1870 to 1879	—	—	—	—	—	—
1880 to 1889	—	—	—	—	—	—
1890 to 1899	—	—	—	—	—	—
1900 to 1909	—	—	—	—	—	—
1910 to 1919	—	—	—	—	—	—
1920 to 1929	—	—	4,627	—	—	—
1930 to 1939	1,067	50	1,468	347	1,027	244
1940 to 1949	3,108	893	3,653	1,320	3,454	2,207
1950 to 1959	16,346	2,759	11,547	4,669	15,567	8,574
1960 to 1969	49,384	6,205	29,238	12,384	68,371	34,107
1970 to 1979	30,303	5,635	18,600	15,032	71,265	47,464
1980 to 1989	23,442	9,798	22,944	19,749	105,494	48,015
1990 to 1999	30,065	18,111	50,744	18,200	137,985	81,358
2000 to 2007	37,113	16,782	89,163	15,564	180,000	84,353

SOURCE: Data from Table 2.2.

national or local level. As we will discuss, however, South Americans have more recently come to the United States for nonpolitical reasons, especially from Brazil.

U.S. Government Policy Responses Since the 1980s

Given the increased movement of people to the United States since the 1980s, how has the U.S. government reacted? The first major response took place in 1986, with the Immigration Reform and Control Act.

Guyana	Paraguay	Peru	Suriname	Uruguay	Venezuela	Other South America
—	—	—	—	—	405	
—	—	—	—	—	—	957
—	—	—	—	—	—	1,062
—	—	—	—	—	—	3,569
—	—	—	—	—	—	1,536
—	—	—	—	—	—	1,109
—	—	—	—	—	—	1,954
—	—	—	—	—	—	1,389
—	—	—	—	—	—	15,253
—	—	—	—	—	—	39,938
—	—	—	—	—	—	38,398
131	33	321	25	112	1,155	4,010
596	85	1,273	130	754	2,182	7
1,131	576	5,980	299	1,026	9,927	17
4,546	1,249	19,783	612	4,089	20,758	28
38,278	1,486	25,311	714	8,416	11,007	97
85,886	3,518	49,958	1,357	7,235	22,405	61
74,407	6,082	110,117	2,285	6,062	35,180	28
57,745	3,583	106,035	1,924	6,720	60,006	68

IRCA

Into the 1980s, public opinion polls showed a marked rise in restrictionist sentiment among Americans, and the public began to favor stricter immigration laws.[64] The end of the Vietnam War was followed by a large-scale influx of southeast Asian refugees, in addition to the increasing numbers of immigrants as a result of the 1965 amendments to the Immigration and Nationality Act. A generation of Americans that had grown up with very little experience of foreigners in their midst—only 5 percent of the population was foreign-born in 1970—was suddenly finding itself surrounded by strangers. Many of these strangers were undocumented immigrants from Mexico whose labor was still in demand, but for whom there were very few legal routes into the country. And just as the foreign-born population began to increase, so did the U.S.-born population of young people, driven by the baby boomlet of the 1970s. This was a perfect storm for a return to nativism.

Rhetoric took on the hue of natural disaster and warfare, with warnings of floods, inundation, hordes, and invasion, while President Reagan gave speeches about "losing control."[65] In this political context Senator Alan Simpson (Republican, Wyoming) and Representative Peter Rodino (Democrat, New Jersey) cosponsored the Immigration Reform and Control Act (IRCA). Technically, it amended the Immigration and Nationality Act, and its essential thrust was to provide a path toward citizenship for illegal immigrants who had remained in the United States since before January 1, 1982, and then to "shut the door" behind them by imposing penalties on companies that hired undocumented workers.

The rhetoric of congressional supporters also established a pattern that would recur, almost verbatim, over the next two decades. Following a "don't allow the perfect to become the enemy of the good" logic, members of Congress reasoned that *some* type of legislation must pass, or the immigration "problem" would simply become worse.

The emphasis on workplace enforcement created a stir; business groups protested, arguing that it imposed unfair burdens, essentially transforming them into de facto immigration agents. In response, Congress lowered the bar for determining whether a given document was real. Verification was as follows:

> (1) the employer to attest, on a form developed by the Attorney General, that the employee's work status has been verified by examination of a passport, birth certificate, social security card, alien documentation papers, or other proof; (2) the worker to similarly attest that he or she is a U.S. citizen or national, or authorized alien; and (3) the employer to keep such records for three years in the case of referral or recruitment, or the later of three years or one year after employment termination in the case of hiring.[66]

Thus, if an employer asked the employee if he or she was legally eligible for the job, then looked at the individual's documentation, the employer was in full compliance.

The passage of IRCA also transformed the Border Patrol. Although the total number of agents would not increase dramatically until the early 1990s, its role expanded. For example, it became more involved in drug enforcement. Border Patrol agents were deputized ("cross-designated") to enforce laws on drug and contraband smuggling, which had previously been the work of the Drug Enforcement Agency and the Customs Service.[67] That change also entailed permission to carry higher-powered weaponry, such as M-14 and M-16 rifles.

When he signed the IRCA legislation, President Reagan heralded it, saying it would "remove the incentive for illegal immigration by eliminating the job opportunities which drew illegal aliens here."[68] Even further:

> Future generations of Americans will be thankful for our efforts to humanely gain control of our borders and thereby preserve the value of one of the most sacred possessions of our people: American citizenship.[69]

As debate during subsequent administrations would reveal, however, very few would in fact be "thankful" for the effects of IRCA, and it cannot be said to have allowed the United States to "gain control" of its borders.

A few years later, yet another anti-immigrant backlash gained steam. In California, Governor Pete Wilson made a high-profile effort, in the form of Proposition 187 (which passed but was struck down by a federal judge), to deny undocumented immigrants access to any public services of any kind, including schools. Not all Republicans agreed with this idea. Significantly, Texas Governor George W. Bush publicly denounced Proposition 187.[70] That two Republican border governors arrived at opposite positions further highlights the lack of partisan cohesion on the issue. Governor (and later President) Bush's rhetoric was consistently sympathetic to Latino immigrants. Nonetheless, President Bill Clinton (1993–2001) believed that a hard line on immigration would protect him from charges of being "soft" as the 1996 presidential election neared.[71] The result was Operation Gatekeeper.

The core of Operation Gatekeeper was to decrease the number of illegal border crossings with a combination of patrols, technology, and fencing. In the four years after its implementation in 1994, the San Diego sector of the Border Patrol grew from 980 agents to 2,264; the number of INS inspectors from 202 to 504; fencing and walls from 19 to 45 miles in length; underground sensors from 448 to 1,214; and infrared scopes from 12 to 59.[72]

Other similar examples include Operation Hold-the-Line in El Paso (1993), Operation Safeguard in Arizona (1995), and Operation Rio Grande in south Texas (1997). Combined, they represented a new way of thinking about the border, with a much stronger emphasis on defining, delineating, then defending it.

Illegal Immigration Reform and Immigrant Responsibility Act of 1996

In 1994, the Republican Party surged politically and won majorities in both the House of Representatives and the Senate. A major element in the successful Republican electoral strategy was the Contract with America, the core of which was to cut government spending and reduce taxation. Immigrants immediately became a topic for debate, as they were portrayed as receiving government assistance without paying taxes. The Personal Responsibility and Work Opportunity Reconciliation (Welfare Reform) Act of 1996 denied legal immigrants access to most federal means-tested programs for five years and prohibited undocumented immigrants from receiving any federal or state benefits except for medical emergency, disaster relief, and immunizations, though in the following two years Congress quietly passed laws scaling back the most punitive of the measures.

The same year, President Clinton signed the Illegal Immigrant Responsibility and Immigration Reform Act, which was aimed at enhancing border security, increasing the size of the Border Patrol, and raising criminal penalties for companies that hired undocumented immigrants. It also required a legal immigrant wishing to sponsor family members to sign a document promising to support those family members at 125 percent or more of the poverty line and to prove having sufficient income. Despite a strong emphasis on enforcement and security, nothing in the legislation significantly affected the number of immigrants who could legally enter the country.

The Effects of Immigration Reform and the South

The Immigration Reform and Control Act coincided with the initiation of the increase of Latino immigration to the U.S. South. The irony is palpable. The legislation that was intended to bring immigrants out of the shadows and then prevent further illegal immigration actually encouraged more immigration and illegal activity beyond immigration, and brought immigrants to new parts of the country. The law had three key consequences—all of them unforeseen by its backers—that, when viewed with other economic, demographic, and political factors, explain how Latino migrants began arriving in the South.

First, it spawned a thriving black market for false documents. Since business owners needed only to make a good faith effort to examine documents, these documents had only to endure passing scrutiny. Soon, counterfeit social security cards could be found at local flea markets. If a manager was shown a reasonable-looking document, he or she could then plausibly claim that the company assumed the individual was in the country legally. It also encouraged subcontracting, as companies could avoid scrutiny by hiring other firms to do certain types of work. These smaller subcontracted firms were therefore in a position to reap the benefits—a steady stream of contracts—by assuming the risk.

Second, it provided an incentive for people to stay in the United States rather than move back and forth from their country of origin. As subsequent studies would reveal, IRCA's enforcement aspect (later augmented under the Clinton administration) did not deter anyone from crossing into the United States illegally, but it did discourage making the attempt more than once.[73] The pressures to emigrate remained as strong as ever, so the incentive to take the initial risk remained high. However, once in the United States, IRCA provided a strong disincentive to leave given the difficulties and dangers of trying to re-enter. Undocumented migrants were therefore more likely to stay longer than they would have in the past, given the risks of multiple crossings. Border enforcement effectively turned a pattern of circular migration into a pattern of permanent settlement in the United States—the exact opposite effect of what was intended.

Especially in the context of the worst recession in California in sixty years, which lasted from 1990 until 1993 and during which the state lost approximately 500,000 jobs, it was logical for workers there to look elsewhere for employment. If one had more difficulty finding work in the west, at the same time that the cost of living (especially housing) was increasing in the west, it was only natural to seek new opportunities in hitherto unexplored regions that might offer more propitious opportunities. Cities like Los Angeles and San Diego were crowded and expensive, and jobs were scarce.

Third, IRCA encouraged the development of new eastern points of entry, geographically closer to the South. With the construction of a fence at the popular San Diego–Tijuana border and the increase of border patrol agents, undocumented immigrants went east to the deserts of Arizona and to Texas. Thus, by the late 1980s, the stage was set for eastward movement. Three further factors brought people to the South, all of which we will discuss in Chapter Six.

Economically, southern metropolitan areas began a sustained boom. The "New South" attracted investment and company relocation, which in turn attracted new residents and their money. Economic development in the South was creating a demand for a wide range of products and services. Among other things, this meant manual labor. Buildings, houses, and apartments sprang up quickly, and construction companies eagerly hired Latino workers. Southern cities became popular destinations for the middle and upper classes of other states, which fueled a strong demand for landscaping, home and hotel cleaning, and home repair and remodeling. Jobs were available for both men and women, so the Latino immigrant experience quickly involved families. The economic situation spurred both family reunification and having children in the United States. Immigrants also quickly communicated to friends and family that jobs were plentiful, and social networks—so critical to the growth of immigrant communities—started to develop.

Demographically, the southeastern United States was similar to national trends, with an aging population. Since the economy was growing so robustly, the demand for labor outpaced the number of young workers.

Politically, the South did not have the same baggage as the west, so there was no built-in bias against Latin Americans. Of course, the racial tension between the white and black populations has remained a central political issue. The civil rights movement and court-ordered desegregation of the 1950s and 1960s was followed by often conflictive race relations as African Americans asserted their rights. The issue of race, however, was always binary, white and black, so the introduction of a new group offered both challenge and promise.

The challenge is that the region has little experience with migrants who have no history in the area and who in many cases do not speak English. Much more so than the rest of the country, however, the South has a recent and high-profile history of struggling against discrimination. This may lead to more promising ways of dealing with the inevitable cultural clashes between Latin American immigrants and the "traditional" populations of blacks and whites in the South. For now, the demographic fit between the demand for labor in the U.S. South and the supply of Latin Americans to fit those jobs may not yet be met with a social and political fit.

We have emphasized that Latin American migrants to the United States have largely arrived from countries with young populations in response to the demand for labor in a country that has been aging. These are the same dynamics that are playing out regionally in the Latin American migrant flow into the Southern states. This concept of demographic fit is an important component of the political demography approach that we take in this book, but we have not yet discussed it in detail. It is such an important idea that it deserves its own chapter, which is next.

CHAPTER FOUR

The Demographic Fit

AS YOUNG PEOPLE APPROACH ADULTHOOD, EVERY SOCIETY MUST deal with the question of whether there are enough resources to provide an economic livelihood for this new generation. If the answer is no, then we have the most obvious reason for the migration of young people. But a society may also turn that question around and ask whether there are enough young people to keep the economy going. If the answer to that question is no, then we have the most obvious reason for the recruitment of labor from elsewhere. Population dynamics in Latin America and the United States during the second half of the twentieth century found Mexico and Central America, in particular, answering the first question in the negative, and the United States answering the second question in the negative—producing the demographic fit that has encouraged massive migration to the United States.

By "demographic fit," we mean that the dents in crucial age groups in one society are matched by bumps in those age groups in another society. By "crucial age groups," we refer especially to the young adult ages—people who are in their economically active prime years. It is virtually unheard of, on the other hand, for a society to believe that it has too few older people, or too few people who might otherwise be dependent upon others. Deficiencies of people are almost always considered in terms of workers, since workers are what help to drive the economy, even in a "post-modern," "information-age," "globalized" world.

The Fit Between the United States and Latin America

For some time, the age structures of the United States and those in much of Latin America—especially Mexico and Central America—have shown a clear demographic fit. The United States economy has needed more young workers than natural population growth produced, whereas in the first decade of the twenty-first century, four Latin American countries had more than 60 percent of their populations under the age of 25—Guatemala (63), Haiti (61), Nicaragua (61), and Honduras (60). The entire list is shown in Table 4.1; note that fourteen Latin American countries have at least 50 percent of their population under age 25 and thus are prime candidates to be sending reinforcements to the United States. Moreover, those young Latin Americans are overwhelmingly in countries that are quite close to the United States—Mexico, obviously, but also in Central America and the Caribbean. All of these countries, but especially Mexico, would have an even higher percentage under 25 were it not for the earlier migration of young people out of the country and into the United States.

The United States and Latin America are not unique with respect to demographic fit. Virtually all of the rich countries of the "north" have very low death rates and very low birth rates, leading to rapidly aging populations, whereas almost all developing countries in the "south" have higher death rates and especially higher birth rates, which have produced younger age structures. The term "demographic divide" has sometimes been used to describe these differences, but from our perspective the importance of the divide is that it is bridged by migrants, since the bumps in the age structure of the south fit the demographic dents in the north. Thus, an aging population in Europe has migrants from many former colonies in Africa and Asia. On the other hand, an aging population in Japan has been accompanied by very little immigration. Japan has dealt with its demographic situation largely by shutting out migrants as best it can, because the official government policy is one of maintaining "ethnic homogeneity."[1]

Table 4.1 Percent of the Population Less than 25 Years Old, 2005, Latin America and the Caribbean, Compared to the United States

Latin American and Caribbean Countries	% under 25 in 2005	Country Population 2005
Guatemala	63	12,293,545
Haiti	61	8,308,504
Nicaragua	61	5,570,129
Honduras	60	7,326,496
Belize	58	287,730
Bolivia	57	8,989,046
Dominican Republic	53	9,183,984
El Salvador	52	6,822,378
Ecuador	52	13,547,510
Peru	51	28,302,603
Venezuela	51	25,730,435
Paraguay	51	6,506,464
Mexico	50	107,449,525
Jamaica	50	2,713,130
Colombia	49	43,593,035
Guyana	49	767,245
Panama	48	3,191,319
Costa Rica	48	4,075,261
Brazil	47	188,078,227
Argentina	44	39,921,833
Trinidad & Tobago	42	1,065,842
Chile	42	16,134,219
Uruguay	39	3,431,932
Barbados	34	279,912
United States	*34*	*301,621,157*
US Non-Hispanic Whites	*31*	*192,372,560*
US Hispanics	*46*	*42,603,116*
Canada	*31*	*32,271,000*

SOURCE: U.N. Population Division 2009. Data by ethnicity for the United States are from U.S. Census Bureau, American Community Survey 2005.

The demographic pattern in the United States is characterized by an aging baby boomer population that has not replaced itself through natural reproduction. The average baby boom woman had fewer than two children (the number needed to maintain the population at a stable level), and the birth rate in the United States dropped precipitously from about 1960 to 1980 and has remained low since then. Every country in Latin America has a percent of the population under 25 higher than the United States. Canada, a nation with high levels of immigration, does have a slightly lower percentage, although its 31 percent under 25 is matched by the non-Hispanic white population of the United States. At the same time, you can see in Table 4.1 that the Hispanic population in the United States has a very young age structure—almost as young as in Mexico—which will eventually contribute to an end to the demographic fit. That is, recent Mexican immigrants are filling the ranks of the young.

Figure 4.1 shows the changes in the population at each age group in Mexico and the United States between 1960, just prior to the change in U.S. immigration laws and about when the Bracero program was ending, and the year 2000—the period in which migration from Mexico to the United States accelerated. You can see that in 2000, the United States had about eleven million more people at ages 45 to 49 in the United States than there had been in 1960, but for every younger age group the increase was increasingly smaller. At ages 15 to 19, for example, there were less than four million more in 2000 than in 1960. These "holes" or "dents" in the age structure are important because American society had changed to accommodate the greater numbers of people (the baby boomers) with infrastructure (like schools and hospitals) and services, so when each successive age group after that was smaller than the previous one, a demand was created to fill in the gaps.

The potential supply of young people in Mexico to fill the gap is obvious from Figure 4.1. In Mexico there were nearly seven million more people aged 15 to 19 in 2000 than there had been in 1960. These young people were competing for places in Mexican society in 2000 that were not being vacated by older people because there were only four million more people aged 45 to 49, as an example, than there had been in 1960. Mexican society had not changed enough to accommodate the increase in the younger population (although NAFTA was designed to help that problem, as we discuss later in the chapter), so many of those young

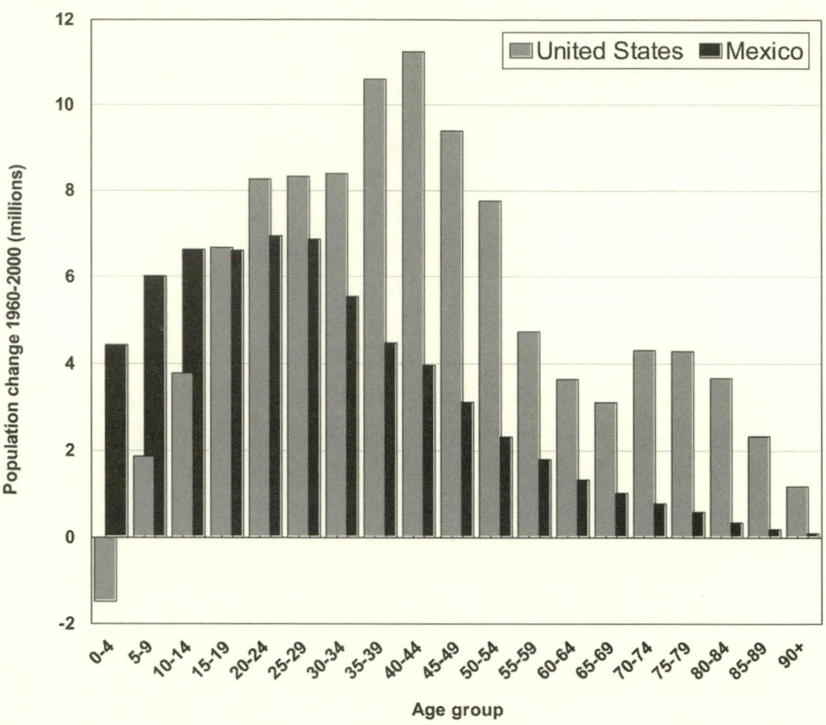

Figure 4.1
Changes in the population by age in Mexico and the United States, 1960–2000

SOURCE: Calculated from U.N. Population Division 2009.

people very naturally looked next door for opportunity. As one Mexican migrant put it,

> Over there [in the United States] you work and you get to eat from that. Better said, your whole family eats. Here, you work hard in hard jobs and sometimes you don't see any food come out of it. There are always dry spells in the job season that leave us with no money.[2]

Especially striking is the fact that in the forty years between 1960 and 2000, the population of Mexico grew from less than 40 million to more than 100 million, a massive increase of 63 million that was facilitated by an officially pronatalist (that is, a policy encouraging reproduction) government policy in Mexico until 1974. To be sure, the United States added 102 million during this same period, but in 1960 the U.S. population was already 179 million—nearly five times the size of Mexico. By 2000, the U.S. population was less than three times that of Mexico. The population of Mexico was growing most quickly in the youngest age groups, as shown in Figure 4.1, whereas in the United States these ages were growing much more slowly than were the middle ages. This is the essence of the demographic fit—the United States age structure was being depleted at the younger ages, while right next door, the Mexican age structure was expanding at those younger ages.

The changes in the U.S. age structure were almost entirely a consequence of demographic shifts within the politically and economically dominant ethnic group, non-Hispanic whites. As can be seen in Figure 4.2, Asians and Blacks experienced a little more growth at the middle ages than at the younger ages (as they too experienced declines in fertility), but the dramatic shifts occurred within the white non-Hispanic population. Although there are millions fewer non-Hispanic whites at the younger ages, there were millions more at the older ages in 2000 than there were in 1960. This has presented a problem for older Americans: Who is going to keep the economy going and pay the taxes that are needed to maintain the health and lifestyle of an increasingly larger number of older people? This question keeps being asked in debates about the funding of Social Security and Medicare, but it rarely surfaces in the immigration debate, perhaps because older people tend to be more opposed to immigration than younger people, so politicians may be unwilling to tie Social Security and Medicare to immigration. Older Americans are generally not receptive to the idea that more immigration is better under any circumstances, since immigration entails embracing unfamiliar "others." The same issues exist in Europe and Japan, where aging populations have created holes in the age structure that threaten the funding of their old age pensions, yet few people in Europe and East Asia seem to want the holes in the labor force to be filled by immigrants.

In essence, the decline in the number of younger non-Hispanic whites in the United States has created a vacuum into which immigrants have flowed. Latin Americans, and mostly Mexicans, have ineluctably responded. Although fertility has recently declined substantially in Mexico, and to a lesser degree in Central America, these declines are much

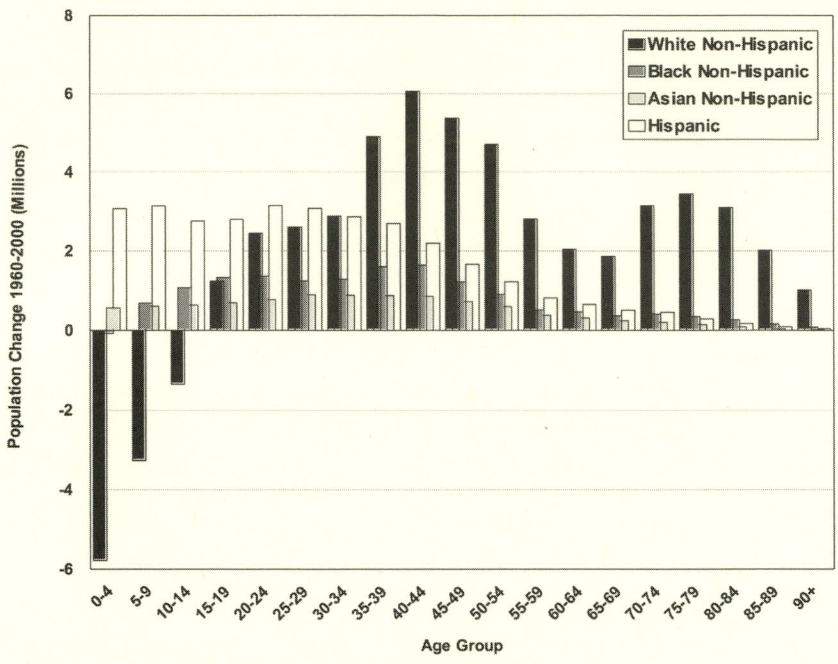

Figure 4.2
Changes in the population by age in the United States by major racial/ethnic groups, 1960–2000

SOURCE: Calculated from U.N. Population Division 2009.

more recent than those in the United States. Between 1960 and 2000, the Mexican population added nearly as many young people as the U.S. non-Hispanic white population was losing. Obviously, not all of those people migrated, but many did, and this cohort and its children who were born in the United States after their parents' immigration are helping to fill in the younger ages in the United States. The size and scope of the demographic fit shown in Figure 4.1 is, in truth, partly obscured by the fact that the population of the United States in 2000 included migrants from Mexico and their children, while, of course, the population of Mexico was less than it might otherwise have been had the migration not taken away millions of young people.

The demographic "replacement" of non-Hispanic whites by Hispanics in the United States can be seen in Figure 4.2, which compares the change in the number of Hispanics in the United States at each age with the number of non-Hispanic whites at each age. At each of the younger ages, the decline in the number of non-Hispanic whites is nearly matched by the increase in the number of Hispanics. Figure 4.2 also shows that the decline in the number of young white non-Hispanics has not been compensated by a rise in the number of Blacks or Asians, but by the increase in the number of Hispanics. In 1960, 45 percent of the non-Hispanic white U.S. population was under the age of 25, but by 2005 that percentage had dropped to 31 (see Table 4.1). The void was there to be filled by immigrants from countries like Mexico with high percentages of young people looking for jobs.

A Longer View of the Demographic Fit with Mexico

We have emphasized the well-known demographic fact that migration is largely the province of the young, and that is an important reason for the demographic fit between the United States and Mexico. The 15–24 age group is particularly prone to migration, and Figure 4.3 shows the average annual rate of growth, in percent, of the population aged 15–24 for Mexico and the United States for a century of five-year time periods, starting with the 1950–1955 period and projecting the population forward to the middle of this century. As we discussed in Chapter Three, labor shortages in the United States during World War II were the major impetus for the Bracero program (1942–1964), and these labor shortages had been a consequence both of men being deployed for war and of the low birth rate in the United States that resulted from the Depression. The low U.S. birth rate just before and during the war meant that the number of people aged 15–24 was still declining in the early 1950s. In Mexico, however, the drop in the death rate starting in the late 1930s, without an accompanying decline in birth rate, meant that the 15–24 age group was growing at a rate of more than 2.5 percent per year. This demographic fit encouraged the maintenance of the Bracero program during this time because employers clamored for workers. There were too few young men in the United States, and so labor was imported, albeit temporarily, from Mexico.

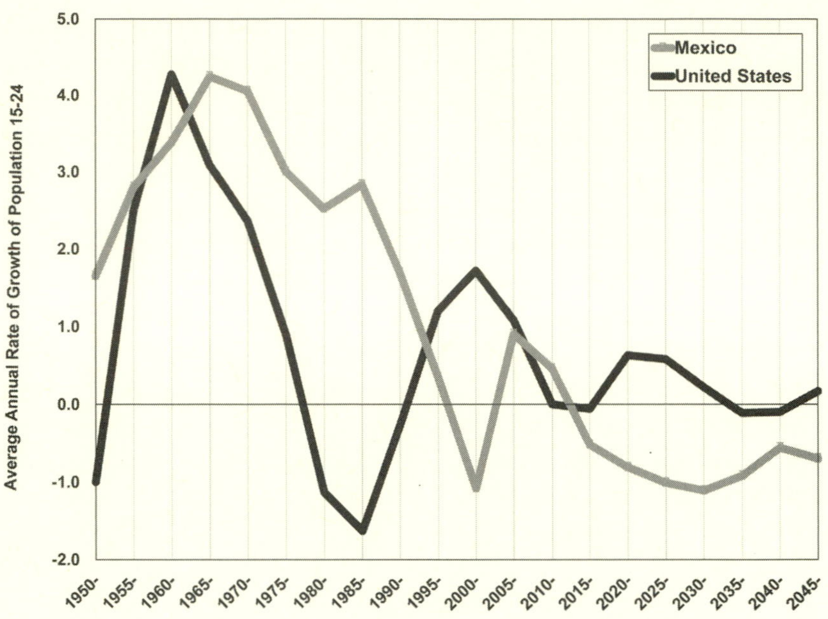

Figure 4.3
The average annual rate of growth of the population aged 15–24, Mexico and the United States, 1950–2050

SOURCE: Calculated from U.N. Population Division 2009.

By 1955–1960 time period, the early baby boomers in the United States were starting to move into the 15–24 age range, and by the 1960–1965 time period, this age group was actually growing more rapidly in the United States than in Mexico. It cannot be a coincidence that the end of the Bracero program came about at exactly the same time as this dramatic demographic shift from fit to no-fit. The labor shortage was shrinking. But this period of no-fit was short-lived, although no one anticipated the end of the baby boom and the steep drop in U.S. birthrates that followed. After the fact, it was decided that the baby boom officially ended in 1964, but that wasn't obvious until several years later.[3]

The U.S. baby boom was followed unexpectedly by the baby bust, so the rate of growth of the 15–24 age group declined steady from the 1965–1970 period through 1990. During most of this period, the rate of growth of the young adult age group remained high in Mexico, and not until the 1985–1990 period did the fertility rate decline in Mexico, which began in the 1970s, start to show its effects in a decreased rate of growth of the 15–24 age group. It is also no coincidence that the period in the chart with a consistent gap between the United States and Mexico in the growth of the 15–24 age group is also the period of most rapid migration of Mexicans to the United States. Despite changes in the U.S. immigration laws in 1965, which for the first time put a numerical limit on the number of legal migrants from the Western Hemisphere, the influx of migrants in the 1990s was enormous, aided to be sure by changes in immigration law in 1996.

By the beginning of the twenty-first century, the demographic fit that pushed immigration levels in the 1990s was much less in effect, and there are two complementary reasons for this: (1) declining fertility in Mexico has slowed the rate of growth of the young adult population; and (2) the previous high rates of immigration of young adults from Mexico to the United States produced a large number of children of immigrants, who have helped to increase the rate of growth of the 15–24 age group in the United States. These trends suggest that the era of demographic fit between the United States and Mexico may now be coming to a close, and that future migration is most apt to be a consequence of the longer-term economic fit between the two countries—young people in Mexico and elsewhere in Latin America seeking higher paying jobs in the United States that they lack at home. A slow rate of population growth in Latin America means a slower flow of people, but the flow is unlikely to stop.

It is probable that the diminishing demographic fit, in the presence of continued underemployment in Mexico and Central America, contributes importantly to the contentiousness of the current policy environment in the United States regarding immigration. There is still a considerable supply of surplus labor among young people in Mexico and Central America, but the demand for this labor in the United States—although still present—is going down, not up.

However, the end of the demographic fit should also mean that the Mexican labor pool, in particular, will be smaller, thereby increasing the chances that a given individual in Mexico will find employment in Mexico, assuming—and this is no sure assumption—that the Mexican economy does not contract. But this is what the Mexican government had in mind when it created family planning policies and launched a public relations campaign including commercials claiming "the small family lives better."[4] That logic has been the driving force of fertility decline in many countries, including the United States.

Mexico is a large country, of course, and a lower birth rate and the subsequent change in the age structure has not occurred evenly in all regions. It has taken place most quickly in the more urban central and northern parts of Mexico, but change has been slower in the southern, rural, and more heavily indigenous areas. Data from the U.S. Border Patrol reveal a shift in the pattern of origin of detainees from Mexico, with increasing proportions of them coming from the southern states of Mexico where birth rates are the highest and the economy is the weakest.[5] Mexico's southern neighbor, Guatemala, is the most populous country of Central America (except for Mexico, of course—which is either in North America or Central America, depending on who you talk to), and as shown earlier in Table 4.1, it has the youngest population in all of Latin America. Guatemalans move to Mexico to find work, and then many look farther north to the United States.

As we have already suggested, the decline and eventual end of the demographic fit does not mean immigration will end. We also noted that other factors—especially economic and political—also play crucial roles in creating incentives for people to make the trek to the United States from Latin America. Those incentives will not disappear, as Latin American economies will remain weaker than the U.S. economy, free market policies will continue to affect rural populations, and political decisions made by Latin American governments as well as the U.S. federal and local governments will influence individuals' calculations about migration.

Further, some types of jobs will remain relatively difficult to fill. Jobs that require intense (and sometimes very unpleasant) physical exertion, are by nature only seasonal, and/or offer no career opportunity, but yet are still critical to the country's economy will very likely still be available. The level of employer demand, however, may at least diminish. In poultry processing, for example, in the past decade about a hundred workers have died and another 300,000 have been injured. At the House of Raeford Farms in eastern North Carolina, thirty chickens come down the line every minute, and they must be quickly gutted, chopped, and sliced.[6] Korina Zorita knew the dangers, but the job paid well enough that she could send $150 back to Mexico every month. Eventually, however, she had to quit because of severe hand and back pain. She was unable even to straighten her fingers. These jobs are the foundation of a huge industry, and their workers are primarily immigrants who cycle in and out because of the hazards.

Economic Factors and Immigration

Demography, then, is very important, but it does not constitute the *only* variable for understanding Latin American migration to the United States. We need also to note the economic and political factors that have contributed to the large increase of Latino immigrants in the past several decades, as well as the political reaction in the United States.

The connection between economic policies and immigration reveals a curious disjuncture between official rhetoric and empirical outcomes. With regard to the former, conventional wisdom is straightforward not only for U.S. policy makers, but also within Latin America itself: Free market–oriented policies, which entail a reduced government role in the economy and greater economic integration between countries, will foster economic growth in Latin America and thereby create employment opportunities, which in turn will give would-be immigrants the option to remain at home. Given the difficulty and risk in reaching the United States, many will take that option to stay home if it is viable. The relationship between economic growth rates and a reduction in emigration is viewed as constant and positive. As President George W. Bush (2001–2009) said in a 2006 interview, "one of the jobs of leadership is to remind people about the benefits, that trade equals jobs, and jobs means people have a chance to realize hopeful dreams."[7]

Disentangling the causal relationships, however, is no simple task. For one thing, we must always remember that the rapid growth of the young population in Latin America means that these economic changes must be significant. Jobs need to appear quickly and in large numbers. Furthermore, the emphasis on free trade is particularly tricky. Free trade is characterized by the elimination of all barriers to trade between countries. The most prominent barrier is a tariff, or tax on imports, but others include government subsidies, import quotas, and import/export licenses. These barriers are intended as shields for particular domestic industries to protect them from foreign competition. So if a previously protected industry must suddenly face foreign competition, it may well have to lay off workers, thus making the unemployment problem worse. If those workers could then go wherever the jobs might be, the problem could be less serious, but that would involve freedom of migration, which policymakers in the United States are unlikely to embrace. Lacking that freedom of legal movement, workers move anyway, but without authorization.

The logic of policy makers in the United States is that the elimination of those trade barriers will decrease undocumented immigration from Latin America by increasing economic growth in Latin America and therefore boosting investment in those economic areas. That investment, in turn, fosters entrepreneurship and job creation. The greater availability of jobs will subsequently change the context for an individual's decision about migration. Since employment is available at home, there is no need to emigrate. Former Mexican President Carlos Salinas (1988–1994) argued that Mexico should be able to export tomatoes rather than tomato pickers.[8] Currently it exports both.

The free trade logic, however, is not so clear cut. As Douglas Massey and others have argued, "The entry of markets and capital-intensive production into nonmarket or premarket societies disrupts existing social and economic arrangements and brings about a displacement of people from customary livelihoods, thus creating a mobile population of workers who actively search for new means of sustenance."[9] Small farming, for example, is deeply affected because competing against large multinational companies is so difficult. That farmer may well decide it is more rational to sell his or her services abroad.

Other researchers have also found a positive correlation between free trade with Mexico and increased migration.[10] Thus the shift from state-led development, where the government actively protects certain industries, and where there are many small farms, to market-driven and capital-intensive (rather than labor-intensive) strategies, such as free trade agreements, disrupts local economies. Especially in the short term, this is inevitable. Free trade agreements are intended to keep governments out of the economy as much as possible, which means the state is not in a position to create new jobs to replace those that disappear due to foreign competition. It takes time, however, for new types of jobs to appear, and for workers to be available and trained to take these jobs. Further, they are not necessarily located near the areas where jobs were lost. In the meantime, workers migrate, either internally or internationally, and once gone, they may never return.

In the case of Mexico, for example, the North American Free Trade Agreement stipulated that by January 2008 (fourteen years after the agreement went into effect) all barriers to the trade of corn would be eliminated. Approximately one-quarter of the Mexican population makes a living by farming, and the majority of these farmers live in poverty. Therefore, many Mexican farmers using traditional, nonmechanized farming practices now must compete with agribusiness—large companies with vast landholdings, using machine-intensive cultivation methods. The corporate farms inside or outside Mexico can grow corn more cheaply than traditional farmers and thus drive down the price of corn, potentially forcing the traditional farmers out of business. Corn exporters in Iowa, for example, have benefited from exporting not only corn but also machinery for Mexican businesses to mechanize further.[11]

From a macroeconomic perspective, this shift simply reflects comparative advantage, which in the long run should foster the greatest economic efficiency, competition, and ideally, sustainable jobs. Capitalism will encourage entrepreneurship and investment, which in turn will create new jobs and force companies to keep prices relatively low. All of these things are positive for national economic growth and for the consumer. As such, they should be a disincentive to migrate to the United States (or any other country). As we have already discussed, migration is a difficult decision most people would rather not make. If there are new jobs to be had, then farmers should logically move to where those jobs are located within their own country.

From a microeconomic perspective, namely the decisions being made at the household level, both the stakes and risks associated with moving are high. The straightforward logic of moving to where new jobs are located often makes little sense for a variety of reasons, not the least of which is simply not knowing where such employment opportunities are. Some farmers may decide to continue subsisting, growing mostly enough for consumption. Many others will migrate to cities with the expectation that jobs will be more plentiful there. As cities within a country swell in population, the competition for jobs becomes more fierce, and the incentive to migrate internationally increases.

An optimistic argument is that the split between theoretical propositions and empirical reality may narrow over time. Once Mexico weathers the short-term upheavals caused by the elimination of trade barriers, and job creation continues in urban areas in the context of decreased growth of the young population, then fewer and fewer Mexican citizens will choose to migrate out of the country. The initial disruption would be replaced by steady job growth, and Mexican workers would gradually adapt to it. If this happens—and it might—it will have been facilitated by the dramatic decrease of the younger population in Mexico, as we saw in Figure 4.3.

This issue is not confined to Mexico. The Central American Free Trade Agreement—which includes Costa Rica, El Salvador, Guatemala, Honduras, Nicaragua, and the Dominican Republic, and is often referred to as CAFTA-DR—was first ratified by El Salvador in 2006, and subsequently by the other countries. Like Mexico, many of these countries have large segments of their populations engaged in small-scale agriculture, which will be affected by free trade. Most also have established migrant streams to the United States, so at least in the short term, it is likely that disruption will encourage emigration to some extent.

In the long term, though, the picture is more optimistic when we take into account the fact that the relationship between economic growth and migration has a powerful demographic component. As family wealth increases, the incentive to have more children decreases. Parental concern about being taken care of in old age is lessened, and enjoyment of disposable income makes it less likely that parents will take on the burden of a large family. As a consequence, even if migration were to decrease as economic growth increases, over the long run this will also be correlated with decreased fertility, which ultimately decreases the competition for scarce jobs. This is the story of the United States, Canada, Western Europe, and Japan, and explains why relatively few people migrate out of those places.

Demography and U.S. Politics

Demography has a direct and significant impact on politics and policies of all kinds. As demographic factors change, so do public perceptions of migration and, in turn, the policy responses of government officials. For example, vacancies in the labor force will compel businesses to pressure policy makers to relax immigration restrictions to allow a new flow of foreign workers. In turn, if the sociodemographic characteristics of those immigrants (race/ethnicity, religion, language, educational levels, and so forth) attract negative attention in the receiving country, public pressure can mount to turn off the immigration spigot. U.S. immigration policy has routinely had to contend with the competing pressures of the economy and society.

The reality of the demographic fit means that the likely effects of U.S. immigration policy on the American economy can be predicted with considerable confidence. Since immigrants from Latin America are still filling the labor gap (even if the gap is diminishing), any policy that attempts to limit the ability of people to join the U.S. labor force will have one or both of the following two consequences. First, it will encourage more inventive (and more dangerous and expensive) ways for illegal immigrants to fill the gap. In practice this has most prominently meant crossing the border in the desert with a coyote. Second, such a policy will result in higher prices if (a) output falls due to insufficient labor, or (b) wages must be increased to attract domestic workers. Over the long term, if those prices remain very high, then the secondary impact will be either inflation (if consumers agree to pay), bankruptcy (if imports replace the product), or mechanization (only if the product is conducive to reduced human labor input).

Thus far, we have only anecdotal evidence to determine what combination of these factors is currently present in the mix of factors influencing migration from Latin America to the United States. Since no enforcement efforts have been successfully implemented in the past, except for very short periods of time, we also cannot use history as a guide. Especially in the wake of the inability to pass immigration reform during the George W. Bush administration, the federal government has focused more on employer raids and border security, while state and local governments have passed laws intended to deter undocumented immigrants from obtaining employment (a topic addressed in more detail in Chapter Six).

Additionally, the federal government has not streamlined or increased the quotas for the H-2A program, which is the "temporary agricultural program established as a means for agricultural employers who anticipate a shortage of domestic workers to bring nonimmigrant foreign workers to the U.S. to perform agricultural labor or services of a temporary or seasonal nature."[12] As a result, even legal workers can be difficult to find for farmers who need seasonal labor at specific times of year. In 2008, Secretary of Homeland Security Michael Chertoff acknowledged that the process had "unnecessarily burdensome restrictions" and the government was proposing possible changes to alleviate them.[13] In 2007, reports emerged that California growers were increasingly moving production to Mexico because of labor shortages.[14] The same year, South Carolina and North Carolina slaughterhouses found it difficult to find and maintain a sufficient workforce after immigration raids.[15] In March 2008, Pennsylvania's largest tomato producer announced he would stop producing tomatoes and pumpkins, and would cut corn production because of a lack of labor.[16] In Vermont, the Agriculture Secretary acknowledged the presence of illegal workers, but police have policies not to bother them about immigration issues because the labor is so badly needed.[17] It reached a point where lawmakers in both Arizona and Colorado proposed their own state-run guest worker programs.[18] Such proposals are only symbolic in nature, because the federal government has never granted such a right to the states, but they reflect the perception of labor scarcity in the face of federal inaction on and antagonism toward legal guest worker programs.

Nonetheless, other studies refute the need for guest workers, arguing that fruit and vegetable production has been rising, that prices are not going up, and that American families have not increased the amount they spend daily on fruits and vegetables.[19] Meanwhile, the Congressional Research Service released a study in 2008 that concluded the following:

> Trends in the agricultural labor market generally do not suggest the existence of a nationwide shortage of domestically available farm workers, in part because the government's databases cover authorized and unauthorized workers. While nonfarm employment generally has increased thus far in the current decade, farm jobs generally have decreased. The length of time hired farm workers are employed has changed little or fallen over the years as well. Their unemployment rate has varied slightly and remains well above the U.S. average. Underemployment among farm workers also remains substantial. In addition, the earnings of farm workers relative to other private sector employees has changed little over time.
>
> This assessment does not preclude the possibility of labor shortages in particular geographic areas at particular times of the year. Some statistical evidence suggests that California growers experienced a tighter labor market in July 2007 compared to peak harvest season a year earlier. It nonetheless appears that the offer of larger wage increases than those of employers in other industries

> contributed to there being sufficient (authorized and unauthorized) workers available to enable California growers to increase employment on their farms in the year ended July 2007.[20]

Demography would suggest, as the Congressional Research Service argues, that as long as unauthorized workers are included, then there may not be a widespread shortage of workers. Undocumented foreign workers continue to fill the labor holes left by the relative scarcity of young (and willing) workers in the United States. This implies that, despite enforcement efforts, the supply of undocumented workers still manages to meet the demand of American businesses. Indeed, a cynic might say that the level of enforcement is just right, since it leads to the appropriate supply of undocumented labor. Regional variation may be related to other factors like local enforcement or even wage levels. Further, as mentioned, as the demographic fit gradually comes to an end, worker shortages will also become more rare as long as wages are reasonable.

The agricultural worker problem is complicated by the seasonality of the work, and by the fact that NAFTA leads to competition from Mexican producers who are likely to be paying lower wages than workers expect to receive in the United States, thus dampening the wages paid by U.S. producers who have to remain competitive to stay in business. These are among several reasons why immigrant workers are found in so many jobs outside of agriculture. According to indirect estimates made by the Pew Hispanic Center, the construction industry employs more unauthorized immigrants than any other industry, followed by the leisure and hospitality industry. Construction and the leisure and hospitality industries combined account for the employment of about 40 percent of all short-term unauthorized workers, followed by building maintenance, cleaning and landscaping, manufacturing, wholesale and retail, education and health services and—lastly—agriculture.[21]

Determining the precise impact of immigration on prices is also extremely difficult. Inflation has many causes, and the rise in oil prices—resulting from a host of different factors—plays a central role because the entire economy is energy dependent, and oil is the main energy source. Especially for agricultural goods, prices also depend upon supplies transported from foreign countries that have free trade agreements with the United States (such as avocados from Mexico or grapes from Chile). Also, the publicized examples of labor scarcity may be at least partially offset by businesses that continue to employ undocumented workers but are not raided by the Department of Homeland Security.

Immigration and Public Policy

Despite criticism from advocates of immigration restriction, since the passage of the Immigration Reform and Control Act (IRCA) in 1986, U.S. policy has acceded—either formally or informally—to the demographic fit. The purpose of IRCA was to provide amnesty and legalization avenues for many immigrants then living in the United States, and to penalize businesses that hired workers illegally in the future, as well as increasing border patrol enforcement to limit future migration. The quotas for legal workers, however, were insufficient, and therefore not only did illegal immigration continue, but it actually increased because of the demand for labor—as noted earlier in the chapter—until the subprime mortgage crisis led to recession in late 2008. At the time that IRCA was passed, some four million unauthorized immigrants were estimated to live in the United States. IRCA legalized about 1.5 million of them, so there was a temporary drop in the number of undocumented immigrants.[22] But then the number increased dramatically in a nearly linear fashion from about 1990 through 2005, when it hit eleven million. The number has grown more slowly since then. Under pressure from business leaders to maintain the flow of labor, Congress ensured that employer enforcement would be lax, regardless of the provisions built into IRCA. In particular, the law would only apply to businesses that "knowingly" hired an undocumented worker. Instead of stemming illegal immigration, the laws facilitated the growth of a large and thriving black market for forged documents.

As it turns out, however, some of those documents, such as social security numbers and legal resident visas (green cards), actually belonged to other people, and this allowed the U.S. government to attempt to prosecute the holders of such documents with identity theft, with conviction leading to a speedy deportation. Thus, people were arrested not for being in the country illegally, but for possessing stolen documents. The push for using these "real" documents, however, has come from the fact that employers can be punished if they hire someone whose Social Security number is not found in the database of valid Social Security numbers. However, in 2009, the U.S. Supreme Court ruled that a person could not be prosecuted for the more serious charge of identity theft (as opposed to the less serious charge of possessing stolen documents) without proof that they knew that the identification number belonged to a real person.

The Immigration Reform and Welfare Reform Acts of 1996 increased the size of the border patrol, funded greater border security measures, and limited the scope of government social programs to which unauthorized immigrants would have access. Given demographic forces, however, workers continued to come and to find jobs. In fact, unemployment rates among Latin American immigrants tend to be low (though it increased across all groups after the 2008 economic crash). For example, Rakesh Kochhar and colleagues note that Mexican migrants who have been in the United States more than six months have an unemployment rate of 5 percent,[23] almost exactly the national average and generally considered full employment. Despite the enforcement measures of the 1996 law, which focused especially on the twin-city areas of San Diego/Tijuana and El Paso/Juarez, workers continued to enter without authorization by shifting their crossings to mountain and desert wastelands, which are generally more dangerous than crossing near large metropolitan areas.[24] Further, government enforcement of existing law remained just as loose as before. Thus, in both 1986 and 1996, demography and economy trumped legislation and enforcement.

Immigration Legislation in the Post-9/11 Era

Early in 2001, President George W. Bush proposed a new immigration policy, the centerpiece of which would be a temporary worker program (TWP), popularly known as a guest worker program, to replace outdated and clearly insufficient quotas. The effects of 9/11 shelved the proposal until 2005 (though he made brief mention of it in January 2004). In the wake of 9/11, the Bush administration shuffled bureaucracies, eliminating the Immigration and Naturalization Service (INS) in 2003, splitting its responsibilities among three new bureaucracies,[25] and placing all under the new Department of Homeland Security.

After President Bush's reelection in 2004, he brought immigration reform to the fore once again. The highest profile legislation in the Senate was initially S. 1033, the Secure America and Orderly Immigration Act, introduced in May 2005 by Senator John McCain (and more commonly dubbed "McCain-Kennedy").[26] The centerpiece of this bill was also a temporary worker program that would initially accommodate up to 400,000 workers, with flexibility to increase if demand remained high.

Workers could stay for three years, with the option of renewing for three more. National registries of employers and workers would be developed, and employers would advertise for a given position, with U.S. citizens being given first refusal. Jobs would then go to registered guest workers. Punishments for infractions would be financial for employers (between $2,000 and $5,000) and deportation for workers. Lacking sufficient political support, the bills were postponed in 2006 until the next congressional session, and instead President Bush signed the Secure Fence Act, intended only to build seven hundred miles of border fence, though it has been plagued by controversy over environmental impact, local political opposition, and lawsuits.

For supporters and opponents alike, the McCain-Kennedy bill became synonymous with comprehensive immigration reform. Subsequent proposals—all unsuccessful to date—used it as a foundation and maintained a similar structure of temporary workers combined with more focus on border security and sanctions. Although President Bush mentioned a temporary worker program numerous times over the first few years of his presidency, he did not offer it as a concrete proposal until February 2006 for the 2007 fiscal year budget. The budget proposal noted that the "U.S. economy has legitimate needs for foreign workers," an argument advanced numerous times by different administration officials over the following months.[27] That "need," of course, is directly correlated to demographic shifts related to the retiring baby boomers in the United States. In 2006, President Bush also called for an expansion of the H-1B temporary (three-year) visa program, which is for occupations requiring more education and training, such as scientists and engineers. In addition, the administration extended temporary protected status for 300,000 Salvadoran, Honduran, and Nicaraguan workers who had been in the country illegally, which in September 2008 was extended for another eighteen months.

There was (and is) considerable opposition to a temporary worker program, most prominently from House Republicans such as Duncan Hunter (California, now retired; although his son won his open Congressional seat and shares his father's view on this issue), James Sensenbrenner (Wisconsin), and Tom Tancredo (Colorado). Sensenbrenner sponsored H.R. 4437, the Border Protection, Antiterrorism, and Illegal Immigration Control Act, which passed the House in December 2005 but was subsequently defeated in the Senate.[28] The legislation rejected the notion that a temporary worker program is necessary at all, and instead centered on enforcement as a means of deporting current illegal immigrants and of deterring such migration in the future. It is perhaps noteworthy that Rep. Hunter was opposed to NAFTA (and can thus be described as isolationist when it comes to the global economy) and was an important force behind the fences already built along the U.S.-Mexico border near his congressional district in San Diego (and can thus be described as isolationist when it comes to immigration). The essence of this argument is that demography is irrelevant and that legal immigrants (in small numbers) and U.S. citizens should be able to fill all available jobs.

After the November 2006 congressional elections, Democrats controlled both houses, and Senate Majority Leader Harry Reid reintroduced a variant of McCain-Kennedy. Had it passed, the Comprehensive Reform Act of 2007 would have combined the legalization avenues of McCain-Kennedy with increased border security, including 370 more miles of border fence. Given the cloture rule (whereby 60 votes are required in the Senate to end debate), the bill never reached the floor for a vote.

Opposition to the bill was very well organized, vocal, and came from various sources. Conservative talk radio hosts encouraged listeners to deluge their elected officials with letters and emails, CNN commentator Lou Dobbs used a national platform to criticize what he called an assault on the middle class. Referring to Mexican President Felipe Calderón (2006–present), Dobbs wrote, "it is President Bush and this Congress who should be most embarrassed, because they are failing to assert rights for Americans in their own country, rights far short of those demanded by Calderón for his citizens living illegally in our nation."[29] At the same time, many pro-immigrant groups complained that the bill was too punitive, would split up families, and did not take human rights of workers—legal or not—into consideration.

Despite Reid's stance, many Democrats were also opposed to the proposed legislation. Many of the Democrats elected in 2006 came from the more conservative wing of the party. For example, North Carolina freshman Democratic Congressman Heath Shuler voted against immigration reform in his conservative district and, in 2008, sponsored a bill that would have tightened employer requirements to verify their workers' immigration status. Speaker of the House Nancy Pelosi opposed Shuler's bill, but eight Democrats joined with Republicans on a vote to bring it to the floor, although ultimately it did not receive enough support for a full vote.[30] Half of those Democrats were from the South. Given the deadlock, legislators turned to other issues, and immigration faded from the congressional radar. Indeed, it was rarely mentioned in the 2008 presidential race between Senators John McCain and Barack Obama.

Since 2006, the federal government has generally increased its enforcement efforts, in large part to refute the charges of being "soft" on the issue of undocumented immigration and to discourage employers from hiring workers without more rigorous examination of identity. High-profile workplace raids became more common. The first big raid in 2006 targeted Swift and Company, a meatpacking company operating in six states. Since then, many other similar operations have taken place across the United States. They are raising a number of moral and ethical questions, particularly with regard to the status of children whose parents are detained and whether detainees are made aware of their constitutional rights. Beyond that, of course, workplace raids do little to address the larger question of push-pull.

The Enforcement Model: The Swift Raids

On December 12, 2006, more than a thousand heavily armed agents from Immigration and Customs Enforcement (ICE) coordinated raids in Swift and Company meat-processing plants in six states (Colorado, Iowa, Minnesota, Nebraska, Texas, and Utah). Department of Homeland Security Secretary Michael Chertoff announced that this largest workplace raid in history was aimed mainly at identity theft, as undocumented workers use real Social Security numbers to obtain work. In all, almost thirteen hundred workers were detained. It marked the beginning of a shift in the federal government's approach to immigration with a newly active enforcement strategy.

In Greeley, Colorado, they were loaded onto buses and driven away, with no word on where they were being taken. The local police refused to take part, as the police chief argued that his participation would make the Latino population fearful of coming to the police.[31] Officials from ICE concentrated on the arrests, and no one informed the remaining friends and families where the detainees were taken or what would happen next. Instead, community volunteers arrived to assist, translate, and locate those who had been arrested. As one volunteer said, "Just this morning

I was with a 16-year-old Guatemalan boy who came here two months ago with his mother . . . He doesn't speak English, he barely speaks Spanish, and he's been living with people who share his apartment. He's in shock. And there's no one, really no one, in charge."[32]

In the Texas panhandle city of Cactus, almost a quarter of the 1,282 detained immigrants were removed from the Swift plant. Ironically, Mayor Luis Aguilar was once an undocumented immigrant who eventually became a citizen through the 1986 amnesty. After the raids, the town's economy was devastated. In Greeley, some fired workers returned to their country of origin, but many others decided to stay in the country (if not the city), arguing that the risk of being found and deported was worth it given the lack of jobs in Guatemala and Mexico.[33]

Another irony is that, since 1997, Swift had participated in the Basic Pilot program, whereby the company voluntarily provided the Social Security numbers of its employees to the federal government. However, if a worker was using an already existing number, the system could not identify it and does not alert the employer to the possibility of identity. Thus, the company became a target anyway. And despite ordering the raid, Secretary Chertoff himself criticized the system and lamented the lack of immigration reform, arguing that a temporary worker program would make such raids unnecessary.

In September 2007, the union of former Swift employees filed a lawsuit against the federal government, arguing that the mass workplace raids represented a violation of the workers' constitutional rights against unreasonable search and seizure.[34] Nonetheless, the Swift raids became a model for future ICE operations across the country, targeting low-skilled industries such as meatpacking and small manufacturing (such as an electrical transformer factory in Laurel, Mississippi) and, on a smaller scale, places such as restaurants and bakeries.

SOURCES: Moreno 2007; Mulkern 2007; Cooper 2007.

Legal Migration

Most of the discussion in this chapter has focused on unauthorized immigration. This is because the family preference philosophy of U.S. immigration laws has always favored family members of current citizens instead of new immigrants. It is not easy for a would-be immigrant to respond legally to the need for labor in the United States. The easiest way to become a legal immigrant is to be a close relative of someone who is already here legally and has become a citizen, although there is a long backlog even of these applications, especially for family members from Mexico and the Philippines.[35] One of the hardest ways to enter legally is to be a relatively low-skilled worker trying to meet the structural needs created by the demographic fit between the United States and Latin America.

In 2007, there were 1,052,415 people admitted legally to the United States. Just under half of these people (494,920) were immediate relatives of U.S. citizens. More importantly, more than half of these immigrants (507,200) were not in the labor force because they were nonworking spouses or older family members. Of those in the labor force, the number whose occupations were in "construction, extraction, maintenance, and repair occupations" was only 9,340.[36] The undocumented immigrants, who number about 500,000 per year, are filling in the holes created by the current system of legal immigration. The United States lets in more legal immigrants than any other country in the world, but not necessarily the people that the economy is demanding. It is for this reason that the issue of undocumented immigration plays such a prominent role in our discussion of the demographic fit.

Immigration and Public Opinion

Members of the media, politicians, and pundits talk quite frequently about what the "American people" think about immigration, sometimes arguing diametrically opposing points. Officials from both the legislative and executive branches, who of course have the task of representing their constituents, deliberate at length regarding about American people.

- "We've tried to address immigration reform in the past by talking about only one aspect of immigration reform. To make it work, to address the concerns of the American people, there must be a comprehensive approach."—President George W. Bush in 2007[37]
- "The American people are rightfully sick and tired of their leaders ignoring their pleas to secure America's borders."—Congressman Tom Feeney, Republican, Florida, in 2008[38]

- "It is my belief that the American people are pro-legal immigration and anti-illegal immigration. It is my belief that the American people are not afraid of an immigration system that is both tough and fair."—Senator Charles Schumer, Democrat, New York, in 2009[39]
- "I believe the American people will only deal with reform if they are convinced that the borders are secure first."—Congressman Robert Aderholt, Republican, Alabama, in 2008[40]
- "The American people want this problem fixed. They want practical, workable solutions."—Secretary of Commerce Carlos Gutierrez in 2007[41]
- "We have a responsibility to create a legal system that works in America. I am afraid this bill didn't do it. That is my problem with the bill [Comprehensive Reform Act of 2007]. I think that the American people agreed."—Senator Jeff Sessions, Republican, Alabama, in 2007[42]

What is it that Americans want? Or do they know? The increased emphasis on border security and workplace raids clearly demonstrates that elected officials tend to believe that Americans support those views. Especially after the failure of the Comprehensive Reform Act of 2007, even presidential candidate John McCain seemed resigned to that fact, quipping in a speech, "By the way, I think the fence is least effective. But I'll build the goddamned fence if they want it."[43] Less colloquial was Senator Jeff Sessions, who opposed the bill: "Senators heard the voices of their constituents and voted accordingly."[44]

Portes and Rumbaut have called this a "game of mirrors," whereby the public view of immigration is guided by surface impressions and very little empirical evidence.[45] When immigration is on the rise, the public is more likely to feel threatened by the "other," particularly if migrants look different and/or speak a different language than the communities into which they move. This can even be true of immigrant children in schools. As one young Mexican immigrant put it, "Especially the girls were really mean, about me not knowing English and not being able to understand what the teacher was saying."[46]

Citizens of any country also tend to become more critical of immigrants—and particularly undocumented immigrants—when the economy sours and/or the perception increases that foreigners are taking jobs that otherwise would be filled by native workers. This is, of course, also affected by demography, since the availability of jobs depends in part upon the number of working-age people searching for a finite number of positions.

Overall, however, Americans tend to hold ambivalent views about immigration and U.S. immigration policy.[47] For example, they might wish to limit further immigration, but not seek to punish those already in the country illegally, particularly those they know personally. This means that such views are not held strongly, especially when compared to other pressing national issues. Even in the mid-1980s, when the call for more border control eventually led to the passage of the Immigration Reform and Control Act, undocumented immigration was routinely viewed as significantly less important than nuclear war, unemployment, or inflation.[48] That lack of intensity has tended to be fairly constant, even at times when a majority expressed opposition to increasing the number of immigrants allowed into the United States.[49]

In the context of post-2006 congressional debates on immigration, it is not at all clear that the "American public" is as concerned as claimed by the elected officials that represent it and the media that covers it. In fact, even though the most recent debate over immigration has generated headlines, Americans tend to view immigration in largely pragmatic terms, seeking neither open borders nor mass deportation. As the demographic fit concludes over the next several years, however, these numbers may well become more negative. As mentioned, this will depend to a large extent on whether the decline of Latin American fertility is combined with economic growth that can provide sufficient employment at reasonable wages.

Public opinion on the issue can be difficult to untangle, and of course the specific wording pollsters use can influence the response. Nonetheless, since 2006, polls have tended to show the following:

- Americans believe undocumented immigration is an important problem.
- Undocumented immigration is not the most pressing problem in the country, and often is listed as fourth or fifth. (The state of the economy and the war in Iraq tend to be first and second.)[50]
- A majority believes that immigrants (including undocumented immigrants) do not take jobs away from U.S. citizens.[51]
- A majority believes there should be a guest worker program.[52]

- A (sometimes slim) majority believes that individuals currently in the United States illegally should be granted some type of route toward legalization.[53]
- Independents are most in support of a legalization route, followed by Democrats and then Republicans.[54]
- Border security should be enhanced.

These views can fluctuate over time and may vary somewhat from region to region. Later we will discuss their relevance in the South. Law professor Peter Schuck argues that most Americans are "pragmatic restrictionists."[55] This means they view immigrants with sympathy, but also consider the problems associated with immigration. They can, however, be convinced of a more expansive policy if the evidence shows that it is not detrimental to communities and the economy. At the same time, though, he argues that there is a "disconnect" between that view and policy makers, with the latter favoring more open immigration policies. The political climate of recent years suggests the opposite may in fact be true. Policy makers tend to believe that the public has a *more* restrictive mood than it really does.

The practical, political importance of these views emerged during the Republican presidential primaries in 2007 and 2008. With the exception of Arizona Senator John McCain, who of course had cosponsored an immigration reform bill with a prominent Democrat, the candidates took a hard line toward undocumented immigrants, arguing that immigration represented one of the most important problems facing the United States. They promised action, to take the form of increasing border security and rejecting either a route to legalization or a temporary worker program. McCain's main rival, former Massachusetts Governor Mitt Romney, routinely emphasized his opposition to any legalization route or to a temporary worker program: "One simple rule: no amnesty."[56] Other candidates also often used the term "amnesty" to demonstrate their opposition to any avenue toward legalization for undocumented workers.

This stance was viewed as popular with the Republican base, meaning the core of registered Republicans who would get out to vote in the party's primaries. However, by March 2008, the last Republican challenger to McCain (former Arkansas Governor Mike Huckabee, who also spoke very strongly about undocumented immigration) had conceded. McCain, who had been ridiculed by fellow Republican challengers for his stance on immigration, became the Republican nominee for President. This could be seen in part as evidence of the ambivalence toward immigration—McCain's views on immigration were not deal-breakers for voters in the Republican primary elections.

It is worth nothing, however, that Huckabee did win in a majority of Southern states; only Mississippi and Virginia voted for McCain. His position on immigration may have contributed to his regional success, though he also garnered support for being the former governor of a southern state and espousing socially conservative views, which is popular with the southern Republican political base, regardless of views on immigration.

Further, as the primaries progressed and even after his victory, Senator McCain maintained a public stance of "enforcement first" and downplayed his previous support for reform. He made only very brief and vague mention in his nomination acceptance speech:

> We believe everyone has something to contribute and deserves the opportunity to reach their God-given potential from the boy whose descendents arrived on the Mayflower to the Latina daughter of migrant workers. We're all God's children and we're all Americans.[57]

His campaign defined his position as follows: "John McCain's top immigration priority is to finish securing our borders in an expedited manner. Governors of border states will be required to certify that the border is secure."[58] Only then, when there is "certification," would any further reform be pursued. Thus, it was very clear that Senator McCain accepted the idea that Americans, but most critically Republican voters, believed that enforcing the border and keeping out undocumented immigrants was one of their most important political goals.

The final months of the presidential race demonstrated that immigration had been moved to the political backburner. The candidates, the Bush administration, and the public were all focused on the financial disaster that led to the $700 billion government bailout of financial institutions hit hard by the collapse of credit and mortgage foreclosures. The American public was watching Wall Street, the U.S. Congress, and the White House for signs of recovery. Immigration reform, very rarely the most crucial question in the public eye, had clearly lost its immediacy. Immigration was not mentioned at all during the three presidential debates in 2008. Although both candidates produced political ads mentioning immigration, the issue was never central to their stump speeches.

According to his campaign declarations, President Obama's position on immigration diverged from McCain's primarily in terms of not requiring "enforcement first" before constructing a temporary worker program and a means by which undocumented immigrants could legalize their status.[59] However, it also emphasized working with Mexico to promote economic development, which represents at least an initial step in recognizing that successful immigration reform requires a coordinated effort.

Policy and the Demographic Fit

We have noted repeatedly that demography is by no means the sole factor in explaining Latin American immigration to the United States and the resulting policy responses, but it is most often neglected in analyses of the subject and requires greater attention. Changes in the demographic structures in the United States and Latin American countries have an important impact on the decision to migrate. Thus, the demographic fit merits close attention, since it also affects how the receiving country—in this case the United States—responds to immigration, and it has an independent effect on the outcomes of U.S. immigration policy.

The popular response to immigration does not always hew to conventional wisdom, in part because the demographic fit has continued to reflect a relative lack of young workers in the United States. In general, U.S. public opinion does not show strong antagonism toward immigration per se, though it clearly considers undocumented immigration to be a problem. As the fit ends, however, that will likely change because the competition for jobs will become more intense.

From a policy perspective, we have thus far focused almost exclusively on how the United States deals with immigration. Indeed, U.S. debate very often ignores Latin American politics, as if governments in the region are passive players, watching their citizens leave the country and doing little else. Chapter Five seeks to counter that assumption by examining the political demography of immigration within Latin America itself. Far from simply being reactive, Latin American governments—of all ideological stripes—have become actively involved in policy reforms intended to advance their own economic and political interests. Far from being irrelevant, these policies have had, and will continue to have, an important impact on the individual decision to move from home to another country.

CHAPTER FIVE

The Latin American Reaction

IN WHAT HAS BECOME A RITUAL FOR SALVADORAN PRESIDENTS, Antonio Saca (2004–2009) traveled regularly to the United States during his term, meeting not only with top U.S. officials but also with Salvadorans and Salvadoran-Americans. After a 2007 visit, President George W. Bush told reporters, "Every time he comes to the Oval Office he's expressed his deep concern and strong support for his citizens that may be here in our country, and I assured him that I was open-minded to his request, but more importantly, I'm working hard to get a comprehensive bill, immigration bill, passed out of the United States Congress."[1] Meanwhile, El Salvador's consul general in Washington went on Spanish-language radio shows, giving out her cell phone number so that Salvadoran immigrants with any sort of problem could reach her directly.[2]

Concern from Latin American governments for their citizens living in the United States isn't entirely new. As discussed in Chapter Three, the Mexican government actively engaged with the United States during the period of repatriation after World War I. Such reactions, however, tended to be short lived and crisis driven, and as a result they never constituted a lasting policy. Once the particular crisis subsided, the Mexican government (like other Latin American governments) once again dissociated itself from the migrants. In addition, they did not include the migrants themselves in policy discussions. However, the first decade of this century has been marked by a heightening of interest, lobbying, and activism on the part of Latin American governments with regard to immigration. Long passive about U.S. immigration policy and emigrant ties, many governments have launched multifaceted strategies to maintain strong—even personal—connections with their citizens (and former citizens).

The connections being forged are part of what is commonly called "transnationalism." It rests on the assertion that, unlike in the past, migrants do not sever ties with the country from which they come. Instead, they maintain contact, which has been facilitated by a global capitalist system that encourages greater integration of national economies.[3] Money and goods move across borders with more speed than ever before, facilitated by free trade agreements and international financial institutions. Technology also provides unprecedented opportunities for travel and communication. Migrants consider transnationalism to be in their best interest, since it offers multiple avenues for shielding themselves from the challenges they face in the host country, such as inequality, racism, and discrimination of various types. The more support an individual can muster, the greater his or her chances of persevering under difficult circumstances.

It is our view that Latin American governments' responses to migrants—and thus the governments' own transnational role—is most usefully viewed in the context of the demographic fit, though it clearly also has political and economic foundations. The demographic changes that contributed to an acceleration of emigration also prompted governments to pay keen attention to the economic and political benefits emigrants could bring.

Foundations of Migrant Connection

By the 1990s, Latin American political leaders recognized that their labor markets could not absorb their large young populations, whereas the U.S. economy was creating lower-skilled jobs at a fast rate without the capacity to fill them. This occurred in the context of slow recovery from a disastrous economic decline in the 1980s (known as the "lost decade" during which many Latin American countries suffered and struggled through an economic depression that followed debt default). In Central America this was also the time just after civil wars concluded (in Guatemala, the final peace pact was not signed until 1996), so demographic change was accompanied by severe social, economic, and political disruptions.

Furthermore, technology was making it easier and cheaper to wire remittances back to family members in the sending country. A broad range of services emerged to capture the market, which reduced the price and expanded the coverage. Before long, even supermarkets across the U.S. south put up bilingual signs and flyers were distributed to suburban homes advertising remittance services. The number of governments interested in their migrants specifically, and migration more generally, has also expanded, and many governments that historically had not engaged the United States in immigration issues have begun to do so. The stakes are high for much of Latin America. The United States has served as a demographic and economic safety valve for many Latin American countries, even if it has also contributed to their political problems at times.

The particular effects of the U.S. Immigration Reform and Control Act also contributed to convincing Latin American policy makers that reaching out to their citizens abroad was more necessary than ever. That and successive U.S. laws created a strong disincentive for return trips among undocumented migrants, since border security made the trip more dangerous and expensive than in the past. It was therefore more necessary than ever to maintain strong contacts with people who otherwise might lose touch with their home country, which might mean losing touch with their money.

Although demography strongly influenced the creation of this newly found activism, it also fosters self-perpetuating forces. Even when the demographic fit closes, and the number of migrants slows, the activism—which is becoming deeply rooted—will certainly continue, though perhaps in more muted form. The embassies and consulates will continue their work, and governments will continue to forge links.

The literature on Latin American migration to the United States has only recently begun to address the Latin American policy response, and the topic generally receives only sporadic reference in studies on immigration. Studies of migration policy have tended to focus on the United States, yet Latin American leaders are especially cognizant of how U.S. immigration policy affects their countries and citizens.

Policy makers in Mexico and Central American countries have, of course, known for some time that migrants to the United States and Canada not only provide a demographic safety valve for a country with a rapidly growing population, they also send back money that keeps the home economy afloat. However, what has become apparent more recently is an inverse relationship between size of remittance and length of time in the United States.[4] Almost seven out of ten migrants from Latin America send money home, but the amount decreases as time goes by, particularly after a decade (though approximately 10 percent of migrants who have been in the United States thirty years or more still send remittances). Consequently, governments must act quickly to catch (and hopefully maintain) remittance income, before migrants reduce the amount they send.

The Inter-American Development Bank estimated that remittances to Latin America from workers abroad in 2008 totaled approximately $45 billion.[5] Not only are these remittances an increasingly large share of Latin American economies, but they come from an exported workforce, since demographic dynamics have led to a bottom-heavy population, which in turn relieves the sending country's government of the need to provide employment. At least for low-wage labor, the easing of unemployment pressures combined with remittance income represents a win-win situation for sending countries, and consequently it is also a strong incentive to keep close ties with migrant communities.

In 2008, as the U.S. economy slowed and inflation crept up, the rate of remittance growth also decreased. The restrictionist climate in the United States certainly contributed, though it is impossible to determine precisely how much. According to the Inter-American Development Bank, between 2006 and 2008, remittances from the United States to Latin America grew by only a bit over 1 percent.[6] In real terms (that is, accounting for inflation), this can be viewed as a decrease.

In addition, there is a humanitarian angle. As the number of workplace raids, detentions, local immigration laws, and other enforcement efforts proliferated after 9/11, Latin American policy makers responded to their citizens' calls for assistance. From the Latin American governments' perspective, there is much to gain and virtually nothing to lose by expanding outreach. For a relatively low cost, governments can demonstrate a commitment to assisting emigrants, which they hope, over time will yield benefits in the form of continued remittances and possibly even the return migration of people who have become more skilled by working in the United States and thus can make valuable additions to the home country economy.

In response to this realization, Latin American political leaders are increasingly trying to engage their fellow citizens living in the United States, exhorting them to continue sending money home (and attempting to facilitate the process), increasing consular services, allowing them to vote from abroad and to obtain dual citizenship, and even seeking their vote. Implicit in this engagement is recognition that, in many ways, the home country benefits greatly when people remain in the United States. As one Salvadoran businessman in Los Angeles put it:

> Our compatriots in El Salvador say, "Emigrant brothers, distant brothers, you are a very important piece of the economy in the country. You are national heroes. But be there, stay there. Send dollars, but don't come."[7]

Governments have concluded that they have a vested interest in ensuring that their citizens living in wealthier countries do not forget about them. With regard to dual nationality, Jones-Correa differentiates between "top-down" policies, where governments change policy without domestic pressure, and "bottom-up" policies, where citizen clamor prompts the change.[8] In twenty-first-century Latin America, it is increasingly difficult to differentiate between the two, since governments respond both to their own citizens and to the economic realities of emigration. As political leaders recognize the clear benefits that emigrants can provide to the home country, they are much more likely to pursue some measure of engagement, regardless of whether citizens were clamoring for it.

Direct Lobbying

The highest profile and most direct manner of political activism is for Latin American presidents and foreign ministers to lobby U.S. government officials in person. However, Latin American governments (indeed, like all governments) also hire high-profile lobbying firms in Washington, D.C. (often referred to as "K Street firms" because of how many companies are on that particular street in the city). So, while Latin American and U.S. presidents and cabinet members meet with each other, professional lobbyists also ply their trade with members of the United States Congress, hoping to influence votes on policy issues important to them. Already by the early 1990s, Mexico had one of the most visible lobbyist presences in Washington, with seventy-one registered with the Department of Justice by late 1991.[9] Even individual Mexican states are involved. In 2007, for example, the government of the northern Mexican state of Sonora hired the Houston lobbying firm J&D International Consulting Services to contact U.S. government officials with regard to border security.[10]

Lobbying for Migrant Rights

Latin American presidents and diplomats have held numerous discussions with their counterparts in the United States since the 1990s. In 1996, representatives from eleven countries (Belize, Canada, Costa Rica, Dominican Republic, El Salvador, Guatemala, Honduras, Mexico, Nicaragua, Panama, and the United States) came together for the first Regional Conference on Migration (RCM; also known as the Puebla Process for the Mexican city where the first meeting took place) to focus on critical issues and discuss possible solutions.

The RCM's stated goals are "the protection and respect for the human rights of migrants, irrespective of their migration status; the promotion of orderly and secure migration; and the dialogue and cooperation among countries, with the active participation of civil society."[11] Thus far, the organization's main accomplishment has been to establish some coordination between national agencies dedicated to immigration policy in each country, and to facilitate the sharing of information on the topic. It holds an annual meeting, and most recently it has focused on issues such as human trafficking.[12]

These efforts have clearly intensified in the post-9/11 era. The wide range of security measures put in place in the wake of the September 11, 2001 attacks reverberated throughout Latin America. In the case of Mexico, for example, the two countries had organized cabinet-level working groups in 2001, and President Bush visited Mexico in February of that year. President Fox then visited Washington, D.C., and the two governments issued a joint statement on September 6, 2001. However, after 9/11 those talks stalled, and the Bush administration did not announce any policy reform until three years later. Mexican Foreign Minister Jorge Castañeda resigned his post in 2003 in part because of his inability to convince the Bush administration to push for immigration reform.[13]

The RCM has been accompanied by other efforts on the part of governments in the hemisphere to forge agreements on immigration. In 2006, diplomats from eleven Latin American countries came together to lobby against restrictionist immigration plans being debated that year in the U.S. Congress.[14] This group included a representative from Mexico, which sends more migrants to the United States than any other country, and Colombia, which sends more migrants to the United States than any other South American country.

Not surprisingly, the Mexican government has been most adamant about U.S. restrictionist policies, especially with regard to the construction of a border wall. President Vicente Fox (2000–2006) was the first to make the issue a lobbying priority.[15] The victory of the National Action Party (PAN) over the Institutional Revolutionary party (PRI) marked the beginning of the heightened valuation of the Mexican migrant community, which in the past had been the object of criticism or had simply been ignored. The PRI had been in power for seven decades, yet had never articulated a policy of reaching out to Mexicans abroad. The PAN, meanwhile, framed them as heroic and central to Mexican economic development. In fact, while running for president, Fox (whose grandfather had been born in the United States) sent hundreds of thousands of dollars worth of calling cards to Mexicans in the United States, encouraging them to call friends and relatives to convince them to vote for him.[16]

In the past, the one-party system dominated by the PRI controlled the political system and had no electoral incentive to reach out to expatriates. As noted, that was combined with the long-held view in Mexico that emigrants' actions ran counter to the ideals of the Mexican revolution. Fox turned that policy on its head and, in fact, openly called U.S. plans to build a border wall "stupid," "discriminatory," and "shameful."[17] Fox's successor, Felipe Calderón (also from the PAN), has followed the same strategy of engagement with migrants and criticisms of the U.S. policies toward them. Similar sentiments came from other countries. In 2006, Guatemalan Vice President Eduardo Stein lamented that the United States wanted trade, but "treats our people as if they were a plague."[18]

It is worth noting that Mexico, for its part, has been criticized for its treatment of Central American migrants crossing its border with Guatemala. Given Guatemala's bloody and lengthy (1960–1996) civil war, migrants fled for years across the border into the southern Mexican state of Chiapas. Subsequently, the lack of jobs pushed Guatemalans northward, primarily to travel through Mexico on their way to the United States. Abuse of the migrants while in Mexico, including beatings, robbery, and rape, has been commonplace, and is often perpetrated by Mexican law enforcement officials.[19]

The Mexican government has responded to these problems, such as in 2006 with President Felipe Calderón's Southern Frontier Rearrangement Plan, which was intended to create a system for documentation of immigrant workers and protection of their rights.[20] Nonetheless, problems persist. An American-run railroad company in southern Mexico had provided "free" transportation northward for many hitch-hiking migrants passing through Mexico. When it stopped operating in 2007, it left thousands of migrants stranded, and the Mexican government sent troops to round them up and deport them.[21] In 2008, the governments of El Salvador and Honduras formally protested the brutal methods used by Mexican officials against migrants from their countries.[22] At the very least, the Mexico-Guatemala border is a constant reminder that Mexico faces similar challenges as the United States, and similarly has been unable to find lasting solutions.

In the United States, the Mexican government opened its forty-seventh consulate in 2007 and works to provide legal advice for undocumented immigrants, particularly in cases where they believe their rights may have been violated.[23] Former Foreign Minister Castañeda relates that U.S. policies ended circular migration, and in the absence of immigration reform in the post-9/11 period, the Mexican government felt it had no choice but to reach out to its expatriates living in the United States.[24] In 2005, the government set up the Institute for Mexicans Abroad with the goal of working with the consulates to forge permanent connections to Mexicans in the United States. The Institute has even provided funding to U.S. schools to teach immigrants literacy in both Spanish and English, through a program known as Plaza Comunitaria, or Community Plaza, which gives $1 million a year to help support literacy programs. As the head of the Institute puts it, "We don't want the Mexicans in the exterior to feel like milk cows being expressed for the resources they were sending back."[25]

During the administration of Vicente Fox, the Mexican government employed a conscious strategy of convincing U.S. banks and other U.S. businesses to accept the Mexican ID card, known as the *matrícula*. This enabled migrants to obtain loans, buy homes, and otherwise engage in normal financial transactions even if they were not in the country legally. As former Foreign Minister Jorge Castañeda noted:

> American immigration conservatives were in a sense right when they began, in 2004, to attack the *matrícula* as an instrument of backdoor amnesty; that was my intention, and I think, though I cannot state it as a fact, that it continued to be Fox's intention after I left his administration.[26]

There were, to be sure, U.S. critics of Mexican lobbying efforts regarding the *matrícula*. The Washington, D.C.,–based Center for Immigration Studies, which is highly critical of undocumented immigration, noted as early as 2003 that the "Mexican government has launched an aggressive grassroots lobbying campaign to win acceptance for its *matrícula* card from state and local jurisdictions and from banks, especially in areas where Mexican illegal aliens are concentrated."[27]

In 2007, the new Mexican Ambassador to the United States, Arturo Sarukhan (whose grandfather was a Russian Armenian immigrant to Mexico), announced that the consulates would be working in tandem with business chambers, civic associations, and other groups to argue for immigration reform.[28] He likened the effort to the successful lobbying in the early 1990s to pass the North American Free Trade Agreement. Given the outcome of the legislative debate, clearly the endeavor was much less successful, since no immigration reform has emerged since the debate began in earnest in 2006. It does mean, however, that future congressional measures will almost certainly be accompanied by active Mexican participation.

As we mentioned in Chapter Three, the continuation of Temporary Protected Status legislation (TPS) has been a major political concern for Central American governments. In 1995, the Salvadoran government initiated a program to assist its citizens in filing for asylum in the United States through its consulates and ad hoc immigration offices.[29] In his first visit to Washington, D.C., in 2008 after his election, Guatemalan President Alvaro Colom (who assumed office in 2008) lobbied to have undocumented Guatemalans in the United States included in TPS legislation.[30] In 2008, Honduran president José Manuel Zelaya Rosales (elected in 2006) traveled to California's Central Valley with other top government officials from El Salvador and Guatemala to discuss the shortage of farm workers in the state and to suggest possible ways to facilitate the temporary migration of Central American workers.[31] Salvadoran presidential candidate Mauricio Funes (eventually elected in 2009) also went to Los Angeles and spoke to expatriates, discussing Salvadoran domestic issues of importance to migrants, such as a 4-cent tax in El Salvador on international phone calls.[32]

Lobbying for Home Country Interests

A related, albeit somewhat complicated, question that merits attention is whether Latin American governments can use their expatriates to further their own foreign policy goals. This rests on the assumptions that (a) governments can articulate their goals effectively to eligible voters living outside the home country, and (b) those voters will be receptive and willing to vote accordingly. To have a substantive impact, governments must also have the organizational capacity and resources to publicize these goals to fellow voters in the United States. Those voters must be U.S. citizens aged eighteen or older, so by definition they will not be undocumented immigrants, nor will they be the most recent legal immigrants (since there is a five-year path to citizenship among legal permanent residents).

These activities (real or perceived—there is little evidence that this is really happening) on the part of foreign governments to influence voting behavior among their former citizens have helped to promote xenophobic conspiracy theories in the United States. For example, rumors of a "North American Union," whereby the sovereignty of the United States would disappear in a merger with Canada and Mexico, gained enough visibility to be mentioned and given credence by Republican presidential candidate Ron Paul.[33] It is given more credence by the fact that Mexican politicians, including former President Fox, have expressed aloud their hope that someday economic integration could expand with the introduction of a "cohesiveness fund" along the lines of the Marshall Plan. Its core would be an investment by the United States in Mexico to build infrastructure, which in the long term would strengthen the Mexican economy and increase Mexican wages so that the economic divergence between the two countries would be greatly diminished. In his memoirs, Fox does not hide how important he believes the idea to be, nor his role in promoting it: "This is a long-term vision. Politicians have to think about the next election, but statesmen think about the next generation."[34]

There is no evidence, however, that the Mexican population has embraced Fox's idea of full integration with the United States. Indeed, as we have noted before, Mexico has spent the past century trying to protect itself from being swallowed up by the United States. It is reasonable to suggest, in fact, that Canada and Mexico are more wary of having their cultures subsumed by the United States than U.S. residents are about being taken over by other cultures. Indeed, the brilliance of America could well be thought of as its ability to absorb other cultures and somehow render them "American."

In the alarmist scenario, immigrants—particularly Mexican—are viewed as lobbyists for foreign governments. Political scientist Samuel Huntington argued that a diaspora population might not serve the best interests of the United States because it will be less able "to define and to pursue its own national interests when these do not correspond with those of other countries that have exported people to America."[35] The "national interest" would thereby be threatened by external influences. This is similar to the concerns expressed by opponents of John F. Kennedy as he was running for President: the fact that he was a Catholic led critics to worry that his view of "national interest" would or could be influenced by the Pope.

There are, however, a number of empirical problems with the argument as it applies to Latin American immigrants, just as there were with respect to Kennedy. Studies have shown, for example, that Latinos often tend not to be happy with the government they left, making them less likely to act in what they perceive as its interests.[36] Alejandro, a young Mexican construction worker who obtained legal residency and works in Oklahoma, put it this way: "I do not like the Mexican government. All political parties are hypocrites. They do not fulfill their promises. They take the money and then they forget about the people. I have always hated politics."[37] Not all migrants necessarily feel the same intensity, but the overall sentiment is not uncommon.

Moreover, the electoral behavior of Latinos shows a pattern of relative partisan disengagement. For example, the number of independents has been rising steadily. A 2007 study by the Pew Hispanic Center found that 25 percent of registered Latino voters considered themselves "independent," up from 20 percent in 2006 and 23 percent in 1999.[38] Such a high percentage of independents is not consistent with engagement in partisan politics to influence policy. Even though 67 percent of Latino voters were reported by CNN exit polls to have voted for Obama in 2008, that does not mean that somehow they were following the dictates of the Mexican government. On the other hand, the clearly anti-immigrant platform of the Republican Party in 2008 undoubtedly did influence the votes of many Latinos, even if that might not have been the most important reason to vote for Obama.

Latino organizations in the United States focus mostly on issues related to Latinos themselves, and not to foreign affairs.[39] Given the tremendous challenges that immigrants—especially, but not exclusively, the recently arrived—face, their top priorities tend to relate to their own wellbeing. Like most voters in the United States, if and when they become citizens and voters, their primary electoral focus is much more oriented toward domestic policies. There is very little incentive (or time) to pursue the foreign policy interests of their home government, even if they were able or willing to do so.

From the perspective of lobbying, the Latino community is neither united nor resource-rich. Although there is certainly considerable wealth within the Latino population, there is currently no indication that wealthier Latinos are more likely to lobby on behalf of the homeland. Studies have shown that once Latin Americans arrive in the United States, they move more toward a panethnic classification, identifying as "Latino" (a term peculiar to the United States, as we previously noted) and not necessarily supporting the policies of their homeland.[40] Rather, they focus on local needs, which often intersect with immigrants from other Latin American countries. This is consistent with our comments earlier in the chapter that the longer Latin American immigrants have lived in the United States, the less likely they are either to send remittances home or to vote in home elections.[41] Once foreign-born Latinos have been in the United States over a decade, almost two-thirds stop sending remittances, which increases to over 80 percent for those who have been in the country more than thirty years.[42]

This does not mean that immigrants completely abandon their political connection to their country of origin. Those who are male, better educated, and have for whatever reason retained strong ties to their country of origin are more likely to engage in cross-border political activity, which can endure even after living in the United States for a number of years.[43] Nonetheless, "the number of immigrants who are regularly involved in cross-border activism is relatively small."[44] In short, the sending country's government cannot count on its expatriates to act as agents of influence in any substantive way.

Cuba, however, is an exception of sorts. United States policy toward revolutionary Cuba was first forged in the Eisenhower administration, but Cuban voters and lobbyists (most notably the Cuban American National Foundation, founded in 1981) became relevant only during the Reagan administration, precisely because organization and resource building requires a high level of coordination, which can take decades to develop. This is why, for example, a similar lobby did not develop among Nicaraguans regarding the Marxist Sandinista government, in power from 1979 to 1990, despite strong support from the Reagan administration to oppose the Sandinistas.

Of course, U.S. policy decisions have sometimes gone against the Cuban diaspora lobbyists' wishes, showing the limits of their influence. For example, in 1999 a young Cuban boy, Elián González, was the lone survivor of an attempt to reach the United States in a raft. His mother died en route, and his Cuban father sought his return to Cuba. Despite highly public and emotional opposition from the Cuban American community in Miami, which included assertions by the mayor of Miami–Dade County that he would not carry out any order to detain the boy, the Clinton Administration did eventually order his repatriation in 2000.[45] And as the 2008 presidential election demonstrated, even the Cuban American community no longer votes as a bloc, as generational change has created greater acceptance of the possibility of political and economic engagement with the Cuban government. During his presidential campaign, Barack Obama found approving audiences for policies regarding more openness with Cuba, even from the Cuban American National Foundation.

Overall, then, it is reasonable to suggest that Latino voters behave like everyone else, namely as rational voters choosing parties and candidates based on issues most relevant to their own lives and immediate circumstances. In fact, in open-ended surveys Latinos rarely place immigration very high on the list of priority issues.[46] Latinos face a host of challenges in the United States, especially when newly arrived—employment, health care, language acquisition, schooling for children, among many others. The demands of the home country are not likely a high priority unless they bear directly on daily life.

Changes in Domestic Laws

In addition to working with and trying to influence government policies in receiving countries, Latin American legislatures have also been passing laws aimed directly at their expatriate populations. Policy changes that allow dual citizenship and the ability to vote abroad are especially indicative of the efforts by Latin American governments to deal with demographic change. When a large proportion of the population is young but also moving out of the country, it is critical not to lose all of their productive capacity. Such legislation has therefore become more common in recent years, paralleling the demographic fit.

Dual Citizenship

Dual citizenship is literally the condition of being a citizen of two countries simultaneously. The vast majority of Latin American countries grant this right to their citizens. Four countries (El Salvador, Panama, Peru, and Uruguay) allowed dual citizenship prior to IRCA in 1986; eight more (Brazil, Colombia, Costa Rica, Dominican Republic, Ecuador, Guatemala, Mexico, and Venezuela) passed new laws in the 1990s.[47] Honduras (2003), Bolivia (2004), and Chile (2004) followed suit in the wake of the more restrictive immigration environment in the United States following the 9/11 attacks.[48] This is by no means a strictly Latin American phenomenon. By 2008, approximately three billion people lived in countries with some sort of dual nationality allowance.[49]

United States law, including the Immigration and Nationality Act, does not mention dual nationality. Officially, through Supreme Court decisions, the U.S. government recognizes that dual nationality exists, but does not encourage it. The State Department notes the ambiguity of the U.S. government's position:

> The U.S. Government recognizes that dual nationality exists but does not encourage it as a matter of policy because of the problems it may cause. Claims of other countries on dual national U.S. citizens may conflict with U.S. law, and dual nationality may limit U.S. Government efforts to assist citizens abroad. The country where a dual national is located generally has a stronger claim to that person's allegiance.[50]

Congress has the authority to legislate immigration, including dual citizenship, but for the reasons noted above has not elected to do so. The government has not even opted to determine how many citizens of the United States are eligible for dual citizenship, or how many obtain it.

In most countries, demand for dual citizenship after 1986 originated with migrant communities that faced new restrictions and argued that citizenship in their current country of residence (the United States) was the most direct means of allowing greater freedom of movement. Thus, migrants to the United States recognized that they would be better off if they became U.S. citizens, but they were at the same time reluctant to throw off their native citizenship. Latin American governments recognized that, paradoxical though it might seem, permitting or even encouraging dual citizenship would also generate a positive relationship with the emigrant community.

Dual citizenship has generated some measure of controversy in the United States. Samuel Huntington referred derisively to "ampersands" and wrote that "the vitality of a democracy depends on the extent to which its citizens participate in civic associations, public life, and politics. Most citizens are stretched to take an interest in and participate in the public affairs of a single community and a single country."[51] There are, after all, only so many hours in a day. How could someone invest themselves fully in the lives of two different countries? The overall thrust of this argument is that it is not possible for an individual to be fully part of two countries at once, and that the United States will inevitably lose culturally and politically as a result. Other, less alarmist, treatments suggest that even if dual citizens are not necessarily "disloyal," they will at least feel conflicted.[52] The issue also often becomes tied to citizenship by birth. According to Representative Lamar Smith (Republican, Texas), it boils down to "burden":

> Congress is long overdue in making sure the 14th amendment is correctly interpreted. Illegal immigration has become a crisis in America. Our borders are overrun. More than 12 million people are in the United States illegally. Passing a law to eliminate birth citizenship would deter illegal immigration and reduce the burden on the taxpayer of paying for Government benefits that go to illegal immigrants.[53]

At the extreme, one might argue, if two countries went to war or otherwise became engaged in a serious protracted international conflict, the loyalty of the individual could be called into question. In the case of Latin America, there has been no such situation in recent years, with the exception of Cuba.

Empirical evidence to sustain the argument with regard to the Hispanic population is, however, mixed. There does appear to be evidence that first-generation dual citizens from Latin American countries feel less civic duty, are less likely to be registered to vote in the United States, and even when registered are less likely to vote than first-generation counterparts who are citizens only of the United States.[54] The focus on first generation, however, obscures assimilation that takes place with the second generation and beyond. In addition, the existence of anti-immigrant legislation, such as that in California in the 1990s, tends to increase electoral participation (including voter registration) among both first- and second-generation immigrants.[55] The political context is therefore important.

Voting, however, is only one facet of civic engagement. As Barreto and Muñoz point out with regard to nonelectoral participation, when it comes to activities such as attending a meeting or rally, volunteering for a campaign, or donating money to a political cause, Mexican noncitizens in the United States are not less likely to participate than either naturalized citizens or the native-born.[56] Since many noncitizens aspire to be citizens but cannot vote, nonelectoral activities become their outlet for integration. Other research, however, calls this conclusion into question for the Latino population as a whole.[57]

A study of Colombians in the United States found that their desire for dual citizenship came directly as a result of desiring to participate more in the civic life of the United States.[58] Not wishing to renounce their Colombian citizenship, they were constrained from fully engaging in their new communities. Alejandro Portes and Rubén Rumbaut note that political activism skills in one context can be transferred to another, and therefore Colombian and Dominican leaders often participate actively both in the United States and in their country of origin.[59] In fact, immigrants who are members of organizations focused on their home country are more likely to be involved in U.S. organizations as well.[60]

It is true, however, that allowing dual citizenship does tend to increase naturalization rates in the receiving country.[61] In other words, those laws do increase the numbers of "ampersands." Whether or not this is desirable will obviously depend upon one's political views. In any event, the promotion of dual citizenship is now spreading across the hemisphere. In the United States, it is not obvious that the phenomenon inflicts any damage or is likely to cause long-term friction. Some people may become more involved in politics, whether through voting or other means, and some may not. Understanding why one choice or the other is made requires contextualization, and therefore defies simple explanation.

Voting from Abroad

Voting from abroad is another means of forging continuous ties with migrants, and refers to the legal right to cast a vote for an election while residing in another country. This typically takes place at a consulate. Eleven Latin American countries (Argentina, Brazil, Colombia, Dominican Republic, Ecuador, Honduras, Mexico, Nicaragua, Panama, Peru, and Venezuela) provide opportunities for their citizens to vote from abroad. The change in law can, in some cases, derive from a particular government believing it would gain political advantage in doing so (for example, Honduras) or because of repeated demands by the citizens themselves (for example, Dominican Republic). In the Nicaraguan case, existing legislation permits the government to do this, but it has not happened as of this writing.[62]

The issue is also being debated elsewhere. In 2005, the Chilean Minister of Foreign Affairs estimated that almost one million Chileans lived abroad (mostly in neighboring Argentina) out of a total population of sixteen million, and over 70 percent of them wished to vote from abroad.[63] Thus far, however, legislation has languished (in fact, the idea was first proposed in 1991) because the political right believes that a majority of ex-pats left the country for political reasons (that is, those who fled the dictatorship of Augusto Pinochet, 1973–1990) and therefore will support the left. Similar debates are occurring in Bolivia and Costa Rica (where the legislatures have considered, but not yet passed bills), El Salvador, and Guatemala.

In the Mexican case, the process was gradual. By the 1980s, presidential and even gubernatorial candidates periodically traveled to the United States, and in the 1990s consulates initiated coordinated efforts to establish relationships with hometown associations in U.S. cities. Migrants then began making demands for their right to vote from abroad, and activists spent a decade lobbying members of the Mexican Congress.[64]

These efforts were unsuccessful for years, as migrants were viewed as possible threats to the PRI's long-standing hold on power. Ultimate success came in large part because Mexico's one-party state was being challenged, and as previously mentioned, a new party, the PAN, won the presidency in 2000.

Colombia offers a unique perspective, since migrants have the right to elect one member of the lower house, who then represents the emigrant community as a "district." The first such election was held in 2002 To be eligible, the voter must prove that he or she has been living outside Colombia for at least five continuous years.[65] Turnout in both the 2002 and 2006 legislative elections were low, approximately 15 percent (versus 40.5 percent for the country overall), though the May 2006 presidential election garnered 38 percent (versus 45 percent overall). Lower turnout is to be expected, but the mere fact that over 300,000 Colombians abroad registered to vote in the 2006 presidential election demonstrates the magnitude of potential political interest from the émigré population.

Latin Americans living in the United States have, as can be seen, become a newly targeted source of votes not only for U.S. elections, but also for elections in the home country. Thus far, however, this pool of potential voters has not been fully tapped. For example, only about 50 percent of registered Brazilians voted from abroad in the 1998, 2002, and 2006 presidential elections (after a brief spike of 70 percent in the 1994 election), even though voting is compulsory and voters must therefore justify their failure to vote.[66] Further, a poll in February 2006 revealed that 55 percent of Mexican nationals living in the United States were unaware that a Mexican presidential election was planned for July.[67] However, Mexican and Central American governments have increasingly sought to influence U.S. immigration policy, thereby taking a more active role and eschewing the traditional "policy of no policy."[68] Brazilians abroad have also successfully lobbied to have immigration addressed more directly by candidates, which is reflected in the efforts of the ruling Brazilian Worker's Party to woo votes in the United States.

The many recent reforms in Latin American countries demonstrate that policy makers have recognized the demographic and economic realities of immigration. It is likely that more countries will enact voting and citizenship reforms in the future, as noted by the debates taking place in several countries on the issue. Future research should focus on the degree to which such reforms encourage migrants to move in the first place, how it affects their length of stay in the United States, and the nature of the Latin American response.

It should be noted, however, that such transnational political linkages can also have unintended domestic political consequences. In 2001, Andrés Bermúdez Viramontes ran for and won the mayorship of the Mexican city of Jerez. Bermúdez was a millionaire dubbed "the tomato king" (for his invention of a tomato transplanting machine) who lived in California and went back to his hometown in the Mexican state of Zacatecas (home to many Mexican migrants to the United States) and ran on a platform that included "make Jerez more like America."[69] The ruling PRI invalidated his victory based on residency requirements. Public outcry led to a change in residency rules, thus opening the door for his and other transnational candidacies. He was in fact elected mayor in 2004. There are signs that a growing number of Mexicans are returning home (or, in the case of Bermúdez, they are binational) and choosing to run for local office, in large part from frustration at the fact that local politics—often dominated by local power structures—have changed very little, even as the country democratized with greater political competition and more free and fair elections at the national level.[70] Bermúdez himself framed emigration as a coping strategy for Mexicans trapped by a corrupt economic and political elite, so that both leaving and returning to the country took on political significance.

In sum, Latin American governments themselves are contributing (if sometimes unintentionally) to transnational political relationships. As a result, the very idea of citizenship is gradually broadening, though the effects are not yet clear. The ties between migrants and their home countries do not correspond either to what critics think, who believe it erodes the sovereignty of the United States, or to what proponents in Latin America believe, who hope migrants will provide concrete political benefits for their home country.

Active Engagement

Another way of engaging with immigrants involves representatives of Latin American governments going to migrant communities in the United States to offer services, advice, and/or to encourage them to stay connected to their homelands. It is a proactive strategy intended to determine which types of services are desired and, from a symbolic standpoint, to demonstrate the sending country's commitment to migrant issues. The most prominent means of doing so is to open consulates and expand their services.

This type of strategy has become common enough that countries are coming together to optimize their resources. For example, in 2008, consulates in New York City from Mexico, Colombia, Costa Rica, Ecuador, El Salvador, Guatemala, Peru, the Dominican Republic, and Uruguay came together to create the "Coalition of Latin American Consulates in New York." As the Consul General from Ecuador noted, "We are no longer just here to sign visas, but to help our communities integrate here while continuing their important role in the development of our countries."[71]

During the 2004 Salvadoran presidential campaign, Antonio Saca and his opponents campaigned personally among the Salvadoran neighborhoods around Washington, D.C. In 2002, Saca's predecessor Francisco Flores Pérez stood next to President Bush, who said, "There's no question there's a lot of hardworking Salvadorans in the United States. And the first thing I want to assure the people of this good country is that we want to make sure they're treated with respect. We want them to be—we recognize—I recognize that family values, something we talk a lot about in America, don't stop at the Rio Bravo."[72]

The Mexican government even went so far as to announce it would print maps so that would-be border crossers would know where to find water and help in the desert on the U.S. side of the border.[73] From a humanitarian perspective, it was intended to reduce the number of deaths in the desert, which had increased in the 1990s. This sparked an outcry in the United States, where it was widely viewed as official encouragement of illegal crossing. It was followed by threats that the maps would be used by mercenaries to track down immigrants, so the Mexican government shelved the plan. The government reiterated, though, that it remained "committed to ensuring that migration into the United States is legal, safe, orderly and respectful of human rights."[74] In many ways this effort was a logical extension of the Grupo Beta program that the Mexican government has funded through its immigration agency since 1990, whose job it is to protect northbound migrants at the U.S.-Mexico border from being preyed upon by criminals on the Mexican side of the border.

Dominican Republic President Leonel Fernández (2004–present) actually grew up in New York City and maintains strong ties there. The Dominican presence in New York City has a long history, with a rapid increase in migration since the 1960s, a time when the long-ruling dictator

Rafael Trujillo was assassinated (1961) and the United States invaded in the wake of the resulting political conflict (1965). After dual citizenship became allowable in 1996, Dominican politicians began routinely to travel to New York to pursue votes. Major political parties also have fund raisers, rallies, and public forums to advance their political messages. The Dominican Revolutionary Party (PRD) has gone so far as to organize community-level committees whose job is to coordinate the party's outreach in the eastern United States.[75] The party relies financially on contributions from Dominicans in the United States, and the government refers to them not as "migrants" but as "Dominicans living abroad."

Hometown associations (HTAs) also represent an important, though understudied, link. They are organizations dedicated to the diaspora, linking migrants to their communities of origin. Estimates of active Mexicans HTAs in the United States range from 600 to 3,000, with an estimated 268 from El Salvador.[76] They have grown exponentially since the passage of the Immigration Reform and Control Act and the resulting policy emphasis on enforcement and deportation. The Mexican government, through its Ministry of Social Development, provides matching funds for any donations (by way of remittances) made to small or medium-sized development projects in the community of origin.[77] The Mexican case also highlights the importance of subnational governments in perpetuating links with migrants. Mexican states have played a central role in implementing programs for matching funds, and rely on transmigrant organizations to carry them out.[78]

From the perspective of migrants, HTAs constitute a source of social networking and advice about employment, immigrant rights, and other pressing issues. The mayor of Valparaíso, Mexico, once drove twenty-six hours to California so he could meet with Valparaíso's emigrants.[79] He brought with him a list of public work projects he hoped to initiate, asking immigrants to contribute. He then traveled to Illinois, where another group of former Valparaíso residents lived. The governor of Zacatecas has done the same, saying "I consider Zacatecas as a binational state."[80] Indeed, there may be more people from Zacatecas living in Los Angeles than there are people in the city of Zacatecas, the capital of the state. The governor began a program whereby the city would match remittances sent home. In 2008 a group of Salvadoran mayors, city councilors, and town administrators arrived in Massachusetts (with side trips into New York and New Jersey), imploring emigrants to invest their money back in El Salvador.[81] This type of lobbying is very personal and face-to-face, with elected officials talking in person to their former constituents.

"Brain Drain" and Latin American Policy

Although Latin American demographic realities have encouraged Latin American governments to seek connections with their citizens abroad, gradually a variant of this strategy has also emerged that differentiates between types of economically active migrants. Highly skilled and wealthier migrants are now being courted, not simply to send money home, but perhaps also to come home—to reverse the brain drain. The "brain drain," of course, refers to the flow of educated migrants who take their skills to other countries—especially the United States—thereby denying the sending country the fruits of those same skills.

Migration tends to be concentrated at the higher and lower ends of the educational spectrum, and this is often thought to be institutionalized by a dual-labor market in richer countries like the United States. The primary sector employs well-educated people, pays them well, and offers them security and benefits, whereas the secondary labor market is characterized by low wages, unstable working conditions, and lack of reasonable prospects for advancement. Perhaps not surprisingly, the countries of origin are especially interested in luring back home those émigrés who are part of the primary labor market. According to data from the U.S. Census Bureau, 18 percent of all migrants from Latin America have a college degree.[82] Further, between 1970 and 1990, the number of professionals and technicians from Latin America living in the United States quadrupled.[83]

Concern about the best and the brightest leaving the country is, of course, not new. The intergovernmental International Organization for Migration, for example, traces its history to the 1950s, when Europe faced the massive displacement in the wake of World War II's devastation. For years, it has run programs like the "Return and Reintegration of Qualified Nationals." The program targets specific countries, which have included El Salvador (hometown association development), the Dominican Republic (increasing the development impact of remittances), Guatemala (return of highly vulnerable migrants), Mexico (assisting voluntary return), and Uruguay (various projects to link with the diaspora).[84]

Scholars now also analyze "network diasporas," or linkages between the country of origin and its skilled workers abroad, which lead to more synergistic relationships.[85] These include professional associations, hometown organizations, training programs, and various types of collaborative initiatives. The ultimate goal is to promote "brain gain" or at least "brain circulation," whereby skilled workers may work abroad for periods of time, but also contribute to economic development in their country of origin.

Of course, brain drain is linked tightly to the loss of revenue from the enterprises and investments of these skilled workers. If their expertise and entrepreneurial skills are benefiting another country, they represent lost economic development. In addition to organizations like the IOM, governments are working independently to develop projects intended to harness the talents of skilled and educated workers abroad.

Brazil and Ecuador in particular have developed targeted programs either to bring the affluent and well-educated back home or to encourage them not to leave in the first place. Although many of these projects are nascent, they provide models for what is likely to continue spreading across the rest of the region.

The Brazilian government has actively worked to increase higher education opportunities and research capacity as a way to keep highly skilled Brazilians in the country, with an explicitly demographic rationale. As the president of Brazil's National Commission for Population and Development noted, brain drain would likely become a hot issue, given the correlation between high levels of education and low fertility.[86] The central strategy of the Brazilian government has been to invest in higher education, thereby greatly reducing the need for Brazilian students to travel (and then possibly reside long-term) in countries like the United States with a broad range of doctoral programs. In 1985, more than 40 percent of Brazilians with doctorates received them in foreign universities, but by 2004 that had dropped to less than 10 percent.[87] One of the unintended consequences has actually been an increase in doctoral students from other Latin American countries, thereby encouraging a brain drain to Brazil, rather than from it.

Much of the Ecuadorian government's active engagement has consisted of Plan Retorno (Return Plan), which seeks to entice middle- and upper-class citizens to bring their expertise, money, and goods back into the country. The government estimated that between 2003 and 2007, 403,000 Ecuadoreans left the country and did not return, and President Rafael Correa (2007–present) has labeled mass emigration a "national tragedy."[88]

Begun in 2008, Plan Retorno raises or eliminates ceilings and tariffs on capital and goods (such as cars) coming back to Ecuador and assists with loans to start new businesses.[89] The government has even discussed the creation of a national Migrant Bank. The essential problem, however, is that the demographic and economic pressures that prompted emigration have not disappeared. The Ecuadorean economy has simply been unable to provide the employment opportunities necessary to encourage repatriation. Whether the Ecuadorean plan gains enough adherents to make an economic dent remains to be seen. However, as the demographic fit closes, there will be a greater incentive for Ecuadorians abroad to return. The existence of a program that makes the process easier and reduces its cost will quite possibly make the decision easier.

Plan Retorno

Rafael Correa was elected president of Ecuador in 2006 on a platform of radical change. His policy orientation was primarily economic, since the country was facing serious problems of poverty and inequality, but he also soon focused on migration, since many Ecuadorians emigrated both to the United States and to Spain, sending home remittances that in 2007 totaled just over $3 billion. In 2007, his government announced the launch of Plan Retorno, which would commence the following year. This announcement was followed by news releases, radio shows, and an accompanying web site (including a registration and live chat feature) called the Ecuadorian House to advertise the plan.

The government's position was to encourage the return of both people and money to reintegrate Ecuadorians abroad into their country, which needed their expertise and capital. The plan's stated three-pronged approach is to be voluntary, dignified, and sustainable. Ecuadorian consulates will play a central role, since they maintain contact with migrants. The program focuses especially on the United States (and especially New York City), Spain, and Italy.

The government emphasizes that "return" is not limited to the physical, though returning to Ecuador is indeed facilitated by the elimination of duties on cars, furniture, and equipment related to work. Instead, it means the recuperation of "political, cultural, professional, and economic" capacity of the millions of Ecuadorians living abroad. The economic component is clearly the most critical. To encourage investment, the government is working to provide financial incentives and elimination of bureaucratic red tape. The goal is to stimulate productive investment in Ecuador rather than simply spurring on consumption from remittances.

Phase One, which entailed creating the web site, identifying Ecuadorians abroad, and reforming laws, began in January 2008. Phase Two, which began in July 2008, is intended to strengthen existing institutions by obtaining the opinions of Ecuadorian migrants, creating a Migrant Bank (Banco del Migrante), and implementing other financial incentives.

The government is highly critical of immigration policies in the United States and Europe, arguing that they "want workers but not people." As the Minister for the National Secretariat of the Migrant put it, "we are fixing up the house for their return." As such, it is part of the overall National Plan of Development for 2007–2010.

SOURCES: Ecuadorian government migration web site (http://migranteecuatoriano.gov.ec); Inter-American Development Bank (http://www.iadb.org/mif/remesas_map.cfm?language=English&parid=5). All translations are by the author.

Finally, all countries dealing with a brain drain face the fact that the United States and other potential receiving countries are actively engaged in recruiting skilled labor. In the United States, skilled workers fall under the H-1B program, which offers a three-year period of employment, with the possibility of a three-year extension, as well as the opportunity to apply for permanent residence. After 9/11, the number of accepted petitions dropped, but demand has remained high.[90] Complaints from businesses have led members of Congress to push for legislation that would make it easier for those with advanced degrees to obtain permanent residency, and prominent companies like Google have complained publicly about the rejection of large numbers of petitions.[91]

The Latin American Reaction and Europe

It is worth pointing out, in conclusion, that the expansive Latin American reaction to U.S. immigration policies has prompted increasing attention—sometimes quite vocal—on Europe. Nearly two million migrants from Latin American are estimated to be currently residing in Europe, mainly in Spain, Italy, and Portugal.[92] The demographic fit exists with Europe, perhaps even more so than with the United States, because Europe has a rapidly aging population (because of very low birth rates, even lower than in the United States) and a strong economy that needs labor to keep it going, so there is a considerable amount of available employment for migrants, whether legal or illegal. Thus, despite the distance migrants must travel, especially when compared to the proximity of the United States, Latin American migrants view Europe as a viable and desirable destination.

Europe has been somewhat more ambivalent about accepting immigrants than has the United States, however, and most immigrants to Europe have been from a specific European country's former colonies or close ally (in the case of Germany and its relationship to Turkey). Spain and Portugal were, of course the principal colonizers of Latin America, so the return migration to those countries is understandable. With respect to Italy, the exodus of people from southern Italy in the late nineteenth and early to mid-twentieth centuries sent migrants to South American as well as the United States, so it is understandable that when Argentines, Uruguayans, Peruvians, or Ecuadorians, for example, seeks fortune outside of Latin America, they might head to the land from which their grandparents came.

Remittances from Latin Americans living in Europe, though not reaching the levels of the United States, nonetheless represent an important source of income. Spain has the largest number of migrants and, according to data from the Inter-American Development Bank, also is the source of the greatest amount in remittances—3.7 billion Euros (about 5.2 billion U.S. dollars) to Latin America as of 2006.[93] Ecuador and Colombia are the top two recipient countries.

In a negative response to the rise in undocumented immigration to Europe, France—presiding over the European Union in 2008—pushed for a common immigration policy that would prevent amnesties such as those enacted by Spain in 2005, which permitted as many as 800,000 undocumented immigrants in that country to apply for legal status. The most controversial element in the policy proposed in the EU by France was a so-called returns directive, which would allow countries to hold undocumented immigrants for six months, in some cases extended to a year, before deporting them back to their country of origin.

This was widely criticized in Latin America, with harsh words from South American presidents Hugo Chávez (Venezuela), Rafael Correa

(Ecuador), and Evo Morales (Bolivia).[94] The General Secretary of the Organization of American States (OAS) argued the following:

> The migratory flow of Latin Americans to Europe, just like the flow to North America, will continue to happen as long as the immigrants can find jobs there that are not available to them in their native countries. While on one side they insist upon the positive character of the globalization process, they refuse to accept the movement of people as one of its consequences. For political reasons, they reject a phenomenon produced by economic globalization.[95]

The OAS further announced that the matter would be discussed by the organization's permanent council to determine what, if any, actions should be taken. As of this writing, it had yet to act.

Given the number of Latin Americans in Europe, it is almost certain that targeted lobbying will follow. Strategies that have worked in the United States may well serve as useful models for action in Europe, particularly if policies aimed at undocumented immigration have a strong punitive bent. Governments may consider that fighting for the rights of those migrants makes good economic and electoral sense.

CHAPTER SIX

The Explosion of Growth in the American South

IN 2007, THE CITY OF CHARLOTTE, NORTH CAROLINA, EXPERIENCED a first. The first baby born in the new year was Josue Eduardo Martínez, a hale and hearty 8 pounds and 21.5 inches long. His parents—whose country of origin was not specified—spoke no English.[1] Charlotte was already labeled as a metropolitan area characterized by "hyper-growth" of its Latino population, and thus provides a good example of how Latino immigration has reshaped the Southern socioeconomic and political landscapes. Yet across the entire southeastern United States, the new reality of a growing and more permanent Latino population is evident. When a geographer asked the Mexican owner of a restaurant in Georgia about his future plans, he replied, "I'm fixin' to go back, but I have three kids and I want them to go to school and go to college. But I'd like to die in Mexico."[2] In other words, the respondent was originally from Mexico, but had taken on a southern dialect and had pushed plans for return far into the future.

This chapter will analyze the demographic and economic changes that have taken place in recent years in the South as a result of Latino immigration, along with the regional political response. As we've argued, demography plays a critical role in understanding why migrants from Latin America have been coming to the United States. In the southeastern United States, the economic growth that accelerated in the 1990s revealed the labor gap that resulted from a predominantly older population. There were jobs to be had, and Latinos began to fill them. It is not, however, a permanent set of circumstances, and as the demography of the region undergoes shifts, so will local responses.

As already noted, until recently the South was not a common immigrant destination. A relatively low level of economic development, combined with endemic (and until the 1960s, legally constituted) racism made the area much less hospitable to newcomers. Given the racial tensions that have marked the region, some have argued that the current debate over immigration is racialized, even if race is rarely mentioned directly.[3]

The New Southern Reality

To get an analytical grip on the political demography of the South, we first must answer some of the basic questions about the nature of the changes taking place.

Who is Coming?

A comparison of census data provides a context for the changes taking place. Table 6.1 shows the countries of origin of the foreign-born population for the entire United States, for the West—the traditional settling place for Latinos—and for the South. For the country as a whole, slightly less than 13 percent of the population as of 2007 was foreign born, and the majority of this group (53.6 percent) had been born in Latin America. In the West, one in five was foreign born, and a majority of these (55.0 percent) were from Latin America. The South is still relatively new to receiving foreigners (6.2 percent), as we have noted, but half of them are from Latin America. Importantly, only about half (52.5 percent) of the Latin American immigrants to the South are from Mexico, compared to eight in ten (81 percent) in the West. Other Central American countries, especially El Salvador, Guatemala, and Honduras, are proportionately more important in the South than in the West, as are immigrants from South America, especially Colombia, Peru, and Brazil. This is not surprising from a geographic perspective, of course, since Central and South American

Table 6.1 Latino Foreign-Born Populations in the South Compared with the West and the United States as a Whole, 2007

Foreign-born population	U.S.	West	South
Percent Foreign-born	12.6%	19.9%	6.2%
Percent of foreign-born from Latin America	53.6%	55.0%	49.7%
Percent of those from Latin America from:			
Caribbean:	***16.6%***	***1.5%***	***10.0%***
Barbados	0.3%	0.0%	0.3%
Cuba	4.8%	0.8%	1.9%
Dominican Republic	3.7%	0.2%	1.2%
Haiti	2.6%	0.1%	1.3%
Jamaica	2.9%	0.2%	3.2%
Trinidad and Tobago	1.1%	0.1%	1.1%
Other Caribbean	1.2%	0.1%	1.1%
Central America:	***70.8%***	***93.9%***	***75.8%***
Mexico	57.5%	81.3%	52.5%
Costa Rica	0.4%	0.2%	0.7%
El Salvador	5.4%	6.4%	8.7%
Guatemala	3.4%	3.7%	5.9%
Honduras	2.1%	0.9%	5.6%
Nicaragua	1.1%	0.9%	1.0%
Panama	0.5%	0.2%	1.1%
Other Central America	0.3%	0.3%	0.3%
South America:	***12.6%***	***4.6%***	***14.2%***
Argentina	0.8%	0.6%	0.8%
Bolivia	0.3%	0.1%	1.6%
Brazil	1.7%	0.6%	1.8%
Chile	0.4%	0.4%	0.4%
Colombia	3.0%	0.8%	3.0%
Ecuador	2.0%	0.5%	0.9%
Guyana	1.2%	0.1%	1.0%
Peru	2.0%	1.2%	2.9%
Uruguay	0.2%	0.1%	0.5%
Venezuela	0.8%	0.2%	0.8%
Other South America	0.2%	0.1%	0.4%

Italics indicate sum for regions

SOURCE: Calculations by the authors from U.S. Census Bureau 2007 American Community Survey.

Table 6.2 Latino Foreign-Born Populations in Atlanta and Charlotte, Compared to Los Angeles, Phoenix, and Dallas, 2007

Foreign-born population	**South**		**Southwest**		
	Atlanta	**Charlotte**	**Los Angeles**	**Phoenix**	**Dallas**
Percent foreign-born	12.7%	9.1%	34.9%	17.6%	17.8%
Percent of foreign-born from Latin America	52.4%	55.9%	58.3%	70.6%	68.6%

countries are considerably closer to the states of the South than to the states of the Southwest, and legal migrants are very likely to find a flight to and from their country of origin through Atlanta, which has the nation's busiest airport.

The new pattern of immigration to the South compared to the West is highlighted in Table 6.2, which compares data for major metropolitan areas of the two regions for 2007. Los Angeles, Phoenix, and Dallas have drawn very heavily from Mexico. Indeed, in Phoenix almost all Latinos are from Mexico. In the South there is greater diversity, with higher percentages from South America and from the Caribbean, as well.

Where Are Latinos Living?

The simple and commonsensical answer to where Latinos are living is "where the jobs are." The initial employment attraction in the South was rural. Poultry processing, tobacco, furniture manufacturing, and other southern economic staples brought Latinos from western states, and then directly from Latin America itself. In some cases, this reflected broader economic transformations in the United States. Meat-processing companies, for example, relocated to the South to reduce transportation costs and to take advantage of low rates of unionization, especially compared to cities in the Midwest.[4] Initial research done on Latino immigration to the South focused on rural communities, particularly in Georgia, where immigrants worked primarily in agriculture but to a lesser extent in the carpet business. Southern businesses recruited Latin American labor, particularly in Mexico, to fill their labor needs.

The combination of agriculture work and carpet installation is, in fact, exemplary of what has happened over the years to agriculture in the United States. Despite the classic images of stoop labor (African Americans in the South and Hispanics in the West), most work is now done by machine. The 2007 American Community Survey counts fewer than one million workers (out of a total of 142 million) who list an agricultural occupation. At the same time, Hispanics account for nearly half (48 percent) of all agricultural workers in the United States, even if the absolute number is fairly small.

Furthermore, only a slim majority of agricultural workers (53 percent) live in rural areas. Agriculture that requires hand work, such as fruits and vegetables, tends to be in close proximity to urban markets, so workers for these farms can live in an urban area even though performing what are thought of as rural tasks. That gives them the flexibility to participate in other urban-based occupations such as construction and service jobs.

Putting those ideas together, it is not surprising that in California as long ago as 1990 only 5 percent of Hispanics lived in rural areas, and in Texas, another heavily agricultural state, only 13 percent of Hispanics lived in rural areas. Yet 20 percent of Hispanics in the South lived in rural areas—a considerably higher percentage than in the southwest. By 2007, the proportion of Hispanics living in rural areas in California was still 5 percent, and in Texas it was still 13 percent, but it had grown to 22 percent in the South.

Especially in the context of economic growth, however, it became clear that there were many employment opportunities in larger towns and cities. For Hispanics the downside has been that urbanization has brought their presence to the attention of all Southerners. Instead of living in rural communities and remaining relatively invisible to the majority of the non-Latino South, the move to larger towns and cities literally began to change the landscape. In leafy suburbs, Spanish became more visible—in signs, markets, bumper stickers, churches (both Protestant and Catholic), and other public venues.

Like other migrants from around the United States, regardless of race, ethnicity, or country of origin, Latinos saw that the South offered numerous benefits compared to traditional gateway cities. The cost of living in California in particular had skyrocketed, and the perception of labor market saturation became more widespread. Therefore, the Golden State became a major source of outmigration for the foreign born.

Who is Staying?

The most obvious sign that someone intends to remain in the country is that they become a citizen. In large part because of enforcement efforts, which have made moving back and forth across the border more difficult, the rates of naturalization across the country have increased—and as we saw in Chapter Five, Latin American governments recognize this reality and are facilitating it. For example, from 2005 to 2007, the number of Mexican naturalizations nationally rose from 77,089 to 122,258 annually.[5] This has also been the case in the South. From 1998 to 2007, the total number of naturalizations (from all over the world) in the Atlanta metropolitan area increased from 4,133 to 11,720 per year, and in the Charlotte area from 971 to 1,850 per year.[6]

It is also evident that, although Mexico is by far the top sending country, South America is also an important source of migrants to the U.S. South. According to the Department of Homeland Security, for fiscal year 2006, Mexicans naturalize in the greatest numbers in every Southern state except Louisiana and Virginia. Thousands of Hondurans fled Hurricane Mitch in 1998, and settled in Louisiana, primarily in New Orleans, so that Mexico ranks second in that state in naturalizations. Colombia, however, ranks second to Mexico in Alabama, Georgia, Mississippi, North Carolina, and South Carolina. In North Carolina, Colombia is consistently the second largest source of naturalizations from Latin America, with Ecuador also becoming more prominent. From Central America, El Salvador is consistently the most important source country. In Virginia, Salvadorans naturalize in the greatest numbers, and nationally, they rank fourth in the rate of naturalization, after Mexicans, Dominicans, and Cubans.

It is clear that many immigrants in the South intend to remain permanently. That is, their intention is not to move back to their country of origin or, as might be the case, the state in which they previously resided. As early as 2000, scholars were finding that Mexican communities in small Georgia cities were built around carpet and meatpacking jobs, but also that immigrants created their own small businesses such as grocery stores, restaurants, bars, beauty parlors, jewelry stores, clothing stores, taxi services, and even insurance agencies.[7] A majority of immigrant survey respondents—indeed, three-quarters of those who were parents—wished to remain in their current city of residence for at least the next three years. For many migrants, these local entrepreneurial opportunities were preferable to following seasonal agriculture or making hazardous trips back and forth to their home country.

The emphasis on permanence is also apparent from the rapid arrival of women into Southern immigrant communities, which strongly suggests that families wish to stay in one area. This is true regardless of immigration status. Once households are established, it becomes less likely that families will choose to uproot and relocate. This is even more true when children are born. Of course, if one or both parents are in the United States illegally, then having a child born in the United States will decrease the likelihood of returning to the country of origin, given the risks. It also changes the sociopolitical dynamic since the children are citizens whereas the parents are not.

Traditionally, the literature on immigration focuses on male "pioneers" who arrive, obtain employment, and then eventually send for their families.[8] In classic patriarchal societies, men typically made decisions for the household and were in a better position to endure the potentially hazardous physical conditions that attended both the trip itself (especially if unauthorized) and the low-wage labor the migrant would obtain. There was, therefore, a delay between the arrival of the men and of the women, evidenced by a sizeable gender imbalance. This is evident in the South as well, but across the region the gender gap is slower to close than the above explanation would suggest, largely because of the continuous flow of new migrants. In 2000, 59.7 percent (684,631) of adult (eighteen and older) Latinos in the South were male, and 41.3 percent (462,798) were female. In 2006, 58.2 percent (965,134) of the adult population was male, and 41.8 percent (691,913) was female. However, the total number of adults had increased 44.4 percent. In short, although the gender ratio was closing very slowly, many men and women were still arriving in the South, which has led to a rapid increase in single men *and* in families. The South is also seeing an increase in the number of older Latinos, which suggests that more grandparents are arriving to assist with childcare while mothers work. This is consistent with results from a 2005 survey showing that 72 percent of Mexican immigrants in South Carolina had not returned to Mexico in the previous five years.[9]

Between 1990 and 2000, the greatest percentage increase of births to Hispanic mothers occurred in southern states, with Tennessee first (625 percent), followed by North Carolina (616 percent), Georgia (490 percent), Arkansas (466 percent), and Mississippi (437 percent).[10] Between 2000 and

2003, the percentage growth remained in double digits in every Southern state except for Louisiana and Mississippi. In Mecklenburg County, North Carolina, the most populous county in the state, the number of women of childbearing age has grown dramatically, and by 2005 nearly one in five children in the county had a mother of Hispanic descent.[11]

This follows a more general pattern of the feminization of Latin American migration. In Mexico, for example, one of the consequences of large numbers of men leaving for the United States was that the women left behind began entering the domestic workforce.[12] As a result, women became more autonomous, and therefore more likely to migrate, or at the very least be part of the family's migration decision. As a result, more young women are migrating and then having children in the United States.

Further, the thriving service industry in the southeast created a large number of jobs most commonly taken by women, such as house cleaning. Given the nature of domestic work, which takes place in a private home and may even include childcare (not to mention often being compensated in cash), it is often viewed as not "real work" and therefore is prone to abuse.[13] In 2007, domestic workers organized in Atlanta to form a national alliance to protect their rights.[14] They told stories of having wages withheld, being locked in a basement, or even beaten with bamboo rods and scalded with boiling water.

The fact that many Latino immigrants are taking jobs in the construction and service sectors also contributes to a pattern of long-term settlement. Unlike agriculture, these are jobs that can be performed year round, which encourages staying in one place. Combined with a relatively welcoming environment, cost of living, and the growth of families, it should come as no surprise that many Latinos are choosing not only to remain in the South, but perhaps also to remain in the same town or city.

Furthermore, since the immigrant community is already established, and as word spreads that the South has a number of attractive qualities for immigrants, chain migration will result: "migratory movements, once started, become self-sustaining social processes."[15] The closing of the demographic fit will eventually slow the number of people arriving to join family and friends, but chain migration processes suggest that it will not stop entirely.

Family building within the immigrant Latino population has significant political effects because, under the current set of immigration laws, migrants cannot be viewed simply as sojourners who work for a finite amount of time and then return to their country of origin. Instead, local political leaders quickly come to the realization that their new Latino communities are here to stay, even if they might shrink or swell a bit in the face of changing economic opportunities. This means not only that elected officials are compelled to construct public policy accordingly, but also that political parties are already courting Hispanic registered voters and, ultimately, will put up Hispanic candidates for elected office. Since Latino immigration to the South is a recent phenomenon, political incorporation will take time. For example, in Charlotte only about 7 percent of Latinos are registered to vote.[16] The rest may not yet be citizens, or they may be too young. In Georgia, North Carolina, and South Carolina, there is a wide gulf between latent and actual political power and influence.[17]

Of course, *actual* political power, driven not only by having the right to vote but also by using that right, depends first upon gaining citizenship. In the short term, Latinos are unlikely to become powerful politically. Over the longer term, as children of immigrants (who tend to be born in the United States and thus are automatically U.S. citizens) reach voting age, and as greater numbers of immigrants naturalize as their stay in the country lengthens, the challenge will be to translate citizenship into voting behavior, especially through concerted registration drives.

To generate higher rates of political mobilization, there must be Latino candidates, especially for high-profile positions like mayor.[18] Turnout, participation, and generally positive feelings among Hispanics toward government increase when there is a visible Latino elected official in a city.[19] Of course, this has occurred in a number of cities with more established Latino communities, but not yet in the South. Even then, however, the process took considerable time. In Los Angeles, for example, a prototypical gateway city, the first modern Latino mayor (Antonio Villaraigosa) was not elected until 2005 (the first mayor of Los Angeles was elected in 1872). Other large gateway cities, such as Chicago, New York, and San Diego, have never had Latino mayors. Nonetheless, the list of larger cities that have elected Latino mayors is growing and includes Austin, Denver, Miami, and San Antonio.

Demography will play an important role in the eventual election of more mayors. Nationally, the Hispanic population has already surpassed African Americans as the most numerous minority, and in the South the gap between Latinos and African Americans will also slowly narrow. The national projections released in 2008 suggest that by 2050, the Hispanic population is likely to double from 15 to 30 percent. By contrast, the African American population is projected to increase only slightly from 14 to 15 percent. However, the recency of these demographic shifts has caused the U.S. Census Bureau to delay its state population projections by race and ethnicity, so as of this writing, such projections were not available. At the national level, the Census Bureau projects that the Hispanic population in the United States will nearly double between 2000 and 2050, from 16 to 30 percent. At the same time, however, the non-Hispanic black population is expected to remain at 12 percent of the national total.[20]

Because the immigrant population in the South is more likely to be recently arrived in the United States than in traditional gateway cities, it is also more likely to send remittances. In 2006, the top two states in terms of the percentage of immigrant Latino adults sending money home were Georgia (85 percent) and North Carolina (84 percent).[21] By contrast, in California 63 percent did so and in Texas only 47 percent. Regionally, the South (at 78 percent) was second only to the Mid-Atlantic (88 percent), the latter of course representing another new gateway region. Only 57 percent of immigrants in the Southwest sent money home. As Latinos transition from "migrant" to "resident," more of their money will remain in the region, rather than being sent back to relatives in their country of origin.

Finally, there is a public health consequence. It is well documented that recently arrived migrants are far healthier than their second- or third-generation counterparts.[22] This explains in part why undocumented immigrant use of emergency rooms and hospital services tends to be overstated, since they tend to be healthier to begin with. However, as more migrants settle in the region, more health problems, such as heart disease and diabetes, will likely manifest themselves, thus eliminating the health advantage that migrants from Latin America bring with them.

Political Response to the Latino Presence in the South

In the past half century, Southern cities and towns have seen tumultuous change, as the Civil Rights Act advanced the rights of African Americans, tearing down barriers to voting, providing equal access to public spaces, and creating equality before the law in all areas of life. Given how contentious race has been, one might expect that the reaction to a greater Hispanic presence would parallel past debates. The political response is, however, much more complex. There is certainly conflict, but also much cooperation.

Perception of Economic Drain

A number of southern states have endeavored to fix a dollar amount on the costs of immigration, legal or not (or both) which then becomes a foundation for public policy. In general, however, they do not provide a very solid foundation because of a significant lack of data. Most of the costs associated with immigration are government services, particularly schools and hospitals, but they do not keep records of whether their clients were immigrants or whether they were in the country legally. In addition, it is extremely difficult to pinpoint the tax revenue garnered from illegal immigrants. Many are hired on a cash-only basis, which of course is never recorded. Others, however, have fraudulent documentation (belying the term "undocumented") and consequently have taxes withheld from their paychecks that they will not recoup (and, indeed, federal taxes like social security do not benefit the state in question anyway). How many fall into the latter category is impossible to determine with even minimal accuracy. Researchers are thus left to guess as best they can. This makes such reports a potentially problematic source of public policy, but they are used for that purpose, nonetheless, largely because elected officials are often convinced that undocumented immigrants are a net drain on the public treasury, even if they can't prove it.

In 2006, the State Auditor of Mississippi determined that illegal immigration cost the state $25 million a year.[23] The core expenses were health care, education, and corrections. At the same time, the report noted that the "most significant finding of this report is Mississippi's inability to accurately quantify the costs of illegal immigrants because most state agencies, schools and other government entities do not currently document the actual numbers of illegal immigrants or their use of services."[24]

The Kenan-Flagler Business School at the University of North Carolina at Chapel Hill estimated in 2006 that, whereas the state's Hispanic population contributed $9 billion to the economy, the state incurred $102 per Latino for health care, education, and law enforcement, summing to expenses of $61 million.[25] This estimate was based on a number of assumptions, such as the assertion that Hispanics spent 20 percent of their disposable income on remittances, along with savings and interest payments. If that percentage is skewed slightly one way or the other, the net estimated contribution of Latinos per capita can change dramatically. It also did not distinguish between legal and illegal immigrants.

A 2007 report in Arkansas found that two-thirds of its immigrants were from Latin America, and their positive economic impact was approximately $3 billion.[26] It also acknowledged the demographic reality that immigrants were acting as labor replacement because the state had demand that its own residents could not fill. The report did not estimate the impact of Latino migrants specifically, but immigrants overall represented a net financial gain for the state of $19 million, or $158 per immigrant. Nonetheless, later in the year state agencies testified to the Arkansan legislature that immigrants constituted a net $170 million drain on state coffers, prompting one state legislator to remark, "We must close the barn door before everything's gone."[27] These diverging conclusions stem from the difficulty of obtaining reliable data, which leaves researchers no choice but to make a large number of inferences and estimates.

Alabama took a slightly different tack by appointing a commission to make recommendations based on the assumption that illegal immigrants posed a threat to the state. Grandly named the Joint Interim Patriotic Immigration Commission, it issued a report in February 2008. It recommended that English be the official language of the state, that sanctuary cities should be abolished, and that in general undocumented immigrants "be discouraged from coming to Alabama."[28] This report was consistent with the widespread perception that undocumented immigrants constitute a drag on the economies of southern states.

These negative perceptions put elected officials in a difficult position. Especially at the city and county levels, where budgets are aimed largely at the services that immigrants consume, officials have no political authority to legislate for or against immigration, but find themselves in the crosshairs when angry residents complain about their perception of immigration's negative effects. One political ramification is that state legislatures, as well as local assemblies and councils, are crafting their own laws. These efforts, as well as the controversy over whether they are constitutional, are discussed later in the chapter.

Nonetheless, Southern political leaders also recognize demographic realities, particularly in terms of too few workers, which can also be reflected in local studies. In Charlotte, Mayor Pat McCrory organized the Mayor's Immigration Study Commission in late 2005. Its extensive 2007 report noted, "While illegal immigrants have provided a necessary labor pool, employers and businesses are increasingly finding themselves in a perpetual balancing act to maintain a workforce, yet adhere to all applicable laws, including immigration laws."[29] As in the rest of the country, the aging population in the South has put employers—especially those offering relatively low-wage, physically demanding jobs—in a quandary. Native residents of many states simply do not supply a large enough workforce, which then creates an incentive to hire migrant labor, which itself poses problems regarding verifying the immigrant status of each job applicant. As the demographic fit closes, this dilemma will be alleviated to an important degree, although of course closing the fit will be accomplished in part by a growth in the younger population from the children of immigrants, thus quite literally changing the face of the South—a future most southerners are not yet aware of and have not yet contemplated.

Perception of Threat

Another aspect of the public response to immigration is the perception that immigrants—particularly undocumented—are more likely to be criminals. This is, at times, driven by the assertion that if someone is willing to break the law to enter and/or remain in the country, ipso facto they are more likely to break the law while living in the United States, perhaps even violently. The city of Hazleton, Pennsylvania, explicitly utilized this logic in passing a restrictive local ordinance aimed at reducing the population of undocumented immigrants.

The City of Hazleton and Immigration

The most prominent and widely publicized case involving local efforts to legislate immigration was in Hazleton, Pennsylvania. In 2006, the City Council passed the Illegal Immigration Relief Act Ordinance, which would punish landlords who rented to undocumented immigrants and employers who hired them. It also required every tenant to register at City Hall. The law was quickly challenged, and in 2007 a federal district court overturned it, asserting that it preempted federal law and as such was unconstitutional. Judge James Munley's decision concluded as follows:

> Whatever frustrations officials of the City of Hazleton may feel about the current state of federal immigration enforcement, the nature of the political system in the United States prohibits the City from enacting ordinances that disrupt a carefully drawn federal statutory scheme. Even if federal law did not conflict with Hazleton's measures, the City could not enact an ordinance that violates rights the Constitution guarantees to every person in the United States, whether legal resident or not. The genius of our Constitution is that it provides rights even to those who evoke the least sympathy from the general public. In that way, all in this nation can be confident of equal justice under its laws. Hazleton, in its zeal to control the presence of a group deemed undesirable, violated the rights of such people, as well as others within the community. Since the United States Constitution protects even the disfavored, the ordinances cannot be enforced.[30]

Similar lawsuits have been launched across the country. The Alabama immigration report, in fact, included a recommendation that legislators be very careful not to pass legislation that might lead to lawsuits.

That logic, however, has been challenged by empirical studies showing the opposite to be true. For example, foreign-born men have a much lower rate of incarceration than native-born, and crime levels in the United States have dropped even as the number of undocumented immigrants increased, and even in cities with large immigrant populations.[31] In large part, this is a matter of self-selection. Contrary to popular belief, individuals who choose to emigrate have lower criminal propensities.[32] (This has potentially important implications for the sending countries as well, if the more criminally minded are more likely remain in the country). At the same time, "lower propensity" does not mean that there is no crime among undocumented immigrants. Some crimes are committed by such people, so there is always fodder for exaggerated claims.

One of the serious areas concerning criminal activity among immigrants relates specifically to Latino gangs. By far the largest Latino gang in the South is MS-13. Although it is associated with Salvadorans, its origins are entirely within the United States. It did not arrive with immigrants, rather it emerged among immigrant groups after they arrived in the United States. When Salvadorans fled the civil war in their country in the 1980s, the majority settled in Los Angeles, where in low-income neighborhoods they were immediately confronted with Mexican-American gangs, which, again, were composed largely of U.S.-born children of immigrants, not immigrants themselves. Mara Salvatrucha ("mara" is slang for gang, and "salvatrucha" refers to Salvadoran guerrillas), known as MS-13, was created as a means of protection for newly arrived migrants who were targeted on the basis of their nationality (a reminder that Latinos are not really a homogeneous group).

It has since become transnational, particularly as gang members are deported to El Salvador, where their prison time is spent recruiting new members, who often migrate back to the United States. Concern about the gang therefore is also a major foreign policy concern. As Assistant Secretary of State for Western Hemisphere Affairs Thomas Shannon noted in 2008, "By working with these nations to dismantle such groups and strengthen institutions, we multiply the effectiveness of our own domestic security efforts."[33] MS-13 is also a major source of concern for Central American security forces[34] because it has become infamous for brutality and is one of the most violent gangs in the United States and Central America.

Inevitably, as Latinos moved from west to east in the United States, a gang presence made itself known in the South. In January 2008, the FBI rated the MS-13 threat in the southeast as "moderate to low," but noted a recent influx.[35] In 2008, a federal grand jury indicted twenty-six suspected members of MS-13 in the Charlotte area, and immediately arrested most of them on charges of extortion, drug trafficking, and/or homicide.[36] Similar sweeps occurred in Tennessee and Virginia.[37] At the same time, the Department of Justice noted that Mexican drug-trafficking organizations dominate the drug trade in the Atlanta metropolitan area, including the sale and distribution of cocaine, ice methamphetamine, and marijuana.[38]

Clearly, the increase of Latino gang activity is a real threat. The dilemma for public policy is to formulate policies aimed at gang activity rather than at Latino migrants more generally. This is no easy matter, since it is a local, national, and international problem that requires a high level of coordination to combat. In the South, there are local initiatives, such as awareness forums held in Dalton, Georgia.[39] Organized by the Coalition of Latin Leaders, the purpose of these forums is to demonstrate that the Hispanic community is dedicated to addressing the problem of gangs.

Local Government Initiatives

After President George W. Bush's failed attempts to persuade Congress to pass immigration reform laws, many local governments across the country decided to take the initiative themselves. The essential argument in local government is that the federal government is either unable or unwilling to enact legislation, so it is incumbent upon them to act. Such efforts can take several forms. First, they can embrace immigrants by establishing what is popularly known as "sanctuary" status. Although the precise nature of that status can vary, the distinguishing characteristic is that a town or city agrees not to make immigration status a precondition for receiving any services, and law enforcement will not make an effort to determine a person's status unless the individual has committed a crime. It is the immigration equivalent of "Don't ask, don't tell." Most sanctuary cities have well-established immigrant populations (such as Los Angeles, San Francisco, and New York) though several are more liberal university towns, such as Austin, Madison, and Ann Arbor. They are not common in the South, and those that exist fall into the latter category, namely Durham and Chapel Hill in North Carolina. In fact, in 2008 the Georgia State Legislature began debating a bill that would deny state funds to any city that declared sanctuary status.[40] This was intended to be a preemptive measure, since no city in Georgia had made any such declaration.

Second, local-level reform can be punitive, seeking, for example, to punish apartment owners who rent to undocumented immigrants, companies that hire them, or anyone who acts to reduce the "demand" side. The logic is that if undocumented immigrants cannot safely find either employment or housing, then they will choose not to live in a given location. This extends to higher education, particularly in terms of whether or not to allow undocumented immigrants to attend community colleges, which tend to be funded at the local level and are heavily subsidized by taxpayers. In 2008, the State Board of Community Colleges in North Carolina ruled that they could not attend, whereas in the past they were allowed to do so as nonresidents (that is, with higher out-of-state tuition).[41]

In 2007, state legislatures in every state in the country introduced 1,562 pieces of legislation related to immigration, with 240 enacted.[42]

That number was up from 2006, when 570 were introduced and 84 were enacted. Of the laws enacted, only a very small number (36, or 15 percent) were in the South. Nonetheless, every Southern state did enact at least one law; Virginia had the most with eight, while Louisiana and Tennessee each had six. Most were punitive to some degree, though not all. Arkansas, for example, passed a resolution (HR 1003) requesting the federal government to pass comprehensive immigration reform (though noting specifically that it should not include amnesty).

Western states with long traditions of immigration accounted for a much greater share of the legislation; Arizona and California combined for 27, or 11 percent of the total. Although one might expect that as more immigrants arrive, Southern legislatures would be more likely to pass legislation, thus far the evidence is not firm. In 2006, the South accounted for 17 of the 84 pieces of legislation, or 20.2 percent of the total, compared to 15 percent in 2007.

What do these numbers tell us? It is obvious that state legislators have collectively decided that without action by the federal government, they have no choice but to pass their own legislation. There is a direct correlation between inaction at the federal level since 2006 and the flurry of legislative proposals at the state and local levels. However, aside from high-profile cases like Hazleton, we know far less about immigration-related legislation proposed at the local level, even though laws are being presented and passed on a regular basis. In Nashville, for example, a member of the city council has pushed to make the city English-only, similar to laws already passed in some small communities, including Cherokee County (an Atlanta suburb).[43] In Prince William County, Virginia (a suburb of Washington, D.C.), county commissioners voted to limit or even block access to public services for undocumented immigrants.[44] In Charlotte, Republican county commissioners proposed a total ban on government services for undocumented immigrants in 2005, but have consistently been unable to achieve the majority required to pass the ban.[45] As Commissioner Bill James put it, the county needed to "get medieval" on businesses, and then word would get out.[46] Taken together, these local legislative efforts represent a patchwork of different interpretations and beliefs about the desired amount and type of immigration in local communities, with adjoining cities and counties passing very different types of laws according to the dictates of varying constituencies.

A pressing, yet still unresolved question is whether this type of legislation, at the state or local level, is even constitutional. Since the nineteenth century, three constitutional clauses—the Naturalization Clause, the Foreign Affairs Clause, and the Commerce Clause—have been identified by the U.S. Supreme Court as exclusively federal responsibility, and immigration falls under all three.[47] Historically, local law enforcement could address criminal violations of the law by immigrants, but not civil violations. For example, police in a given city could prosecute the crime of human smuggling, but not lack of legal status.[48] Lacking legal status, that is, being in the United States illegally, is a civil, not a criminal violation of the Immigration and Nationality Act, as we have noted previously. This important difference is often lost in the rhetoric about criminal activity among undocumented immigrants.

Supporters of the constitutional validity of local immigration legislation, including the U.S. Department of Justice after the 9/11 attacks, argue that as sovereign entities each state has "inherent authority" to enforce both civil and criminal immigration laws. As mentioned, local lawmakers have also expressed frustration with their inability to address undocumented immigration in the absence of federal immigration reform. The division between criminal and civil aspects of immigration remains legally fluid and open to interpretation.

From a punitive standpoint, police and sheriffs can also sign agreements that provide federal immigration training for local law enforcement, granting them authority to identify, process, and even detain undocumented immigrants if they have been encountered through normal law enforcement duties. These agreements were made possible by a 1996 amendment to section 287(g) of the Immigration and Nationality Act, and have been adopted in growing numbers. Commonly referred to as "287(g)," these "memoranda of agreement" (MOAs) resolve the problem of inherent authority because the federal government is formally granting local governments that authority. As such, unlike local immigration laws, there are no legal challenges to 287(g).

As of August 2008, U.S. Immigration and Customs Enforcement (ICE) had signed sixty-three MOAs under the 287(g) provisions and had trained more than 840 local law enforcement personnel in dealing with undocumented immigrants.[49] Just under half (twenty-eight) were in the South (in Alabama, Arkansas, Georgia, North Carolina, South Carolina, Tennessee, and Virginia). In fact, in February 2006, the first 287(g) MOA in the South was established in Mecklenburg County, North Carolina, and the Sheriff who did so, James Pendergraph, later became the first Executive Director of ICE's Office of State and Local Coordination.

Although controversial, they are relatively popular in the South. In a December 2007 poll, 72 percent of Arkansans agreed that if an undocumented immigrant were pulled over for a traffic violation, they should be deported.[50] Or, as Davidson County (Tennessee) sheriff Daron Hall put it, "I appreciate the continued support and want to remind you that just over 3,500 criminal aliens have been removed from our community and there is no doubt in my mind we are safer. More than half of those removed have been previously arrested."[51] In congressional testimony, a representative from Alabama's Department of Public Safety stated that "Alabama's MOA with Homeland Security is a reasonable, common-sense platform that results in a win-win outcome both for the law enforcement community and for the citizens whom we serve."[52] For local governments, they offer a fairly low-cost but high-profile means of responding to undocumented immigration, and do not carry the threat of lawsuits in the same way that legislation might.

They are popular enough that making them mandatory became part of the Republican Party's campaign platform for the presidential election of 2008. Republicans argued that the rule of law "means requiring cooperation among federal, state and local law enforcement and real consequences, including the denial of federal funds, for self-described sanctuary cities, which stand in open defiance of the federal and state statutes that expressly prohibit such sanctuary policies, and which endanger the lives of U.S. citizens."[53] Party platforms tend to reflect the ideals of the party's base, so this does not necessarily mean that a majority of party members share the same sentiments. It does, however, show that local enforcement has become a hot issue. The Democratic Party platform in 2008 did not mention state and local immigration law enforcement.

Critics argue that 287(g) programs are discriminatory because they encourage "profiling," whereby local law enforcement officials will target those they believe are Hispanic on the assumption that they may be in the country illegally, even with no probable cause. They can point to comments such as those from Johnston County (North Carolina) Sheriff Steve Bizell, who said that illegal immigrants were "breeding like rabbits" and that "Mexicans are trashy."[54] Furthermore, opponents assert that the possibility that interaction with law enforcement may lead to deportation will make immigrants less likely to seek assistance when they are crime victims. Latino immigrants are already targets for crime because they often carry cash rather than checks and credit cards.

Immigration and Public Opinion in the South

As we've noted, unsuccessful Republican presidential candidate Mike Huckabee, who was opposed to immigration, did well in Southern primaries against John McCain, who had long advocated immigration reform that included a Temporary Worker Program. It was widely argued that McCain's stance on immigration damaged him politically in the South, especially in South Carolina.[55] For this to hold, we would expect Southern voters to consider immigration as an issue of high salience, so much so that they based their votes in large part upon it. How, then, do people in the South view immigration?

One major indicator is the importance southerners place on immigration vis-à-vis other issues when deciding how they will vote. Table 6.3 shows that immigration is only the third or fourth priority for Southerners, behind the war in Iraq, the economy, and national security. Although considerable media attention is focused on undocumented immigration, other issues dominate the minds of Southern voters. This does not suggest, of course, that immigration is not viewed as important, but rather that it

Table 6.3 Salience of Immigration in the South, 2008

State	Importance
Alabama	9%, 3rd (May 2008)
Arkansas	5%, tied 6th (May 2008)
Georgia	10%, 3rd (May 2008)
Louisiana	7%, 4th (May 2008)
Mississippi	10%, Tied 4th (May 2008)
North Carolina	12%, 3rd (May 2008)
South Carolina	No data
Tennessee	9%, 4th (April 2008)
Virginia	10%, 3rd (May 2008)

SOURCE: Rasmussen Reports n.d. (http://www.rasmussenreports.com). The question provides respondents with nine topics, and asks them to name which is most important when they think about how to vote in the presidential election.

does not generate the same amount of political interest. This is consistent with national public opinion which, despite heavy media coverage, rarely considers immigration as a top issue of interest. A USA Today/Gallup poll conducted in September 2008 found immigration sixth on the list of the most important issues for voters (the top five were the economy, Iraq, energy [including gas prices], health care, and terrorism).[56] At most, we can confidently argue that Southerners may perhaps be slightly more focused on immigration compared to other issues than the country as a whole, but still are less interested than commonly portrayed.

Politics, Demography, and Race in the South

Given the region's political and cultural history, race is an important element in understanding how immigrants are received in Southern communities. Because the terms "Latino" and "Hispanic" are ethnic, not racial, categories, there is some confusion regarding what race individuals may belong to. This is especially true of Latin American descendants of slaves, who are "Black" (and perhaps even "African American," given their birth in the Americas) but have little in common with Blacks in the U.S. South besides darker skin. Most Latinos in the South, however, are "mestizo," a broad term referring to a mix of indigenous peoples and their Spanish and Portuguese colonizers. As more migrants of African descent arrive in the South from Brazil, Colombia, and the Caribbean, among other places, the racial and ethnic context will become even more complex.

Western states have long dealt with the clashes inherent in the rapid growth of groups with very different ethnic and linguistic backgrounds (including Asians), and the substantial literature on race relations in the West is largely pessimistic about relations between African Americans and Latinos. In particular, although the two groups face similar challenges, especially discrimination, and so should be natural allies, they also compete for scarce resources. As legal scholar Nicolás Vaca writes, "in the real world the ostensible moral and philosophical bases for coalition politics have largely fallen apart because of competing self-interests."[57] It is worth asking, however, whether there is a unique confluence of race and immigration in the Southern experience. Racism and racial tension have emerged across the country, of course, but the legacies of slavery put race more prominently on the political agenda in the South. How does the African American community respond to Latino immigration, and what does this mean for the future of race relations in the region? There are two competing hypotheses.

The first and most common hypothesis holds that African Americans consider Latinos a threat. Despite the common refrain that immigrants take jobs that no one wants, the threat hypothesis considers job displacement a serious problem. A study of poultry processing in five Southern states concluded that immigrants were clearly taking jobs that had been filled by African Americans.[58] It may not be that African Americans no longer want the jobs, but rather that employers have changed their rationale for hiring, moving toward a docile workforce that will consistently accept low wages and poor conditions without becoming restive or joining unions.

Further, the argument goes, not only do immigrants compete for low-wage jobs, but immigrant labor drives those wages down further.[59] The increased size of the low-wage labor pool means that employers have the luxury of offering lower wages. The Latino population also receives a share of finite social services at the local level, in competition with other low-income groups, including African Americans. This was a problem in Los Angeles, where friction developed in the 1990s when California fell into recession, and many African Americans felt overwhelmed and pushed aside by newly arrived Latinos.[60] Despite facing similar problems, having similarly strong and largely conservative religious beliefs, and living near each other, very often there was almost no interaction between Latinos and blacks, and there remained a divide that proved difficult to bridge.

A study in Durham, North Carolina, found that African Americans were split about whether Hispanics took jobs from Blacks: 47 percent agreed that this was the case, 53 percent disagreed.[61] These responses cut across all income levels, so were not necessarily related to whether an individual was concerned about economic competition for themselves. However, 61 percent of African Americans felt "concerned" or "somewhat concerned" at the growth of the Latino population, compared with 41 percent of white respondents. Anecdotally, researchers encountered responses from African Americans such as "I don't fool with no Mexicans at all; want them to get back on the ship" and "Hispanics should all just swim home, don't know why they came to Durham."[62] This combines fear of job loss and wage reduction with the commonly held assumption (by people of all races) that all Latinos are in the country illegally; or perhaps it is a more generalized xenophobia.

These sentiments are exacerbated by commonly held perceptions that African Americans do not work as hard as Latino immigrants. After a

2007 raid by federal immigration agents at a Stillmore, Georgia, poultry processing plant, for example, African Americans came to fill the vacated positions. Many quickly left, citing dangerous working conditions, abusive management, and failure to pay promised wages. In the opinion of one Latino worker, "The blacks sit in the cafeteria and don't come to the line until the chickens are brought in, but the Hispanics, we spend the time cleaning and doing things that need to be done."[63]

A study of editors of African American newspapers in the South found what the authors call "empathetic rejectionism."[64] This means the editors empathize with the Latino population and feel that affirmative action laws should protect them, but still tend not to publish many articles about them, knowing their African American readers view immigration with ambivalence.

The second hypothesis is that African Americans generally embrace Latinos, viewing them as fellow minorities who suffer from many of the same prejudices at the hands of the majority white population. As such, there is a solid basis for cooperation. Therefore we can expect relations between the two groups to be largely free of serious conflict, though clear cultural and linguistic differences remain. This is based on national studies showing that, contrary to conventional wisdom, African Americans were more sympathetic toward Latinos than were Anglo Americans.[65]

In Alabama, for example, African American community and religious groups have reached out to the Latino population, and as a result the relationship has been largely positive, even during economic lulls.[66] A study of rural Georgia similarly found that the atmosphere was welcoming for the most part, especially since the growth of the immigrant community meant greater prosperity, though it notes that racial tension might increase if the economy slowed.[67] As one senior African American policy maker in Charlotte, North Carolina, noted, there should be important points of agreement between Blacks and Latinos in terms of civil rights, particularly since illegal immigrants work under a "new system of slavery."[68]

There may, in fact, be less effect on wages than often argued.[69] Studies have shown that even in new destinations like Raleigh-Durham, wages of natives are not much affected, though there is no consensus about precisely how labor markets adapt to the change of the labor pool's size.[70] It should be noted, however, that from a political perspective, *perceptions* matter much more than statistical studies. If people believe their wages are being affected, then this will have social as well as public policy repercussions.

Regardless of which of the two competing hypotheses you might think is more reasonable, the growth of the Latino population has created new racial undertones to national politics. Although Latinos outnumber Blacks nationally, this is not yet the case in the South, where there are 15.3 million Latinos and 21.5 million Blacks, but the combination of immigration (even when it slows as the demographic fit closes) and fertility will continue to close the gap. This will probably spark political competition between the two groups, as each constituency seeks attention for themselves from candidates and political parties. Since many Latinos are not registered voters, this competition is not yet keen, but if an African American–Hispanic cultural division persists, it may well translate into more intense political rivalry. For the time being, however, the competition—to the extent that it exists—is much more economic than political.

Latinos and Settlement in the South

Another unique aspect of Latino migration to the South is that settlement has not followed the traditional patterns of gateway cities. In Western states like California, Latinos tended to group in specific parts of a city, particularly in and around downtown areas. These neighborhoods would then be identified in cultural and linguistic terms, with signs in Spanish, grocery stores catering to specific ethnic tastes, and other signs of entrepreneurship aimed at that audience.

Over time, the more affluent have gradually moved toward the suburbs, but the delineated areas remain. Studies have shown that Latin American immigrants, especially the newly arrived, are more likely to get a job in an enclave, particularly in an immigrant-owned business.[71] Renewal of the enclave labor force through sustained immigration further strengthens the enclave itself,[72] leading critics to worry that immigrants concentrated in these areas will be much less likely to assimilate and become more "American."[73]

In the South, the development of enclaves is less evident. Latinos have been moving more directly to the suburbs, rather than to city centers and their periphery. This is a development that one scholar has dubbed the "suburban immigrant nation," since "the outer city is no longer 'sub' to the 'urb' in any traditional sense of the word."[74] Rather than living in well-defined ethnic neighborhoods, they live in many different suburban areas, defying the traditional process of enclave consolidation. According to the 2007 American Community Survey, 36.9 percent of Hispanics in the South live in the suburbs (defined as "metro area, outside central city"), compared to 30.6 percent outside the South. In fact, in the South a greater percentage of the Latino population lives in the suburbs than either whites (25.6 percent) or blacks (21.7 percent). Further, only 12.7 percent of Hispanics live in the center city in the South, compared to 25 percent outside the South. In the South, a much greater percentage of Hispanics (21.3 percent) live outside metropolitan areas compared to their counterparts outside the South (6.6 percent).[75]

What this demonstrates is that agricultural jobs remain plentiful, so many Latinos are working in more rural areas in the South than in the rest of the country. In all areas of the country, however, the settlement pattern is to move out of rural areas and into cities once an individual has made contacts and linkages to migrant communities (such as with family members, friends, and hometown associations). Once Latinos move to cities, they tend to go directly to the suburbs.

The employment opportunities in Southern cities, such as construction, landscaping, and housekeeping, are found more commonly in suburban areas rather than city centers. It therefore makes economic sense to settle near the job location, and this also happens to be where the least expensive housing—apartments—are located.[76] Housing is often more expensive in downtown areas, particularly if gentrification projects are underway, and public transportation is typically inadequate to convey employees to their jobs.

In fact, in the case of Charlotte, the Latino population has largely avoided the city center, residing instead in the ring of suburbs that surround it. Figure 6.1 utilizes 2006 birth data to map where Latinos are living in Mecklenburg County. Ironically, city leaders were accustomed to having lower-income groups clustered downtown, so government agencies offering social services are located there, far away from the Latino component of their target population. Although public transportation is available, this spatial mismatch has meant that many migrants are unable or unwilling to take advantage of service provisions.[77]

In both social and political terms, this is significant. Although clusters do develop, they do not become enclaves. In other words, dispersal is part of the overall settlement pattern, rather than the secondary effect of generational change. This can create conflict as native residents react to the changes taking place in their neighborhoods, but in the longer term this pattern will likely contribute to quicker assimilation. As the case of Charlotte reveals, service providers will be required to reconsider the ways

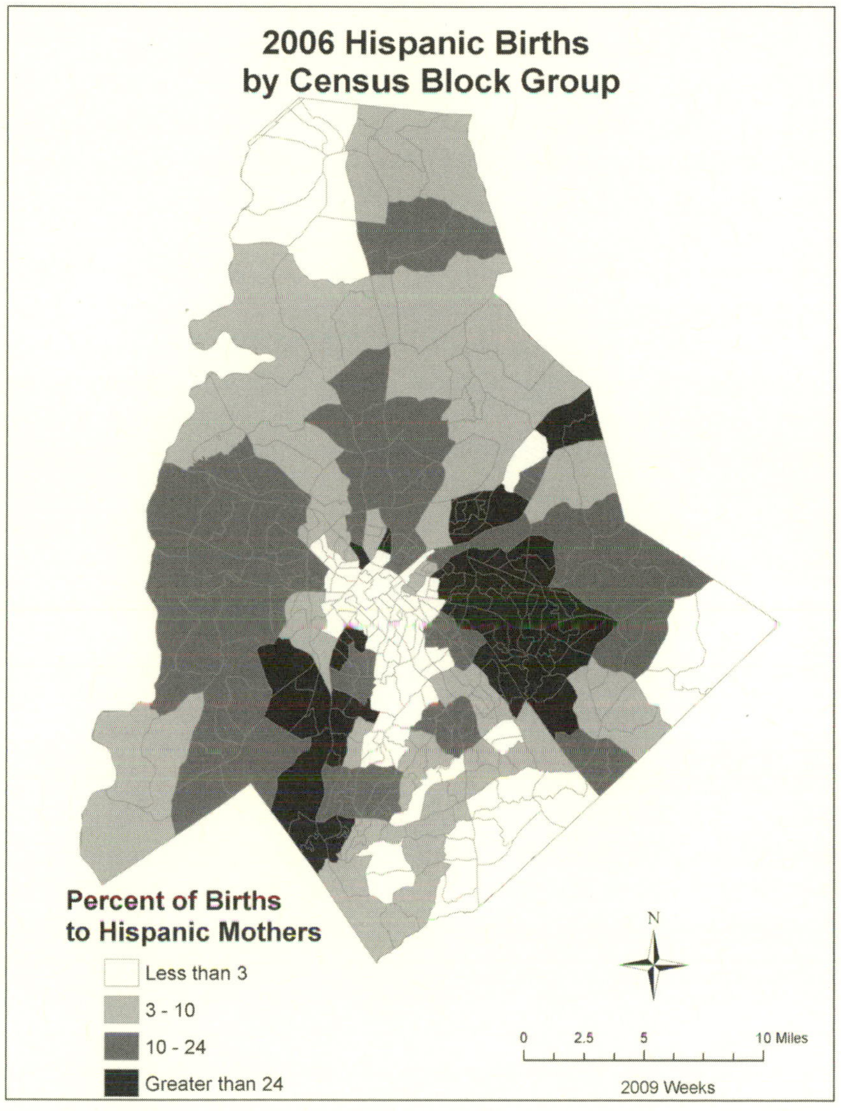

Figure 6.1

Births to Hispanic mothers in Mecklenburg County by census block group, 2006

SOURCE: Prepared by Amy Weeks from unpublished data provided to the authors by the Mecklenburg County Department of Health.

in which they offer services, since the Latino population will be found all across towns and cities, making it much more difficult to develop any centralized system.[78]

Suburbanization also increases the visibility of the Latino population, which forces local elected officials all across metropolitan areas to address the issue. The impact of immigration is not isolated in a downtown area, which could increase the chance of its being ignored by wealthier suburban political leaders. In cultural terms, it means non-Latino residents are being introduced to Latin America, especially with regard to food. Suburban supermarkets in the South have expanded their selection of Latin American, particularly Mexican, foods. This is buttressed by a near explosion of Mexican restaurants throughout the South. Supermarkets also tap into the remittance market, with Western Union and other companies setting up highly visible bilingual signs and distributing advertising in suburban neighborhoods to capture some of the profit from wiring money.

The Future of Latinos in the South

Particularly after the passage of IRCA, and especially since the 1990s, the South has experienced a large demand for all types of labor. Banks, high-tech firms, and companies of all sorts were moving to the area, which led to a boom in construction jobs and low-skilled service work. Meanwhile, traditional agriculture and poultry processing in the region had a constant need for workers, who were less and less likely to come from the local population. Stable employment, a good climate, and low cost of living also convinced many migrants to stay. As mentioned in Chapter One, this has largely remained the case despite the recession.

If there is anything certain about this phenomenon, it is this: even if the Latino population in the South levels out, it is highly unlikely to decrease anytime soon. The demographic fit is coming to a close, and the migrant flow will likely slow, but Latinos will not disappear as a result. Latinos already in the region are having children and bringing family members to join them through chain migration. The number of people will eventually outstrip the number of available jobs, and local political responses will reach a higher pitch as a consequence. In the next and final chapter, we consider what the future looks like for the United States as a whole and the South in particular as a result of Latin American immigration, and we analyze the public policy implications of these demographic changes.

CHAPTER SEVEN

Where Are We Going?

THE TERM "NEW SOUTH" CAME INTO USAGE AFTER THE CIVIL WAR, as a way to denote the shift from a slave-based plantation economy to one that was, at least in theory, becoming more industrialized and modern. Since the 1980s, it has been used to describe the economic boom in the region, accompanied by extensive and lasting migration from other states. Migrants have viewed the area as an attractive place to live and work, with a mild climate and low cost of living. As we've seen, however, the New South was opening up not only to the rest of the country, but to the rest of the world as well. It is, as historian Raymond Mohl has argued, the "Nuevo New South."[1] The U.S. South is now well into a new era of economic development, cultural evolution, and public policy, marked in part, of course, by the dramatic growth of the Latino population. In this final chapter, we summarize the implications of these changes and the policy challenges that accompany them.

How can we best understand the dynamics and processes of immigration to the United States, and to the South in particular? A central argument of this book is that the politics of Latin American immigration cannot be divorced from demography. Although this fact is only rarely raised during the all-too-often bloviated debates over immigration, it is empirically unavoidable and should always be taken into consideration. Political decisions made in the United States with regard to immigration cannot immediately alter demographic realities, and so at particular moments demographic pressures will play an important role in determining whether given policies can succeed in achieving their goals. In addition, Latin American governments are increasingly aware of the dynamics of demographic change in their own countries, and have responded accordingly.

The assertion that demography is a critical component does not mean it is the only component, to be viewed in isolation from economic and political factors. In a critique of demographic analyses, demographer Michael Teitelbaum argues that "demography-driven explanations, while enlightening, have not succeeded in addressing the rather messy realities and complexities inherent in the patterns of international migration."[2] Along similar lines, another scholar of migration writes that demographic explanations of illegal immigration have been largely discarded, and that "[e]mployment creation, rather than simple population increases, will be the crucial determinant of future immigration pressures."[3] Critics of a demographic approach tend to view the study of immigration in demographic terms as necessarily separated from other disciplines and explanations. Although some past works have shown that type of disciplinary isolation, as we noted in Chapter Two, it is a mistake to throw the conceptual baby out with the bath water.

The truth is that no explanation—regardless of discipline—has succeeded in capturing all the messiness inherent in the mass movement of people from one country to another. There is no grand theory that encompasses every last aspect of the passage of people from Latin America to the United States, or their movement within it. Our contention is simply that demography provides an explanatory power that other hypotheses in isolation cannot offer. It also offers insight not only into why people move, but also into the development of immigration policy, both in the United States and in Latin America.

Employment creation, for example, may be a critical part of understanding migration pressures, but it cannot be divorced from the demographic context in which jobs are created. Even a relatively high rate of job creation may not be high enough to bring all new job aspirants into the local economy, and that will encourage outmigration. At the same time, it is easier to "create" jobs by preserving them when there are a lot of older workers leaving the job market through retirement (such as in the United States) than when a very young labor force requires that virtually all jobs be created "from scratch" (as is true in Mexico, Central America, and northwestern South America). It is not population growth per se that matters, but rather the rate of growth of different age groups, especially the young adult ages at which people migrate.

Although the demographic composition of Latin American countries and their governments' response to the movement of people may seem distant and even irrelevant to residents of the U.S. South, these will continue to have a very real and important impact on southern economics, politics, and even culture. This is because another central assertion of this book is that the Latino population in the South is there to stay. Families are arriving or being created by young adult migrants after their arrival. Immigrants are having children, and not only are these children U.S. citizens by virtue of the Fourteenth Amendment to the Constitution (which, of course, does not protect their parents from deportation), but their parents are also naturalizing at increasing rates. The so-called hyper-growth of the Latino population will not persist, of course. There is now a large population base, and as the demographic fit closes, there will be fewer employment opportunities for newly arrived immigrants, so growth is slowing. But those who have already relocated are not simply seasonal laborers who follow crop harvests, and they are not all temporary sojourners who will return to their country of origin when they can. They are taking stable jobs, living in the suburbs of southern cities, and raising their children.

The economic recession that emerged in the United States in 2007, and led to the financial crises in the latter part of 2008, will not mean an emptying of Latino neighborhoods in the South or anywhere else in the United States. It may slow the rate of increase, but that is not the same as a massive exodus of Latin Americans. A report late in 2008 by the Pew Hispanic Center showed that, between 2007 and 2008, the unemployment rate went up more for Hispanics than for non-Hispanics, and that, after adjusting for people who withdrew from the labor force, it was higher for Latino immigrants than for Latinos born in the United States.[4] The construction industry, in which many Latinos are employed, led the regional job losses. Nonetheless, unemployment rates for all groups remained below

7 percent, the level reached in 2003, and there was no evidence from either the United States or Latin America (especially Mexico) that the recession had led to a significant return migration.

Immigration: Myth and Reality

So where does the United States, and the South in particular, go from here? To begin answering this question, we can look at the issues that politicians, pundits, and concerned citizens alike often raise with regard to immigration and its effects. It is all too tempting to believe that demographic pressures can be controlled (at least in a democratic system), legislated away, or ignored outright. This may well be one of the most widespread myths about immigration. These demographic forces, however, are irresistible, and efforts to address immigration will likely fail, or even engender unexpected—and probably unwanted—consequences if policy makers and the public at large cannot grasp that essential fact.

Periodically, published studies emphasize the persistence of myths about the Hispanic population and immigration policy, seeking to puncture conventional wisdom about the negative impact of immigration and the habits of immigrants themselves.[5] Such studies are useful, since they serve to dispel commonly held negative notions about Latinos. None, however, has addressed the particular dynamics of the "*Nuevo* New South."

Assimilation and Threat

The question of assimilation has been politicized and often used in arguments favoring limited legal immigration and strict enforcement of illegal immigration. As we've mentioned previously, Samuel Huntington argued that because Latinos come in constant (and large) numbers rather than in different waves, live in enclaves, live very near their countries of origin, and as a consequence can remain largely within their native culture, they are less likely to assimilate. In short, they fail to complete the "critical first phase" of assimilation, which is "the acceptance by the immigrants and their descendants of the culture and values of American society."[6] If newcomers don't become like "us," then what of our collective future? Alarm rests on the assumption that Latin American immigrants have no plans for learning English and adapting to U.S. cultural, political, or even legal norms. Given the histories of their countries of origin, maybe they do not even value freedom and democracy in the same way.

Such concerns are age-old, as old as the movement of people itself, and were in evidence as Italians, Germans, Poles, Chinese, and other large immigrant groups came to the United States and settled in the nineteenth and early twentieth centuries. Worry is also rooted in public policy: if Latinos do not assimilate, then what is the associated cultural cost of enclaves or the public cost of providing bilingual services? What we have argued is that these fears, although understandable, are simply not supported by empirical evidence.[7] Nonetheless, these fears are prevalent and distinct from those of the past. Anthropologist Leo Chavez refers to what he calls the "Latino Threat Narrative":

> The Latino Threat Narrative posits that Latinos are not like previous immigrant groups, who ultimately become part of the nation. According to the assumptions and taken-for-granted "truths" inherent in this narrative, Latinos are unwilling or incapable of integrating, of becoming part of the national community. Rather, they are part of an invading force from south of the border that is bent on reconquering land that was formerly theirs (the U.S. Southwest) and destroying the American way of life. Although Mexicans are often the focus of the Latino Threat Narrative, public discourse . . . often includes immigration from Latin America in general, as well as U.S.-born Americans of Latin American descent.[8]

The fact that Latin America is so close, and that a large chunk of the western United States used to belong to Mexico (even if relatively few Mexicans lived there), makes the question of Latino immigration all the more sensitive and vulnerable to misinformation. In particular, irrespective of whether Huntington's hypothesis holds for other parts of the country, Southern cities are experiencing different housing patterns than traditional gateways. Rather than being concentrated in enclaves near city centers, the Latino population is dispersed around suburbia. This largely reflects the location of employment opportunities, which tend not to be in city centers. Since there is ample affordable housing—especially apartments—in the suburbs (indeed, often much cheaper than in urban centers), initial settlement logically occurs there. This settlement pattern facilitates assimilation, since newly arrived immigrants and native residents alike live in relatively close proximity, often even shopping at the same supermarkets and eating at the same restaurants, while their children attend the same schools and play together.

In fact, it is ironic that one of the most important public policy challenges—not only in the South but in the nation as a whole—is to ensure that Latinos do not assimilate *too much*. The "Latino health paradox" has been amply documented, demonstrating that recent immigrants have better health outcomes than the native born, but that these positive indicators disappear as people adopt the less healthy lifestyles of the United States. This is particularly salient for the South, where the Latino population is quite young and therefore in a better position to adopt preventative measures before health problems set in. Steps should be taken to maintain the more healthy outcomes—for pregnancy, birth, drug and alcohol abuse, heart diseases, diabetes, among others—that plague the second generation and beyond, just as they plague all Americans to a degree not suffered by the recently arrived. Conversely, it would be worth highlighting the immigrant diets that have led to their better health outcomes and encourage U.S. citizens to take lessons from the nutritional behavior of immigrants.

Ideally, newly arrived immigrants should also resist assimilating with regard to criminality, and in fact, recently arrived migrants, especially those in the country illegally, are less likely to commit crimes than others. Thus, another irony is that individuals who entered the country illegally adhere to U.S. laws more closely than those who have lived in the country for years, though it is important to remember that breaking immigration laws is a civil, not a criminal offence. A rise in criminal behavior, as we noted with respect to gang activity, seems to come with acculturation in the United States, rather than the other way around.

Assimilating too much is an issue that communities in Latin America have contended with for some time. Despite their contribution to local economies, migrants returning home from the United States are often viewed as bringing with them new habits of drinking more, taking drugs, driving faster, and generally representing a corrupting influence.[9] Compared to much of Latin America, the United States is more secular and more permissive, so immigrant acculturation to the United States can become like a virus and spread back into the societies from which the migrants came. Americanization is not always good for your health.

Another component of assimilation and the threat scenario centers on politics. As a bloc, the Hispanic population could theoretically either follow the dictates of its home governments or indeed even seek to take back the southwestern United States through a *reconquista* of what had been taken after the Mexican-American War of 1846–1848. That there is no evidence for either supposition seems not to diminish its persistent reappearance. Yet the suppositions rest on the threat narrative, namely that Latinos, and especially recently arrived immigrants, are primarily focused on where they came from rather than where they are and where they plan to stay.

This negative viewpoint toward Latin American immigrants even considers democracy as a contributing factor to crisis. If unassimilated immigrants become citizens and vote, then they will vote in ways inimical to the traditional "American" (that is, native-born) population. The empirical problem is that, in the South or elsewhere, Latinos do not form a unified political bloc, they pay relatively little attention to the political needs of the government of their home countries, and they evince no interest in taking over any part of the United States. A majority do vote for the Democratic Party, but for widely varying reasons. In the South, these fears are even more weakly grounded, since very few Latinos are yet registered to vote.

From a public policy standpoint, focus should be directed not only on the nuts and bolts of integration and assimilation, such as language acquisition and education, but also on the conditions that lead new immigrants astray. Those core issues are, of course, critically important, but Southern towns and cities—with a disproportionately recent immigrant population—are especially tasked with avoiding the social ills that bedevil traditional gateways. This will require coordinated efforts among elected officials, local government agencies and bureaucracies, law enforcement, and community organizations. Of course, such coordination must include implementation of programs intended to prevent children of immigrants from joining gangs, which are now spread across borders and have become international syndicates deeply involved in drug trafficking, extortion, robbery, and murder. This is all the more important because the existence of gangs, especially Hispanic gangs like MS-13, casts a negative light on all immigrants, who are viewed as potential—if not actual—violent offenders.

It is difficult to imagine U.S. immigration policy achieving its stated goals without an integrated approach that includes Latin American policy makers. The most important player in this is, of course, the Mexican government. Bilateral relations have been strained, since immigration policy is most typically viewed in the United States as a unilateral affair in which Mexicans have no input. However, as one Mexican scholar has argued, immigration policy may require not only binational coordination, but also the inclusion of state governors and other relevant domestic political actors.[10]

Health Care

Another prominent worry is that immigrants abuse the health care system in the United States. Since emergency rooms do not require proof of citizenship before providing care, critics argue that immigrants will take advantage and then never pay the bill. This argument is also extended to births, asserting that women routinely cross the border not only for the purpose of receiving better services, but also to ensure that their child will be a United States citizen by virtue of being born on U.S. soil. The derogatory term "anchor baby" has come into popular usage, referring to the idea that parents in the country illegally can use the child as a lever to achieve residency or citizenship in the future, as a result of the long-standing family preference system within U.S. immigration laws. Since 2006, the immigration debate at the federal level has included proposals, such as the Birthright Citizenship Act of 2007, to require at least one parent to be a U.S. citizen or legal permanent resident for a baby to enjoy the same status (though, in fact, children born in the United States cannot even begin assisting their parents to become citizens until they are twenty-one years old).[11]

The U.S. General Accounting Office has determined that the burden of undocumented immigrants on hospitals cannot be determined given a lack of data.[12] But estimates are that only about 20 percent of the uninsured in hospitals are immigrants, legal or not.[13] As already noted, recent immigrants tend to be healthier than the rest of the population, so the overall burden of undocumented immigrants is certainly less than conventional wisdom believes it to be. In general, the foreign born use public health services much less than the native born.[14]

Nonetheless, local governments do shoulder a disproportionate share of the fiscal burden of undocumented immigration because they are the ones who tend to provide whatever services those individuals need, but the taxes paid by undocumented immigrants tend to go disproportionately to the federal government rather than to local governments. Consequently, legislation should focus on establishing a means by which those governments could petition the federal government for compensation. The only long-term solution is to provide avenues for legal migration, which will ensure that individuals can obtain health care (especially preventative) through normal means and not primarily through emergency rooms.

Learning English

Another prevalent assumption that we have discussed is that Latino immigrants are less likely than other immigrants to learn English. As mentioned above, the hypothesis holds that, especially since Latinos live in concentrated enclaves and have access to Spanish-language media (such as national cable channels like Univision and local newspapers, or even the internet for the more affluent), they feel less need to learn English.

That this myth persists is particularly unfortunate, since numerous studies have dispelled it. The use of Spanish drops off rapidly with the second generation.[15] As Alejandro Portes and Rubén Rumbaut point out, "Immigrants in California and elsewhere overwhelm English classes in the belief that acquisition of the language is the ticket to upward mobility for themselves and their children."[16] If anything, the threat is primarily to the foreign language, as first-generation immigrants watch it disappear from their children and grandchildren. Indeed, a study in Dallas found that immigrant parents "overwhelmingly view bilingualism as the ideal, yet many parents especially those who are English-dominant or bilingual, find it difficult to maintain Spanish at home because of outside pressures that prioritize English and concerns about their children's English-language acquisition."[17] Sociologists Tomás Jiménez and David Fitzgerald refer to this as "dissimilation," as migrants move further away culturally from their communities of origin.[18]

A 2006 Pew Hispanic Center poll found that 92 percent of Latinos (and 96 percent of foreign-born Hispanics) agreed it was "very important" to teach English to children of immigrant families.[19] The South is no different. For example, in 2000, 51.3 percent of Hispanics in North Carolina spoke English "very well," and by 2007, that had risen to 55.2 percent.[20] For perspective, 61.7 percent of Latinos in California spoke English "very well" in 2000, compared with 65.0 percent in 2007. Since a greater proportion of the Latino population in the South is recently arrived, the difference is not surprising. However, the trends are very clear. Over time, the percentage of Latinos learning English has been rising. This results largely from the fact that more are born in the United States and therefore are growing up bilingual. In 2000, 64.3 percent of Latinos in North Carolina were foreign born, compared with 54.9 percent in 2007. In California, the percentage had fallen from 45.1 to 41.4 percent.

In short, it is no mystery to the Latino immigrant population that success in the United States requires fluency in English. The foreign born in particular are acutely aware of this fact. They made the difficult choice to emigrate—which if legal is a lengthy, costly, bureaucratic adventure, and if illegal is expensive and fraught with danger—to improve their own situation, and realize that moving up the socioeconomic ladder, achieving some measure of the American Dream, is virtually impossible with only Spanish. The myth of Spanish-only remains firmly embedded in the public consciousness, but it is not borne out by any empirical data.

In terms of political response, given the strong interest immigrants have in becoming fluent in English, it is therefore important to create an environment within which immigrants can learn English as quickly as possible. The demand throughout the country for English as a Second Language (ESL) classes confirms that immigrants understand the importance of learning English, and it is crucial that communities have the resources to meet this need, especially through community colleges. It is also important, however, to emphasize that learning English does not entail making Spanish disappear. Even if later generations tend to speak it less, Spanish will not—and should not—be viewed as a threat. But the fact that Spanish is still used and remains "visible," so to speak, does not automatically mean that people do not speak English.[21] Instead, the South will be creating a larger pool of bilingual residents.

Social Security

Baby boomers are beginning to retire, and the cost of their retirement benefits will be enormous. It is what demographer Dowell Myers calls a "demographic tsunami."[22] Nonetheless, social security reform has been as elusive and highly politicized as immigration reform. In fact, President George W. Bush proposed reforms in both areas but failed to convince Congress to pass either. A 2007 Congressional Research Service report noted starkly that "in the future the program is financially unsustainable under current policy."[23] Despite periodic dire warnings about the consequences of inaction, few Americans consider it a pressing problem, and there is a general sense that the problem will either go away or somehow otherwise resolve itself. Paradoxically, a majority of Americans believe the system will eventually go bankrupt, but only a minority believe this constitutes a crisis.[24] The issue never entered into the 2008 presidential campaigns.

Young immigrants, however, can help fill the demographic gap. As Myers points out, immigration can alleviate other related economic strains like an insufficient labor force and too few young home buyers to satisfy the number of older sellers. The demographic fit therefore offers part of the solution, since there is a ready pool of workers able and willing to contribute to the U.S. economy and pay into the Social Security system, providing the income stream for older retirees. Strangely enough, the social security system has already benefited greatly from undocumented workers with falsified social security numbers. The Social Security Administration estimated a total of $500 billion in unclaimed funds in 2008.[25]

From a policy perspective, increasing the number of immigrant workers will require expanding the temporary low-skilled work visa programs. There is no legal limit to H-2A visas, but the government generally allows no more than about 30,000 annually, whereas the H-2B nonagricultural visas are capped at 66,000. Neither quota comes close to filling the demand; for example, in 2008, the H-1B visas were filled by July. Meanwhile, permanent low-skilled work visas are limited only to 5,000. For all categories, these are migrants with specific job opportunities who would immediately be contributing to virtually all aspects of the economy.

The Power of Legislation

It is important also to challenge the myth that the political will to enforce existing immigration laws can repair the broken immigration system. As Congressman and one-time presidential candidate Tom Tancredo writes, "Our borders are porous because we lack the political will to close them. The amazing thing is we have the technology and resources to secure our border tomorrow, but we lack the will to do it."[26] In this line of thinking, it is necessary only that politicians and the country at large *want* to stop undocumented immigration.

There can be no doubt that political will is a necessary component of effective immigration reform. What we have argued, however, is that demographic realities demonstrate that the movement of peoples from Latin America into the United States cannot be willed away, that other powerful forces at work cannot be ignored. Technology and legislation cannot trump demography. Ultimately, it may take more political will to acknowledge the importance of demography and to forge policies that recognize it as an independent driving force.

The demographic fit, however, is not permanent, as of course demographic shifts never are. As the ranks of the young are filled in the United States, especially with the children of immigrants, the need for workers to support the aging baby boomers will abate. At the same time, rates of fertility in Latin America are dropping, so that the pool of the working age cohort will become smaller and potentially more absorbable by Latin American economies. Former Mexican Foreign Minister Jorge Castañeda once joked with officials in the George W. Bush administration that eventually they [Mexico] wouldn't have enough Mexicans.[27] Indeed, as you read this there are fewer Mexicans under the age of fifteen than there were five years ago.

At the same time, it is important to emphasize the fact that the closing of the demographic fit will not mean the end of immigration. Even though the pool of workers in Latin American countries will shrink, weak economies will likely still not absorb all of them (though they will certainly absorb a higher percentage than before). At least in the short term, the effects of free trade agreements will still spark both internal and external migration. Further, family reunification will inevitably continue, a phenomenon that will likely be pronounced in the southeastern United States because the immigrant population is relatively new.

The Future Face of the South

Understanding where the South is going must involve recognition that it is already permanently altered. The growth of the Latino population in the South will affect its cultural characteristics, its racial and ethnic features, and the nature of political competition for constituencies from remote rural areas to the largest cities. The latest incarnation of the New South will have—indeed, already has—a Latin American flavor.

As we've discussed, in contrast to the classic pattern of seasonal migration of Latino immigrants within other parts of the country (notably the Midwest), in the South are clear signs that people intend to stay. The new South has attractions for migrants that traditional destinations cannot always match. For all of the reasons outlined above, many people (of all races, origins, and nationalities) view it as a destination not only for work but for raising families. And, indeed, Latino families are growing relative to other ethnic and racial groups, though not necessarily at the very high rates in popular imagination. The image of Hispanics having very large families is a long-held nugget of conventional wisdom that is no longer accurate.

As recently as 1980, the average woman in Mexico had five children, which decreased to 2.2 by 2005, and in Mexico City the birth rate is now below replacement level.[28] Thus, recent immigrants to the United States from Mexico are coming from a country with a new set of low fertility norms. In 1990, the average woman in Mexico had 3.2 children, and Latinas in the United States had 3.0 children[29]; in 2000, those rates had dropped to 2.4 children in Mexico and 2.7 children in the United States. In 2007, the most recent data available at this writing, the birth rate among Latinas had actually risen a bit, to almost 3.0 children each.[30] It is not clear yet what is behind this trend, but we are nonetheless in an unexpected transition period in which foreign-born Latinas are experiencing fertility levels that are higher than currently prevail in Mexico. Looked at in absolute terms, the Hispanic population accounted for 15 percent of the total U.S. population in 2006, but births to Hispanic women represented 24 percent of babies born in that year, and of women having their fourth child (or more), 31 percent were Hispanic.

In the South, only 5 percent of the total population was Hispanic as of 2007, but 11 percent of births were to foreign-born Latinas. Already, then, a unique generation of Southerners is being born and entering the public school system. By birth, the majority of the youth are United States citizens and will forever be part of the country, though Latin American governments will continue to do what they can to maintain ties to them. From a cultural perspective, they will be transnational, since they, like all other children of immigrants, will have ties to their parents' country of origin, though those ties will weaken over time, just as the use of Spanish will decline. This new generation will in a real sense redefine what "Southern" means.

This has some obvious public policy implications. Although the rate of immigration will slow, as a new destination the South has a relatively high proportion of recently arrived immigrants. Further, chain migration will continue. As families become established, they will let friends and families—both in other parts of the United States and in their country of origin—know that the South offers opportunities they may not find elsewhere.

As a consequence, there are several immediate challenges. The recently arrived are more likely to be poor. Although the per capita income of Latinos in the South is increasing, the increase is slow. As mentioned, the idea that immigrants overwhelm "free" health care is a myth, but there is no doubt about the public cost of providing education to children who speak little English and whose own parents are not well educated. Federal courts have consistently ruled that immigration is the exclusive domain of the federal government, so that laws passed at the state and local level often have a very tenuous existence, with the more controversial immediately challenged in court, and in some cases abandoned as a result. For the time being, local communities will be compelled to address the fiscal impact of immigration with little or no alleviation from the federal government.

Unfortunately, one potential outcome is an increasingly uneasy relationship between the Latino population and local law enforcement, an inevitable consequence of the 287(g) program discussed in the previous chapter. According to a 2008 Pew Hispanic Center study, 8 percent of native-born U.S. citizens and 10 percent of immigrants said that in the previous year they had been stopped by authorities and asked about their immigration status.[31] An overwhelming majority of Americans, however—81 percent—believe that immigration enforcement is a job for the federal government alone. For the undocumented, the obvious concern is detention and deportation. Even immigrants in the country legally and long-term residents bear some resentment about simply being stereotyped and pigeon-holed ("profiled") as a potential threatening "alien" and therefore subjected to mistreatment.

The other sensitive issue stemming from the demographic transformation of the South relates to race relations. For literally centuries, race in the region has been binary: black and white. Policy makers at all levels must recognize the tension that has emerged in some—though not all—parts of the South. Some African Americans are concerned about the increase of the Latino population, fearing that they will take jobs and depress wages. Analysis of current data is inconclusive and contested. Regardless, public policy must take race and ethnicity into account and encourage coalition building, because resentment can easily result from policies that shift scarce public resources away from one group to aid another. In attempts to avoid this, there are efforts like the 2009 African-American Latino Unity Summit in Charlotte.

Tied to this is the political future of the South. Only a small percentage of the Latino population in the South is registered to vote at this time, primarily because fewer people have achieved citizenship relative to other states. For example, North Carolina is the twelfth largest state in the country but has less than 1 percent of all Hispanic voters, and only 2 percent of registered voters in the state are Latino.[32] Over the next generation, this will change—the Hispanic vote will become more central to elections, and we will begin to see Latinos running for state and local elected offices. In the 2008 presidential campaign, Barack Obama and John McCain both produced ads in Spanish for swing states with established Latino populations, particularly Colorado, Florida, Nevada, and New Mexico. In the future, the same will by done for the South. This will likely create competition with the African American community. Thousands of African Americans are in elected positions across the South, and are in those positions only after decades of social and political battles to overcome both de facto and de jure segregation. The more that policies today focus on cooperation and common goals, the more likely it is that future political competition will be productive rather than destructive.

Taken from another angle, the increase of Latino voters in the South will have important national political implications. In the 2008 presidential election, Southern states like Virginia (where a Democrat had not won since 1964) and North Carolina (last going for a Democrat in 1976), normally Republican bastions, became battleground states. Eventual winner Barack Obama's campaign employed considerable resources and won both states. Since a majority of Latinos lean toward the Democratic Party, the future may see more Southern states consistently up for grabs in presidential contests. This is by no means inevitable. As recently as 2004, exit polls estimated that George W. Bush garnered somewhere between 33 and 44 percent of the Latino vote nationally. However, the shift in rhetoric after his election toward the idea that Latinos are a national threat certainly pushed many Hispanics out of the Republican Party.

Given the relative youth of the Latino population in the South and the fact that many Latino citizens in the region are children, changes in political party allegiance will not have an immediate impact. In another generation, however, the political picture will look much different. The African American vote is already closely tied to the Democratic Party, and if the

Hispanic vote follows the same pattern, then combined they will represent a formidable challenge to the Republican Party's hold on Southern states in presidential elections. That hold dates to the administration of Richard Nixon, and demography may well erode it.

Nonetheless, as elsewhere in the United States, it is important to remember that Latinos will not necessarily constitute a unified political bloc. Since Mexico is a large country and borders the United States, the majority of Latinos will be of Mexican descent, but the population is quite diverse. There are differences in social class, social conservatism (for example, many religious conservatives favor the Republican Party), length of residency in the United States, and cultural differences based on migrants' origins in different areas of Mexico. The challenge for political parties and candidates will be to emphasize commonalities.

Finally, a positive outcome of these political shifts is that an increased Latino political presence will further accelerate assimilation and integration. Gaining a political voice is an important step toward working with other groups on an equal basis and having a stake in the success of the political process. This will not erase sociocultural differences, but it will reduce them.

The Future of Immigration Policy

Given legislative inaction at the federal level, where despite extended debate Congress has not passed significant legislation with regard to immigration, the policy response has increasingly moved to the state and local levels. Now more than ever, policy makers in the South require a firm conceptual and empirical foundation for making decisions on the issue. From a policy perspective, there is a central fact that policy makers must recognize: the Latino population cannot be legislated away. The demographic changes taking place in the South are inescapable and irresistible. As mentioned, this does not mean that high rates of growth will continue. But legislators at both the state and local levels must craft policies that acknowledge Latinos as an integral part of the region's—and the country's—common future.

All too often, lawmakers consider policy options that involve enacting laws intended to dissuade undocumented immigrants from remaining. These include penalizing employers, blocking access to community colleges, creating 287(g) agreements with the federal government to deputize local law enforcement as a way to hasten deportation of anyone arrested, and cracking down on apartment owners who do not check the immigration status of their renters. These policies are detrimental to the state because they sour relations between law enforcement and the immigrant population, they block young people from reaching their educational potential (which directly affects the state's well-being), and they generally create a climate of mistrust and fear. Instead, attention should be shifted toward helping the Latino community prosper and thereby become better integrated.

Policies designed to discourage undocumented immigrants also suffer from an ignorance of how demography and politics have combined to create a situation in which immigrants who are responding to the demand for labor in the United States wind up in a tenuous legal situation. In 2007 (the most recent year available at this writing), the United States accepted 1,052,415 legal permanent residents into the country. Of these, however, only 162,176 (15 percent) were admitted for employment-based reasons. The vast majority of legal immigrants (689,820—66 percent) were admitted because they were relatives of U.S. citizens or noncitizen legal permanent residents. Family reunification was a major part of the Immigration and Nationality Act passed in 1965, and it has remained the centerpiece of U.S. immigration policy since that time. Because of the huge volume of demand from this category of immigrant (with long backlogs, especially from the Philippines and Mexico), there has been little movement toward increasing the employment-based categories of immigrants. Yet, the demographic fit that has been driving much of the migration in the first place is an employment-based phenomenon having nothing to do with family reunification. It is this conundrum that has, in essence, created the category of undocumented or illegal immigrant.

Despite the intensity of the rhetoric during the 2008 presidential primaries, immigration as a campaign issue quickly dropped from sight. In part, this resulted from the relative similarity of the positions of Senators Barack Obama and John McCain. The stated policy views of each candidate did not diverge much, and during the campaign their prescriptions for immigration were not often mentioned. Further, the economic crisis that hit the United States in September and October of 2008 eclipsed most other policy areas. Nonetheless, in speeches Obama pledged to tackle immigration reform quickly: "The time to fix our broken immigration system is now."[33]

If there is to be such a thing as comprehensive immigration reform, it must incorporate changes in immigration law that recognize the demographic realities behind the movement of peoples and the resulting need for young workers, as well as the logistical impossibility of deporting the roughly twelve million people already residing in the United States illegally, in addition to the need for effective and enforced border security. One of the core dilemmas for passing such legislation is that both the Democratic and Republican parties face deep internal splits. Any reform will require not only bipartisan support, but will risk the partisan backlash from those who end up on the wrong side of the party leadership, or whose views diverge from their constituents.

This does not paint a rosy picture for the chances of achieving a reformed immigration system that establishes coordination at the international, national, state, and local levels. As one prominent analysis put it, such a system is like machinery: "Blindly tinkering with a gear here or a cog there, or adding new levers simply because they 'look good,' is to invite a host of unintended consequences, and perhaps to cause a calamity that no one expected or desired."[34] The construction of such a machine is no mean feat, particularly in such a complex political environment. It cannot function unless it accounts for the demographic and economic contexts in both the United States and Latin America, the labor needs of different states, and the effects of immigration at the local level.

In poll after poll, the American public has shown itself to be mostly pragmatic with regard to immigration. Americans have more pressing issues to think about, and the majority favor reform that is neither open border nor enforcement only. However, the very fact that most do not consider immigration the first, second, or even necessarily the third most important issue facing the country means that very vocal minorities hold considerable sway. In the context of congressional politics, where the possibility of a filibuster in the Senate requires 60 votes to get legislation passed (which Democrats did not reach in the 2008 senatorial elections, and lost another in the special election after the death of Senator Edward Kennedy), the chances of success are slim.

Unfortunately, demography does not offer much short-term solace, at least in terms of helping to pass some type of comprehensive legislation that addresses all the different angles of immigration policy. As we transition away from a demographic fit between the United States and Latin America, the ranks of the young will be growing in the

United States and competition for jobs will intensify, potentially turning up the heat under the immigration debate. Furthermore, a number of prominent think tanks are dedicated to lobbying Congress and swaying public opinion in opposition to current levels of immigration (legal or not). These include the Federation for American Immigration Reform, the Center for Immigration Studies, the Immigration Reform Law Institute, NumbersUSA, and ProjectUSA. They are well organized and have enough funding to ensure a significant impact on any proposed legislation.

The reaction can also, of course, be exacerbated by economic downturns, which squeeze the job market even more. The pool of working-age Latin Americans will also decline, and the extent to which they find employment in their home economy will affect how bitter the debate becomes, and this may be significantly affected by U.S. responses to the economic needs of Latin American nations. Current and future policy decisions would benefit greatly from an understanding of the demographic changes both in the United States and in Latin America, and policy makers' acknowledgment that such changes are—by their very definition—never static. Policies that may have been appropriate in the past will not necessarily work in the present or future because the demographic and political contexts are shifting.

The Role of Latin American Governments

Fears about immigration are heightened when news stories periodically emerge that discuss strategies employed by Latin American governments to assist their citizens abroad. It can be easy to envision conspiracies and to assume that those governments are plotting against the best interests of the United States. Although, like all governments, they are pursuing policies they believe to be optimal for their own citizens, there are many areas in which international cooperation is both possible and necessary.

For example, Latin American governments will have to be more involved with the massive trade in human smuggling and falsified documents. Despite the popular perception that immigrants should simply "get in line" and come into the country legally, it is prohibitively difficult and expensive for many. In his novel *American Visa*, Bolivian author Juan de Recacoechea captures the scene at a United States consulate in La Paz:

> I began to notice intermittent wails coming from the other side of the room. Applicants for visas who didn't have their papers in order were sent to a confessional booth, where they tried to explain everything to the consul himself, who had the final say in the matter. About one in every three people was sent over to chat with the big boss. If he had any doubts about you, *ciao*—you were out on the streets.[35]

For the poorest individuals, even such a visit represents an immense and most likely an insurmountable obstacle. In the absence of legal avenues, getting to the United States requires entering the illegal and extremely dangerous world of coyotes, desert crossings, and forgery. After the border crackdowns in the 1990s, particularly in California, migrants opted for ever more perilous crossing points in the desert. The violence surrounding crossing the border has even led to new illicit businesses, such as "virtual kidnappings" whereby extortionists in Mexico call relatives of immigrants crossing illegally and falsely claim that they will be killed or maimed unless they are paid thousands of dollars.[36]

As previously detailed, Latin American governments are increasingly enacting laws aimed at maintaining links with emigrants. For immigration reform to succeed, U.S. policy makers will to remain cognizant that reform does not exist in a domestic political bubble, but is tightly bound to political, economic, and of course demographic currents within Latin America. Immigration should therefore rise higher on the political agenda for U.S.–Latin American relations.

Conclusion

The central thesis of this book is that migration is an irresistible force best understood by examining both demographics and politics in tandem with one another. Our political demographic perspective also recognizes that population movements can, in and of themselves, become political issues. This is not an automatic function of migration, but is tied to the social reality that people who are different in some way are frequently targeted for abuse and discrimination. Latin American immigrants to the United States tend to be different linguistically and educationally from the average U.S. resident, and in the South the fact that they are neither "white" nor "black" creates an unprecedented dilemma for local communities. As the demographic reality of the emerging Latino population in the South takes hold, public perceptions of migration will shift and, in turn, so will the policy responses of government officials.

Demography is a critical, though by no means sole, factor in understanding why people move to the United States from Latin America, how easily they find employment when they arrive, why federal immigration reform passes or not, and how pitched the debate becomes. But as we have argued, it is also an important factor for explaining the political future of the South.

The power of myths (largely negative, as a result of xenophobia) surrounding Latino immigration remain strong and are repeated through media outlets, political speeches, and simple word of mouth. Meanwhile, political solutions at all levels of government have tended not to acknowledge the demographic roots of migration, nor the demographic consequences of current migration policies. Irresistible forces are thus treated as problems that can be legislated away, as opposed to phenomena that will inevitably affect communities regardless of legislative attempts to avoid them. As a new immigrant gateway region, the future of the South will hinge at least partly on how it incorporates and successfully integrates the existing and latent political, economic, and cultural strengths of the Latino population.

Notes

Chapter One

1. Associated Press 2009.
2. Papademetriou and Terrazas 2009.
3. CNN 2009.
4. Stock 2008.
5. *Seattle Times* 2008.
6. Echávarri 2009.
7. Papademetriou and Terrazas 2009.
8. Llana 2008.
9. Lopez, Livingston, and Kochhar 2009.
10. Díaz 2007, 271.
11. Ruzich 2009.
12. Gonzales 2009.
13. McWhirter and Pickel 2009.
14. Weeks 2008.
15. Lacy 2009, 1.
16. Quoted in Sweet 2009.
17. Wayne Cooper, Honorary Consul to Mexico, interview with GBW, October 13, 2008.
18. Swarns 2006.

19. Gonzales 2009.
20. Smith and Furuseth 2004, 163.
21. See Orner 2008, 19–30.
22. Stephens 2008.

Chapter Two

1. The number of farms in the United States producing tobacco fell from 512,000 in 1950 to 56,997 in 2002 (Capehart 2004, 3).
2. As will be discussed in subsequent chapters, although there are no numerical limits on the number of H2A visas available, on an annual basis the U.S. government approves very few of them (generally from 10,000 to 33,000).
3. Hummel 2005.
4. This book will utilize the terms "illegal," "undocumented," and "unauthorized" interchangeably to describe such immigrants. All three refer to an individual from another country who does not have legal permission to reside and work in the United States.
5. "Latin America" is a vague term, but usually refers to those countries in the western hemisphere that are former colonies of Spain and Portugal. This book will follow that convention, but to a limited extent will also examine other countries in the hemisphere, such as Haiti, which are closely bound to Latin America and follow similar migratory patterns. "Hispanic" is a term used by the United States Census Bureau, whereby respondents self-identify as being "Mexican, Puerto Rican, Cuban, Central or South American, or some other Hispanic origin."
6. This book will use "Latino" and "Hispanic" as synonyms. The former enjoys more popular usage, while the latter is associated with the parlance of the U.S. government bureaucracy, such as the Office of Management and Budget and the Census Bureau.
7. Getis and Getis 1995.
8. For a survey of recent research, see Kugler and Swaminathan 2006.
9. Weeks 2008.
10. Malthus 1992 [1798], 14.
11. Ehrlich 1968, 17. Emphasis in the original.
12. Note that Marxism, including that practiced in the People's Republic of China, is adamantly anti-Malthusian, so the idea that the one-child policy is Malthusian is rejected in China. For more on this, see Lee and Feng 1999.
13. Plato 1960 [360 B.C.], 122.
14. Smith 1999, 598.

15. For a recent discussion, see Urdal 2006.
16. Westoff 2007, 166.
17. Wiener and Teitelbaum 2001, 10.
18. Durand and Massey 2004.
19. Davis 1963.
20. Massey and Espinosa 1997; Massey, Durand, and Malone 2002.
21. For example, see Borjas 2003.
22. Huntington 2004.
23. For a discussion by a participant in the political debate, see Castañeda 2007.
24. Warren and Passel 1987.
25. Passel and Cohn 2008.
26. Hoefer, Rytina, and Baker 2008.
27. U.S. Census Bureau 2009.
28. Hoefer, Rytina, and Baker 2008.
29. U.S. Census Bureau 2009.
30. U.S. Census Bureau 2009.
31. Weeks 2008.
32. U.N. Population Division 2009.
33. Wallerstein 1974; Sassen 2001.
34. Asthana 2005.
35. Urrea 2005, 167–168.
36. Massey, Durand, and Malone 2002.
37. Castillo 2008.

Chapter Three

1. Snipp 1989.
2. Massey, Durand, and Malone 2002, 25.
3. Proffitt 1994, 100.
4. Mitchell 1992, 10.
5. Mitchell 1992, 11.
6. Quoted in Daniels 2004, 32.
7. Daniels 2004, 29.
8. Daniels 2004, 50.
9. Proffitt 1994, 149.
10. Cardoso 1980, 5.

11. Quoted in Cardoso 1980, 6.
12. Buchenau 2004, 42.
13. Instituto Nacional de Estadística y Geografía 1994.
14. Cardoso 1980, 22.
15. García y Griego 1983, 50.
16. García y Griego 1983, 55.
17. Cardoso 1980, 30–31.
18. Aguilar Camín and Meyer 1993, 10.
19. Walsh 2000, 7.
20. Verduzco 1995, 574–575.
21. Cardoso 1980, 96.
22. Cardoso 1980, 108.
23. Quoted in García y Griego 1983, 53.
24. Cardoso 1980, 147.
25. Quoted in Daniels 2004, 64.
26. Boggs 1940, 73.
27. Boggs 1940, 72.
28. U.S. Census Bureau 2009.
29. Quoted in Fitzgerald 2005, 7.
30. Political Database of the Americas 2004.
31. Galaraza 1964, 46–48.
32. In 2008, Braceros who worked from 1942 to 1946 won a class action suit in the United States, claiming they had never been repaid, and the Mexican government set up a fund to finally process those payments. See Black 2008.
33. Nelson 1975, 286.
34. García y Griego 1983, 57.
35. García y Griego 1983, 58.
36. Craig 1971, 17.
37. Quoted in García y Griego 1983, 63.
38. Calavita 1992, 54.
39. García y Griego 1990.
40. Craig 1971, 188–191.
41. See Watts 2002.
42. U.S. Department of State 1964, Documents 346 and 352.
43. Sklair 1989, 28–29.
44. Quoted in Sklair 1989, 45.
45. *Congressional Record* 1965, 21791.

46. Johnson 1966, 546.
47. Woodward 1999, 100–101.
48. Lundquist and Massey 2005.
49. García 2006, 48.
50. Coutin 2004.
51. Booth, Wade, and Walker 2006.
52. Menjívar 2000.
53. Coutin 2004.
54. Arana 2005.
55. Díaz-Briquets 1989, 35.
56. Stycos 1971.
57. Díaz-Briquets and Perez 1981; Hollerbach 1980.
58. Greenhill 2002.
59. Konczal and Stepick 2007, 447.
60. Arriaga 1970.
61. Alchon 1997.
62. Arriaga 1970.
63. Wright and Zúñiga 2007, 38.
64. Mitchell 1992, 16–17.
65. Weeks, G., 2008, 203.
66. For a summary of the bill and other details, see Immigration Reform and Control Act 1986.
67. Dunn 1996, 53.
68. Reagan 1989, 1522.
69. Reagan 1989, 1524.
70. Daniels 2004, 244.
71. Cornelius 2005, 778.
72. Nevins 2002, 4.
73. For example, see Massey, Durand, and Malone 2002.

Chapter Four

1. Castles and Miller 2003, 164.
2. Martell, Pineda, and Tapia 2007, 51.
3. Weeks, J., 2008.
4. Kronholz and Lyons 2006.

5. Weeks, Jankowski, and Stoler 2009.
6. St. Onge, Ordoñez, Hall, and Alexander 2008.
7. Bush 2006.
8. Quoted in Andreas 2000, 104.
9. Massey, Durand, and Malone 2002, 21.
10. For example, see Boucher, Smith, Taylor, and Yúnez-Naude 2007.
11. Elbert 2008.
12. U.S. Department of Labor.
13. U.S. Department of Homeland Security 2008.
14. Preston 2007.
15. Greenhouse 2007.
16. *Capitol Press* 2008.
17. Ring 2009.
18. Billeaud 2008a.
19. Martin 2007.
20. Levine 2008, Summary.
21. Pew Hispanic Center 2006c.
22. Passel 2006.
23. Kochhar, Suro, and Tafoya 2005.
24. Massey, Durand, and Malone 2002.
25. These are the Bureau of Customs and Border Protection (BCBP), the Bureau of Immigration and Customs Enforcement (BICE), and the Bureau of Citizenship and Immigration Services (BCIS).
26. Secure America and Orderly Immigration Act 2005.
27. Office of Management and Budget 2007.
28. Immigration and Nationality Act 2005.
29. Dobbs 2007.
30. Soraghan 2008.
31. "Grand Island Police Refuse to Help with Raid," *KETV Omaha*, http://www.ketv.com/newsarchive/10516610/detail.html.
32. Cooper 2007.
33. Quintero 2007.
34. Solis 2007.
35. Hayes and Hill 2008.
36. U.S. Department of Homeland Security 2008.
37. Bush 2007.
38. Feeney 2008.

39. Schumer 2009.
40. Aderholt 2008.
41. Gutierrez 2007.
42. Sessions 2007.
43. Purdum 2007.
44. Pear 2007.
45. Portes and Rumbaut 2006, 346–347.
46. Quoted in Orner 2008, 188.
47. Pantoja 2006.
48. Harwood 1986, 208.
49. Daniels 2004, 232–234.
50. For a selection of different polls for 2007 and 2008 on this point, such as CNN, NBC News, the *Wall Street Journal*, and the *New York Times*, see PollingReport.com, http://www.pollingreport.com/prioriti.htm.
51. Pew Hispanic Center 2006d; Benac 2006.
52. For example, NBC/Wall Street Journal poll, June 2006, http://msnbcmedia.msn.com/i/msnbc/sections/news/060614_NBC-WSJ_Poll.pdf; Schulman and Regan 2006.
53. Preston and Connelly 2007; Johnston and Simon 2006; Glazer 2007, 76.
54. For example, see the 2006 Times/Bloomberg Poll in Brownstein 2006. See also Jacobe 2008.
55. Schuck 2007, 21.
56. Davenport 2007.
57. For a full text of the speech, McCain 2008.
58. Quoted in Leggiere 2008.
59. See the Obama-Biden Web site, http://www.barackobama.com/issues/immigration/.

Chapter Five

1. Associated Press 2007.
2. Aizenman 2007.
3. Smith 2006, 6.
4. Inter-American Development Bank 2005, 20.
5. Inter-American Development Bank 2008a.
6. Inter-American Development Bank 2008b.
7. Quoted in Coutin 2008, 73.

8. Jones-Correa 2001.
9. Dresser 1993, 93
10. U.S. Department of Justice 2007, 145.
11. Regional Conference on Migration 2010.
12. Ibid.
13. Storrs 2006, 5.
14. De Leon 2006.
15. Imaz 2007.
16. Smith 2003, 330.
17. Harman 2006.
18. Tobar 2006.
19. For a vivid depiction, see Nazario 2007.
20. See Shepard-Durni 2008.
21. Stevenson 2007.
22. *Chicago Tribune* 2008.
23. Archibold 2007.
24. Castañeda 2007.
25. Quoted in Wides-Munoz 2008.
26. Castañeda 2007, 149.
27. Dinerstein 2003, 1.
28. *USA Today* 2007.
29. Carvajal 1995.
30. Constable 2008.
31. Keeler 2008.
32. Ellingwood 2008.
33. Paul 2006.
34. Fox and Allyn 2007, 150.
35. Huntington 2004, 91.
36. Domínguez 2007.
37. Quoted in Chiu and Gutiérrez 2007, 159.
38. Taylor and Fry 2007.
39. De la Garza, Pachon, Orozco, and Pantoja 2000, 46.
40. Masuoka 2008.
41. Waldinger 2008, 18.
42. Inter-American Development Bank 2004b, 20.
43. Guarnizo, Portes and Haller 2003, 1211–1248.

44. Ibid., 1238.
45. For an overview of the case, see PBS NewsHour 2000.
46. Leal, Nuño, Lee, and de la Garza 2008.
47. Jones-Correa 2001; Embassy and Consulate Web sites.
48. Escobar 2007.
49. Sejersen 2008.
50. U.S. Department of State, n.d.
51. Huntington 2004, 212.
52. Renshon 2001.
53. U.S. House of Representatives 2005a, 3.
54. Staton, Jackson, and Canache 2007; Cain and Doherty 2006.
55. Ramakrishnan and Espenshade 2001.
56. Bareto and Muñoz 2003.
57. Leal 2002.
58. Escobar 2004.
59. Portes and Rumbaut 2006, 138.
60. DeSipio 2006; Pantoja 2005.
61. Jones-Correa 2001; Mazzolari 2005.
62. Navarro Fierro, Morales, and Gratschew 2007. U.S. citizens living abroad can vote in elections by obtaining an absentee ballot from the county within the United States where they are registered to vote. Canada has a similar mail-in ballot that is available for people who have maintained a permanent address in Canada while living abroad.
63. *Santiago Times* 2005.
64. Smith and Bakker 2008, 132–134.
65. Restrepo de Acosta 2007.
66. Calderón-Chelius 2007.
67. Suro and Escobar 2006.
68. Rosenblum 2004.
69. Thompson 2004; Smith and Bakker 2008, 109–130.
70. Schwartz 2008.
71. Henry 2008.
72. *Weekly Compilation of Presidential Documents* 2002, 507.
73. *Los Angeles Times* 2006.
74. Quoted in Storrs 2006, 10.
75. Levitt 2007, 407.
76. Somerville, Durana, and Terrazas 2008, 2.

77. Ibid., 5.
78. Goldring 2002.
79. Thompson 2005.
80. Ibid.
81. Sacchetti 2008.
82. Özden 2005, 6.
83. Pellegrino 2001, 116.
84. Interational Organization for Migration, n.d.
85. For example, Kuznetsov 2006.
86. Rios-Neto 2005, 14.
87. Saravia and Miranda 2004.
88. *El Comercio* (Ecuador) 2007.
89. Mindlin 2007.
90. Kapur and McHale 2005, 58.
91. Thibodeau 2008.
92. Padilla and Peixoto 2007.
93. Inter-American Development Bank 2007.
94. MercoPress 2008.
95. Organization of American States 2008.

Chapter Six

1. *Charlotte Observer* 2007.
2. Quoted in Guthey 2001, 59.
3. Winders 2007.
4. Kandel and Parrado 2005.
5. Rytina and Caldera 2008.
6. U.S. Department of Homeland Security 2007, Table 21.
7. Hernández-León and Zúñiga 2000, 58.
8. Castles and Miller 2003.
9. Woodward 2006, 9.
10. Sutton and Mathews 2006.
11. Weeks, Weeks, and Weeks 2006–2007, 56–57.
12. Hondagneu-Sotelo 1994, 12–14.
13. Hondagneu-Sotelo 2001, 10.
14. Domestic Workers United 2007.

15. Castles and Miller 2003, 26.
16. Calculated from the Mecklenburg County Board of Elections; UNC–Charlotte Urban Institute 2006.
17. Bullock and Hood 2006.
18. Barreto 2007.
19. Kaufmann 2003.
20. U.S. Census Bureau 2009.
21. Inter-American Development Bank 2006, 40.
22. Weeks, Rumbaut, and Ojeda 1999; Cho, Frisbie, Hummer, and Rogers 2004.
23. Bryant 2006.
24. Ibid., cover letter.
25. Kasarda and Johnson 2006.
26. Capps et al. 2007.
27. Wiest 2007.
28. For the text of the report, see Sims 2008.
29. Mayor's Immigration Study Commission 2007, 36–37.
30. *Lolazno v. Hazleton* 2007.
31. Rumbaut and Ewing 2007; see also Hagan, Levi, and Dinovitzer 2008.
32. Butcher and Piehl 2007.
33. Shannon 2008.
34. Brevé 2007.
35. Federal Bureau of Investigation 2008.
36. Cherrie 2008.
37. Echegaray 2008; *Richmond-Times Dispatch* 2008.
38. National Drug Intelligence Center 2008.
39. Fuchs 2008.
40. Pickel 2008.
41. *News & Observer* 2008.
42. National Conference of State Legislatures 2008.
43. Loller 2008.
44. *Washington Post* 2007.
45. Morrill 2005.
46. Interview with GBW, February 9, 2006.
47. See Pham 2005.
48. Seghetti, Viña, and Ester 2006, 1.
49. U.S. Immigration and Customs Enforcement 2008.

50. Rassmussen Reports 2007.
51. Hall 2008.
52. U.S. House of Representatives 2005b, 20.
53. Republican National Committee 2008, 13.
54. Perez 2008.
55. Shear 2007.
56. USA Today/Gallup 2008.
57. Vaca 2004, 188. For a good overview of the literature and its generally negative outlook, see Betancur 2005.
58. Schwartzman 2008.
59. For example, Borjas 2003.
60. Suro 1998, 243–264.
61. McClain et al. 2007, 108.
62. Ibid., 112.
63. Pérez and Dade 2007.
64. Weill and Castañeda 2004.
65. Cummings and Lambert 1997.
66. Mohl 2002, 273.
67. Studstill and Nieto-Studstill 2001.
68. Interview with GBW, January 11, 2006, Charlotte, North Carolina.
69. For example, Simon 1999.
70. Card and Lewis 2007.
71. Bohon 2001, 118.
72. Wilson and Portes 1980.
73. Huntington 2004.
74. Hardwick 2008, 31.
75. U.S. Census Bureau 2009.
76. Smith and Furuseth 2004.
77. University of North Carolina at Charlotte Urban Institute 2006.
78. See Weeks, Weeks, and Weeks 2006–2007.

Chapter Seven

1. Mohl 2005.
2. Teitelbaum 2008, 54
3. Baldwin-Edwards 2008, 1454.

4. Kochhar 2008.
5. For example, Sullivan 2000; Martin 2008; Valenzuela 2007.
6. Huntingon 2004, 183.
7. For a good overview of the assimilation controversy with regard to Mexican migrants, see Saenz, Filoteo, and Murga 2007.
8. Chavez 2008, 2.
9. For an excellent discussion of a Mexican community, see Fitzgerald 2009, chapter 5.
10. Escobar 2008.
11. See Chavez 2008, 89.
12. U.S. General Accounting Office 2004.
13. Okie 2007.
14. Goldman, Smith, and Sood 2006.
15. Citrin, Lerman, Murakami, and Pearson 2007; see also Davila and Mora 2000.
16. Portes and Rumbaut 2006, 119.
17. Lutz 2007–2008, 37.
18. Jiménez and Fitzgerald 2007.
19. Pew Hispanic Center 2006b.
20. Tabulations by the authors from unpublished census data: Census 2000 PUMS data are courtesy of www.ipums.org; ACS 2007 PUMS data are from www.factfinder.gov.
21. Linton 2004.
22. Myers 2008, 2.
23. Gravelle and Labonte 2007, 1.
24. Morin and Russakoff 2005.
25. U.S. Social Security Administration 2008.
26. Tancredo 2006, 127–128.
27. Conversation with GBW, August 1, 2008.
28. Consejo Nacional de la Población 2006.
29. Hamilton, Sutton, and Ventura 2003, Table 2.
30. Hamilton, Martin, and Ventura 2009, Table 5.
31. Lopez and Minushkin 2008.
32. Pew Hispanic Center 2008.
33. See Obama 2008.
34. Massey, Durand, and Malone 2002, 1.
35. De Recacoechea 2007, 46.
36. Billeaud 2008b.

Bibliography

Aderholt, Robert B. 2008. http://aderholt.house.gov/index.cfm?sectionid=99§iontree=4,25,99.

Aguilar Camín, Héctor, and Lorenzo Meyer. 1993. *In the Shadow of the Mexican Revolution: Contemporary Mexican History, 1910–198.9* Austin: University of Texas Press.

Aizenman, N. C. 2007. "The Face of El Salvador's Charm Offensive," *Washington Post*, January 9.

Alchon, Suzanne Austin. 1997. "The Great Killers in Precolumbian America: A Hemispheric Perspective." *Latin American Population History Bulletin* 27 (Fall): 2–11.

Andreas, Peter. 2000. *Border Games: Policing the U.S.-Mexico Divide*. Ithaca, NY: Cornell University Press.

Arana, Ana. 2005. "How the Street Gangs Took Central America," *Foreign Affairs* 84, 3 (May/June): 98–110.

Archibold, Randal C. 2007. "Debate Raging, Mexico Adds to Consulates in U.S." *New York Times*, May 23.

Arriaga, Eduardo E. 1970. *Mortality Decline and its Demographic Effects in Latin America*. Berkeley: Institute of International Studies, University of California.

Associated Press. 2009. "Exodus of Migrants from Mexico Falls by Half." *New York Daily News*, February 21.

Associated Press. 2007. "Bush, Saca Discuss Immigration Reforms." *Washington Post*, February 27.

Associated Press. 2004. "U.S., Mexicans to Meet Over Reparations." *New York Times*, February 8.

Asthana, Anushka. 2005. "The Polish Plumber Who Fixed the Vote." *The Guardian*, May 29. http://politics.guardian.co.uk/eu/story/0,9061,1495098,00.html.

Baldwin-Edwards, Martin. 2008. "Toward a Theory of Illegal Migration: Historical and Structural Components." *Third World Quarterly* 29, 7: 1449–1459.

Bankston III, Carl L. 2007. "New People in the New South: An Overview of Southern Immigration." *Southern Cultures* 31, 4: 24–44.

Barreto, Matt A. 2007. "Sí Se Puede! Latino Candidates and the Mobilization of Latino Voters." *American Political Science Review* 101, 3 (August): 425–441.

Barreto, Matt A., and José A. Muñoz. 2003. "Re-examining the 'Politics of In-Between': Political Participation among Mexican Immigrants in the United States." *Hispanic Journal of Behavioral Sciences* 25, 4: 427–447.

Benac, Nancy. 2006. "Poll: Most Open to Letting Immigrants Stay." *USA Today*, April 3.

Betancur, John J. 2005. "Framing the Discussion of African American-Latino Relations: A Review and Analysis." In Anani Dzidzienyo and Suzanne Oboler (eds.). *Neither Enemies Nor Friends: Latinos, Blacks, Afro-Latinos*. New York: Palgrave Macillan, 159–172.

Billeaud, Jacques. 2008a. "2 States Consider Guest Worker Programs." Associated Press, March 14.

Billeaud, Jacques. 2008b. "'Virtual Kidnappers' Target Immigrant Families." Associated Press, September 22.

Black, Thomas. 2008. "Mexicans Can Seek Payments for U.S. Work in 1940s, Judge Rules." *Bloomberg.com*, October 14. http://www.bloomberg.com/apps/news?pid=20601086&sid=aHGOZhilTGZU&refer=latin_america.

Boggs, S. Whittemore. 1940. *International Boundaries: A Study of Boundary Functions and Problems*. New York: Columbia University Press.

Bohon, Stephanie. 2001. *Latinos in Ethnic Enclaves: Immigrant Workers and the Competition for Jobs*. New York: Garland Publishing.

Booth, John A., Christine J. Wade, and Thomas W. Walker. 2006. *Understanding Central America: Global Forces, Rebellion, and Change*. Boulder, CO: Westview Press.

Borjas, George J. 2003. "The Labor Demand Curve is Downward Sloping: Reexamining the Impact of Immigration on the Labor Market." *Quarterly Review of Economics* 118, 4 (November): 1335–1374.

Boucher, Stephen, Aaron Smith, J. Edward Taylor, and Antonio Yúnez-Naude. 2007. "Impacts of Policy Reforms on the Supply of Mexican Labor to U.S. Farms: New Evidence From Mexico." *Review of Agricultural Economics* 29, 1: 4–16.

Brevé, Federico. 2007. "The Maras: A Menace to the Americas." *Military Review* 87, 4 (July/August): 88–95.

Brownstein, Ronald. 2006. "Most Back Tighter Border and a Guest-Worker Program." *Los Angeles Times*, April 13.

Bryant, Phil. 2006. *The Impact of Illegal Immigration on Mississippi: Costs and Population Trends*. A Report from the Performance Audit Division #102, February 21. http://www.osa.state.ms.us/documents/performance/illegal-immigration.pdf.

Buchenau, Jürgen. 2004. *Tools of Progress: A German Merchant Family in Mexico City, 1865–Present*. Albuquerque: University of New Mexico Press.

Bullock III, Charles S., and M. V. Hood III. 2006. "A Mile-Wide Gap: The Evolution of Hispanic Political Emergence in the Deep South." *Social Science Quarterly* 87, 5 (December): 1117–1135.

Bush, George W. 2006. Quoted in Lynn Sweet, "Bush Leaves This Afternoon for Cancun." *Chicago Sun-Times*, March 29. http://blogs.suntimes.com/sweet/2006/03/bush_leaves_this_afternoon_for.html.

Bush, George W. 2007. "Immigration Reform," Address in Glynco, Georgia, May 29. http://www.presidentialrhetoric.com/speeches/05.29.07.html.

Butcher, Kristin F., and Anne Morrison Piehl. 2007. *Why are Immigrants' Incarceration Rates so Low? Evidence on Selective Immigration, Deterrence, and Deportation*. National Bureau of Economic Research, Working Paper 13229 (July).

Cain, Bruce, and Brendan Doherty. 2006. "The Impact of Dual Nationality on Political Participation." In Taeku Lee, S. Karthick Ramakrishnan, and Ricardo Ramírez (eds.). *Transforming Politics, Transforming America: The Political and Civic Incorporation of Immigrants in the United States*. Charlottesville: University of Virginia Press, 89–105.

Calavita, Kitty. 1992. *Inside the State: The Bracero Program, Immigration and the INS*. New York: Routledge.

Calderón-Chelius, Leticia. 2007. "Compulsory Voting and Renewed Interest among External Voters." In *Voting from Abroad: The International IDEA Handbook*. Stockholm: International Institute for Democracy and Electoral Assistance, 128–131.

Capehart, Tom. 2004. "Trends in U.S. Tobacco Farming." United States Department of Agriculture, Outlook Report TBS257–02 (November).

Capitol Press. 2008. "Farmer Stops Producing Tomatoes, Blames Lack of Migrant Labor." Editorial, March 26.

Capps, Randy, Everett Henderson, John D. Kasarda, James H. Johnson Jr., Stephen J. Appold, Derrek L. Croney, Donald J. Hernandez, and Michael Fix. 2007. *A Profile of Immigrants in Arkansas: Executive Summary*. Little Rock, AK: The Winthrop Rockefeller Foundation (April). http://www.urban.org/UploadedPDF/411441_Arkansas_complete.pdf.

Card, David, and Ethan G. Lewis. 2007. "The Diffusion of Mexican Immigrants during the 1990s: Explanations and Impacts." In George J. Borjas (ed.). *Mexican Immigration to the United States*. Chicago: The University of Chicago Press, 193–227.

Cardoso, Lawrence A. 1980. *Mexican Emigration to the United States: 1897–1931*. Tucson: The University of Arizona Press.

Carvajal, Doreen. 1995. "Salvador Helps Refugees Filing for Asylum in U.S." *New York Times*, October 27.

Castañeda, Jorge G. 2007. *Ex Mex: From Migrants to Immigrants*. New York: The Free Press.

Castillo, E. Eduardo. 2008. "Mexico, US Find no al-Qaida Links since 9/11." Associated Press, September 12.

Castillo, Miguel Angel. 2003. "Migraciones en el hemisferio: Consecuencias y relación con las políticas socials." Centro Latinoamericano y Caribeño de Demografía (CELADE), May. http://www.eclac.cl/publicaciones/Poblacion/8/LCL1908P/lc11908-p.pdf.

Castles, Stephen, and Mark J. Miller. 2003. *The Age of Migration: International Population Movements in the Modern World*, 3rd ed. New York: The Guilford Press.

Charlotte Observer. 2007. "City Welcomes 1st Baby of '07, Josue Eduardo Martinez Callejas." January 2.

Chavez, Leo R. 2008. *The Latino Threat: Constructing Immigrants, Citizens, and the Nation*. Stanford, CA: Stanford University Press.

Cherrie, Victoria. 2008. "Dozens Held in Gang Sweep." *Charlotte Observer*, June 25.

Chicago Tribune. 2008. "Central American Immigrants Seek Rights in Mexico." May 1.

Chiu, William, and Marisol Raquel Gutiérrez. 2007. "Migration and Political Involvement." In Wayne A. Cornelius and Jessa M. Lewis (eds.). *Impacts of Border Enforcement on Mexican Migration: The View from Sending Communities*. La Jolla, CA: Center for Comparative Immigration Studies, UCSD, 149–162.

Cho, Y., W. Frisbie, R. Hummer, and R. Rogers. 2004. "Nativity, Duration of Residence, and the Health of Hispanic Adults in the United States." *International Migration Review* 38 (1): 184–211.

Citrin, Jack, Amy Lerman, Michael Murakami, and Kathryn Pearson. 2007. "Testing Huntington: Is Hispanic Immigration a Threat to American Identity?" *Perspectives on Politics* 5, 1 (March): 31–48.

CNN. 2009. "Bad Economy Forcing Immigrants to Reconsider U.S." February 10. http://www.cnn.com/2009/US/02/10/immigrants.economy/index.html.

CNN. 2001. "Special Report: War Against Terror." http://edition.cnn.com/SPECIALS/2001/trade.center/victims.section.html.

Congressional Record. August 25, 1965.

Consejo Nacional de Población. 2006. *Cuadernos de salud reproductiva, Republica Mexicana*. CONAPO. http://www.conapo.gob.mx/publicaciones/inicios/002.htm.

Constable, Pamela. 2008. "Guatemalan Stresses Immigrant Sacrifices." *Washington Post*, April 30.

Cooper, Marc. 2007. "Lockdown in Greeley." *The Nation*, February 26.

Cornelius, Wayne A., and Marc Rosenblum. 2005. "Immigration and Politics." *Annual Review of Political Science* 8: 99–119.

Coutin, Susan Bibler. 2008. *Nations of Emigrants: Shifting Boundaries of Citizenship in El Salvador and the United States*. Ithaca, NY: Cornell University Press.

Coutin, Susan. 2004. "The Odyssey of Salvadoran Asylum Seekers." *NACLA Report on the Americas* 37, 6 (May/June): 38–41.

Craig, Richard B. 1971. *The Bracero Program: Interest Groups and Foreign Policy*. Austin: University of Texas Press.

Cummings, Scott, and Thomas Lambert. 1997. "Anti-Hispanic and Anti-Asian Sentiments among African-Americans." *Social Science Quarterly* 78, 2: 338–353.

Daniels, Roger. 2004. *Guarding the Golden Door: American Immigration Policy and Immigrants Since 1882*. New York: Hill and Wang.

Davenport, Jim. 2007. "Mitt Romney Slams Immigration Plan." *San Francisco Chronicle*, May 19.

Davila, Alberto, and Marie T. Mora. 2000. "The English-Skill Acquisition of Hispanic Americans during the 1980s." *Social Science Quarterly* 81, 1 (March): 261–275.

Davis, Kinglsey. 1963. "The Theory of Change and Response in Modern Demographic History." *Population Index* 29 (4): 345–366.

De la Garza, Rodolfo O., Harry P. Pachon, Manuel Orozco, and Adrián Pantoja. 2000. "Family Ties and Ethnic Lobbies." In Rodolfo de la Garza and Harry P. Pachon (eds.). *Latinos and U.S. Foreign Policy: Representing the "Homeland"?* Lanham, MD: Rowman and Littlefield Publishers, Inc.

De Leon, Sergio. 2006. "11 Countries Plan to Lobby Against U.S. Immigration Law." *Miami Herald*, February 14.

Dell'orto, Giovanna. 2001. "14 Illegal Immigrants Die in Desert." *Washington Post*, May 24.

DeSipio, Louis. 2006. "Transnational Politics and Civic Engagement: Do Home-Country Political Ties Limit Latino Immigrant Pursuit of U.S. Civic Engagement and Citizenship?" In Taeku Lee, S. Karthick Ramakrishnan, and Ricardo Ramírez (eds.). *Transforming Politics, Transforming America: The Political and Civic Incorporation of Immigrants in the United States*. Charlottesville: University of Virginia Press, 106–126.

Díaz, Junot. 2007. *The Brief Wondrous Life of Oscar Wao*. New York: Riverhead Books.

Díaz-Briquets, Sergio. 1989. "The Central American Demographic Situation: Trends and Implication." In Frank D. Bean, Jurgen Schmandt, and Sidney Weintraub (eds.). *Mexican and Central American Population and U.S. Immigration Policy*. Austin, TX: The Center for Mexican American Studies, 33–64.

Díaz-Briquets, Sergio, and Lisandro Pérez. 1981. "Cuba: The Demography of Revolution." *Population Bulletin* 36, 1: 1–41.

Dinerstein, Marti. 2003. "IDs for Illegals: The 'Matricula Consular' Advances Mexico's Immigration Agenda." *Center for Immigration Studies Backgrounder* (January).

Dobbs, Lou. 2007. "Mexican President's Blatant Hypocrisy," CNN.com, September 5. http://www.cnn.com/2007/US/09/04/Dobbs.Sept5/index.html.

Domestic Workers United. 2007. "Domestic Workers Take U.S. Social Forum by Storm; Form National Alliance," July 16. http://www.domesticworkersunited.org/shownews/5.

Domínguez, Jorge I. 2007. "Latino Impact on U.S. Immigration and Foreign Policy." Paper presented at the conference of the International Studies Association.

Dresser, Denise. 1993. "Exporting Conflict: Transboundary Consequences of Mexican Politics." In Abraham F. Lowenthal and Katrina Burgess (eds.). *The California-Mexico Connection*. Stanford, CA: Stanford University Press, 82–112.

Dunn, Timothy J. 1996. *The Militarization of the U.S.-Mexico Border, 1978–1992*. Austin, TX: The Center for Mexican American Studies.

Durand, Jorge, and Douglas Massey (eds.). 2004. *Crossing the Border: Research From the Mexican Migration Project*. New York: Russell Sage Foundation.

Echávarri, Fernanda. 2009. "Employer Sanctions Law, Recession Spur Decline in Day Laborers." *Tucson Citizen*, March 2.

Echegaray, Chris. 2008. "Middle Tennessee Gang Leaders Plead Guilty." *The Tennessean*, July 29.

The Economist. 2005a. "Emerging Market Indicators." April 2.

The Economist. 2005b. "Sport in Brazil: Footloose." January 22.

Ehrlich, Paul. 1968. *The Population Bomb (Revised)*. Rivercity, MA: Rivercity Press.

Elbert, David. 2008. "Iowa's World Exports Double in Five Years." *Des Moines Register*, March 9.

El Comercio (Ecuador). 2007. "403,000 emigrantes salieron del Ecuador en cuatro años." December 22.

Ellingwood, Ken. 2008. "In El Salvador, Journalist May Lead Leftists to Center Stage." *Los Angeles Times*, June 26.

Escobar, Cristina. 2007. "Extraterritorial Political Rights and Dual Citizenship in Latin America." *Latin American Research Review* 42, 3: 43–75.

Escobar, Cristina. 2004. "Dual Citizenship and Political Participation: Migrants in the Interplay of United States and Colombian Politics." *Latino Studies* 2, 1: 45–69.

Escobar Latapí, Agustín. 2008. "Mexico Policy and Mexico-U.S. Migration." The Center for Comparative Immigration Studies, University of California at San Diego, Working Paper 167 (May).

Federal Bureau of Investigation. 2008. "The MS-13 Threat: A National Assessment." January 14. http://www.fbi.gov/page2/jan08/ms13_011408.html.

Feeney, Tom. 2008. http://www.tomfeeney.com/position-statements/immigration/.

Fitzgerald, David. 2009. *A Nation of Emigrants: How Mexico Manages its Migration*. Berkeley: University of California Press.

Fitzgerald, David. 2005. "State and Emigration: A Century of Emigration Policy in Mexico." The Center for Comparative Immigration Studies, University of California at San Diego, Working Paper 123 (September).

Fox, Vicente, and Rob Allyn. 2007. *Revolution of Hope: The Life, Faith, and Dreams of a Mexican President*. New York: Viking.

Fuchs, Erin. 2008. "Dalton Hispanics Confront Gang Problem." *Chattanooga Times Free Press*, March 30.

Galarza, Ernesto. 1964. *Merchants of Labor: The Mexican Bracero Story*. Charlotte, NC, and Santa Barbara, CA: McNally & Loftin, Publishers.

García, María Cristina. 2006. *Seeking Refuge: Central American Migration to Mexico, the United States, and Canada*. Berkeley: University of California Press.

García y Griego, Manuel. 1983. "The Importation of Mexican Contract Laborers to the United States, 1942–1964: Antecedents, Operation, and Legacy." In Peter G. Brown and Henry Shue (eds.). *The Border That Joins: Mexican Migrants and U.S. Responsibility*. Totowa, NJ: Rowman and Littlefield, 49–98.

Garcia y Griego, M., J. R. Weeks, and R. Ham-Chande. 1990. "Mexico." In W. J. Serow, C. B. Nam, D. F. Sly, and R. H. Weller (eds.). *Handbook on International Migration*. New York: Greenwood Press.

Getis, A., and J. Getis. 1995. *United States & Canada: The Land and the People*. Dubuque, IA: William C. Brown Communications.

Glazer, Gwen. 2007. "Immigration." *National Journal* 39, 20 (May 19): 76.

Goerman, Patricia L. 2006. *The Promised Land? The Lives and Voices of Hispanic Immigrants in the New South*. New York: Routledge.

Goldman, Dana P., James P. Smith, and Neeraj Sood. 2006. "Immigrants and the Cost of Medical Care." *Health Affairs* 25, 6: 1700–1711.

Goldring, Luin. 2002. "The Mexican State and Transmigrant Organizations: Negotiating the Boundaries of Membership and Participation." *Latin American Research Review* 37, 3: 55–99.

Gonzales, John Moreno. 2009. "Mixed Signals Along South's 'Immigrant Highway.'" *Washington Post*, March 10.

Gravelle, Jane, and Marc Labonte. 2007. *Social Security Reform: Economic Issues*. Congressional Research Service, CRS Report for Congress, RL31498 (January 31).

Greenhill, Kelly M. 2002. "Engineered Migration and the Use of Refugees as Political Weapons: A Case Study of the 1994 Cuban Balseros Crisis." *International Migration* 40, 4: 39–74.

Greenhouse, Steven. 2007. "Crackdown Upends Slaughterhouse's Work Force," *New York Times*, October 12.

Guarnizo, Luis Eduardo, Alejandro Portes, and William Haller. 2003. "Assimilation and Transnationalism: Determinants of Transnational Political Action among Contemporary Migrants." *American Journal of Sociology* 108, 6 (May): 1221–1248.

Guthey, Greig. 2001. "Mexican Places in Southern Spaces: Globalization, Work, and Daily Life in and around the North Georgia Poultry Industry." In Arthur D. Murphy, Colleen Blanchard, and Jennifer A. Hill (eds.). *Latino Workers in the Contemporary South*. Athens: The University of Georgia Press, 57–67.

Gutierrez, Carlos M. 2007. Speech to Associated General Contractors of America, San Antonio, Texas, March 22. http://www.commerce.gov/NewsRoom/SecretarySpeeches/PROD01_002824.

Hagan, John, Ron Levi, and Ronit Dinovitzer. 2008. "The Symbolic Violence of the Crime-Immigration Nexus: Migrant Mythologies in the Americas." *Criminology and Public Policy* 7, 1: 95–112.

Hall, Daron. 2008. "The 287(g) Program is Working and Residents Are Safer Because of it." *The Tennessean*, August 12. http://www.tennessean.com/apps/pbcs.dll/article?AID=/20080812/OPINION03/808120370/1008/OPINION01.

Hamilton, B. E., J. A. Martin, and S. J. Ventura. 2009. *Births: Preliminary Data for 2007*. National Vital Statistics Reports, 57, 7. Hyattsville, MD: National Center for Health Statistics. http://www.cdc.gov/nchs/data/nvsr/nvsr57/nvsr57_12.pdf.

Hamilton, B. E., P. D. Sutton, and S. J. Ventura. 2003. *Revised Birth and Fertility Rates for the 1990s and New Rates for Hispanic Populations, 2000 and 2001: United States*. National Vital Statistics Reports 51, 12. Hyattsville, MD: National Center for Health Statistics. http://www.cdc.gov/nchs/data/nvsr/nvsr51/nvsr51_12.pdf.

Hardwick, Susan. 2008. "Toward a Suburban Immigrant Nation." In Audrey Singer, Susan W. Hardwick, and Caroline B. Brettell (eds.). *Twenty-First Century Gateways: Immigrant Incorporation in Suburban America*. Washington, DC: Brookings Institution Press, 31–50.

Harman, Danna. 2006. "Latin Leaders Balk at US 'Wall.'" *Christian Science Monitor*, March 27.

Harwood, Edwin. 1986. "American Public Opinion and U.S. Immigration Policy." *Annals of the American Academy of Political and Social Science* 487 (September): 201–212.

Hayes, Joseph M., and Laura E. Hill. 2008. "Immigrant Pathways to Legal Permanent Residence: Now and Under a Merit-Based System." San Francisco: Public Policy Institute of California.

Henry, Samantha. 2008. "Latin Consulates Ally to Assist NY Area Immigrants." Associated Press, June 17.

Hernández, Kelly Lytle. 2006. "The Crimes and Consequences of Illegal Immigration: A Cross-Border Examination of Operation Wetback, 1943–1954." *Western Historical Quarterly* 37, 4 (Winter): 421–444.

Hernández-León, Rubén, and Víctor Zúñiga. 2000. "'Making Carpet by the Mile': The Emergence of a Mexican Immigrant Community in an Industrial Region of the U.S. Historic South." *Social Science Quarterly* 81, 1 (March): 49–66.

Hoefer, M., N. Rytina, and B. C. Baker. 2008. "Estimates of the Unauthorized Immigrant Population Residing in the United States: January 2007." *Population Estimates* (September). http://www.dhs.gov/xlibrary/assets/statistics/publications/ois_ill_pe_2007.pdf.

Hollerbach, P. 1980. "Recent Trends in Fertility, Abortion, and Contraception in Cuba." *International Family Planning Perspectives* 6, 3: 97–106.

Hondagneu-Sotelo, Pierrette (ed.). 2003. *Gender and U.S. Immigration: Contemporary Trends*. Berkeley: University of California Press.

Hondagneu-Sotelo, Pierrette. 2001. *Doméstica: Immigrant Workers Cleaning and Caring in the Shadows of Affluence*. Berkeley: University of California Press.

Hondagneu-Sotelo, Pierrette. 1994. *Gendered Transitions: Mexican Experiences of Immigration*. Berkeley: University of California Press.

Hummel, Marta. 2005. "N.C. Farming Has a Labor Crisis." *Greensboro News & Record*, October 30.

Hunter, Desiree. 2008. "Board Policy Bars Illegal Immigrants From 2-Year Schools." *Montgomery Advertiser*, September 26.

Huntington, Samuel P. 2004. *Who Are We? The Challenges to America's National Identity*, New York: Simon and Schuster.

Imaz Bayona, Cecilia. 2007. "Percepciones de la migración en México y Estados Unidos." *Metapolítica* 51, 11 (Enero-Febrero). meme.phpwebhosting.com/~migracion/rimd/documentos_miembros/13005art-metapolitica-ene-feb2007.doc.

Immigration and Nationality Act. 2005. "Amendment to strengthen enforcement of the immigration laws, to enhance border security, and for other purposes," H.R. 4437, December 17. http://frwebgate.access.gpo.gov/cgi-bin/getdoc.cgi?dbname=109_cong_bills&docid=f:h4437rfs.txt.pdf.

Immigration Reform and Control Act. 1986. "Amendment to effectively control unauthorized immigration into the United States, and for other purposes," S. 1200, Conference report, October 14. http://thomas.loc.gov/cgi-bin/bdquery/z?d099:SN01200:@@@L&summ2=m&|TOM:/bss/d099query.html|#major%20actions.

Instituto Nacional de Estadística y Geografía. 1994. *Estadísticas Históricas de Mexico, Tomo I.* Aguascalientes: INEGI.

Inter-American Development Bank. 2008a. "Fewer Latin Americans Sending Money Home from the United States, Survey Finds." Press Release, April 30. http://www.iadb.org/news/articledetail.cfm?artid=4595&language=English.

Inter-American Development Bank. 2008b. *The Changing Pattern of Remittances: 2008 Survey of the Remittances From the United States to Latin America* (April). http://idbdocs.iadb.org/wsdocs/getdocument.aspx?docnum=1418521.

Inter-American Development Bank. 2007. "Immigrants sent 3.7 billion euros from Spain to Latin America in 2006," June 5. http://www.iadb.org/news/detail.cfm?language=English&id=3883.

Inter-American Development Bank. 2006. "Public Opinion Research Study of Latin American Remittance Senders in the United States." Multilateral Investment Fund Document, October 18. http://idbdocs.iadb.org/wsdocs/getdocument.aspx?docnum=826095.

Inter-American Development Bank. 2005. *Sending Money Home: Remittance to Latin America and the Caribbean* (May).

Inter-American Development Bank. 2004a. *Receptores de Remesas en América Latina: El Caso Colombiano* (September).

Inter-American Development Bank. 2004b. *Sending Money Home: Remittance to Latin America and the Caribbean* (May).

International Organization for Migration. n.d. "Americas." http://www.iom.int/jahia/Jahia/pid/250.

Jacobe, Dennis. 2008. "Economy Widely Viewed as Most Important Problem." Gallup.com, March 13. http://www.gallup.com/poll/104959/Economy-Widely-Viewed-Most-Important-Problem.aspx.

Jiménez, Tomás R., and David Fitzgerald. 2007. "Mexican Assimilation." *Du Bois Review* 4, 2 (September): 337–354.

Johnson, Lyndon Baines. 1966. *Public Papers of the President of the United States, Lyndon Baines Johnson, Book II—June 1 to December 31, 1965.* Washington, DC: United States Government Printing Office.

Johnston, Nicholas, and Roger Simon. 2006. "Immigration Debate Splits Republican Politicians, Not Voters." Bloomberg.com, April 13. http://www.bloomberg.com/apps/news?pid=10000103&sid=asHdTQGmf_DM&refer=us.

Jones-Correa, Michael. 2001. "Under Two Flags: Dual Nationality in Latin America and Its Consequences for Naturalization in the United States." *International Migration Review* 35, 4 (Winter): 997–1029.

Kandel, William, and Emilio A. Parrado. 2005. "Restructuring of the U.S. Meat Processing Industry and New Hispanic Migrant Destinations." *Population and Development* 31, 3: 447–471.

Kapur, Devesh, and John McHale. 2005. *Give Us Your Best and Brightest: The Global Hunt for Talent and Its Impact on the Developing World.* Washington, DC: Center for Global Development.

Kasarda, John D., and James H. Johnson Jr. 2006. *The Economic Impact of the Hispanic Population on the State of North Carolina.* Chapel Hill: Kenan-Flagler Business School, University of North Carolina, January. http://www.kenan-flagler.unc.edu/assets/documents/2006_KenanInstitute_HispanicStudy.pdf.

Kaufmann, Karen M. 2003. "Black and Latino Voters in Denver: Responses to Each Other's Political Leadership." *Political Science Quarterly* 118, 1 (Spring): 107–125.

Keeler, Guy. 2008. "Top Central America Figures in Valley." *Fresno Bee*, June 7. http://www.fresnobee.com/263/story/653637.html.

Kochhar, R. 2008. *Latino Workers in the Ongoing Recession: 2007 to 2008.* Washington, DC: Pew Hispanic Center.

Kochhar, Rakesh, Robert Suro, and Sonya Tafoya. 2005. *The New Latino South: The Context and Consequences of Rapid Population Growth.* Washington, DC: Pew Hispanic Center July 26.

Konczal, Lisa, and Alex Stepick. 2007. "Haiti." In May C. Waters and Reed Ueda (eds.). *The New Americans: A Guide to Immigration since 1965.* Cambridge, MA: Harvard University Press, 445–457.

Kosnett, Jeffrey R. 2004. "I Fought for Families of Foreign Victims Killed on 9/11." *Kiplinger's Personal Finance* 58, 9 (September): 104.

Kronholz, June, and John Lyons. 2006. "Population Shift: As Families Shrink in Mexico, the U.S. May Feel Impact." *Wall Street Journal*, April 28.

Kugler, Tadeusz, and Siddharth Swaminathan. 2006. "The Politics of Population." *International Studies Review* 8: 581–596.

Kuznetsov, Yevgeny (ed.). 2006. *Diaspora Networks and the International Migration of Skills: How Countries Can Draw on Their Talent Abroad.* Washington, DC: World Bank).

Lacy, Elaine. 2009. "Cultural Enclaves and Transnational Ties: Mexican Immigration and Settlement in South Carolina." In Mary E. Odem and Elaine Lacy (eds.). *Latino Immigrants and the Transformation of the U.S. South.* Athens: University of Georgia Press, 1–17.

Leal, David L. 2002. "Political Participation by Latino Noncitizens in the United States." *British Journal of Political Science* 32: 353–370.

Leal, David L., Stephen A. Nuño, Jongho Lee, and Rodolfo O. de la Garza. 2008. "Latinos, Immigration, and the 2006 Midterm Elections." *PS: Political Science and Politics* XLI, 2 (April): 309–317.

Lee, James, and Wang Feng. 1999. *One Quarter of Humanity, Malthusian Mythology and Chinese Realities 1700–2000.* Cambridge, MA: Harvard University Press.

Leggiere, Phil. 2008. "McCain and Homeland Security." *Homeland Security Today*, September 30. http://www.hstoday.us/content/view/5404/201/1/1/.

Levitt, Peggy. 2007. "Dominican Republic." In Mary C. Waters and Reed Ueda, with Helen B. Marrow (eds.). *The New Americans: A Guide to Immigration Since 1965*. Cambridge, MA: Harvard University Press, 319–412.

Levitt, Peggy, and Rafael de la Dehesa. 2003. "Transnational Migration and the Redefinition of the State: Variations and Explanations." *Ethnic and Racial Studies* 26, 4 (July): 587–611.

Levine, Linda. 2008. "Farm Labor Shortages and Immigration Policy," Congressional Research Service, CRS Report for Congress, RL30396 (January 17).

Linton, A. 2004. "A Critical Mass Model of Bilingualism among U.S.-Born Hispanics." *Social Forces* 83, 1: 279–314.

Llana, Sara Miller. 2008. "Recession Slows Mexican Immigrants' Holiday Trips Home." *McClatchy.com*, December 23. http://www.mcclatchydc.com/world/story/58379.html.

Loller, Travis. 2008. "English-only Movement Targets Nashville, Tenn." *Business Week*, August 11.

Lopez, Mark Hugo. 2008. *The Hispanic Vote in 2008*. Washington, DC: Pew Hispanic Center, November.

Lopez, Mark Hugo, and Susan Minushkin. 2008. *2008 National Survey of Latinos: Hispanics See Their Situation in U.S. Deteriorating; Oppose Key Immigration Enforcement Measures*. Washington, DC: Pew Hispanic Center, September 18. http://pewhispanic.org/reports/report.php?ReportID=93.

Lopez, Mark Hugo, Gretchen Livingston, and Rakesh Kochhar. 2009. *Hispanics and the Economic Downturn: Housing Woes and Remittance Cuts*. Washington, DC: Pew Hispanic Center, January 8. http://pewhispanic.org/files/reports/100.pdf.

Los Angeles Times. 2006. "Mexico Won't Give Maps to Migrants." January 27.

Lozano v. Hazleton. 2007. *Pedro Lolazno et al. v. City of Hazleton*. Case 3:06-cv-01586-JMM, July 26, 188–189. http://www.aclu.org/pdfs/immigrants/hazleton_decision.pdf.

Lundquist, Jennifer H., and Douglas S. Massey. 2005. "Politics or Economics? International Migration during the Nicaraguan Contra War." *Journal of Latin American Studies* 37: 29–53.

Lutz, Amy. 2007–2008. "Negotiating Home Language: Spanish Maintenance and Loss in Latino Famlies." *Latino/a Research Review* 6, 3: 37–64.

Malthus, T. R. 1992 [1798]. *An Essay on the Principle of Population*. Cambridge: Cambridge University Press.

Marklein, Mary Beth. 2008. "Illegal Immigrants Face Threat of No College." *USA Today*, July 7.

Martell, Alpha, Maribel Pineda, and Luis Tapia. 2007. "The Contemporary Migration Process." In Wayne Cornelius, David Fitzgerald, and Pedro Lewin Fischer (eds.). *Mayan Journeys: The New Migration from Yucatán to the United*

States. La Jolla, CA: Center for Comparative Immigration Studies, University of California, San Diego, 49–70.

Martin, David A. 2008. "Eight Myths about Immigration Enforcement." Public Law and Legal Theory Working Paper Series, Paper 83. Charlottesville: University of Virginia Law School.

Martin, Philip. 2007. "Farm Labor Shortages: How Real? What Response?" Center for Immigration Studies Backgrounder, November. http://www.cis.org/articles/2007/back907.pdf.

Massey, Douglas, and Kristen Espinosa. 1997. "What's Driving Mexico-U.S. Migration? A Theoretical, Empirical, and Policy Analysis." *American Journal of Sociology* 102, 4: 939–999.

Massey, Douglas S., Jorge Durand, and Nolan J. Malone. 2002. *Beyond Smoke and Mirrors: Mexican Immigration in an Era of Economic Integration*. New York: Russell Sage Foundation.

Masuoka, Natalie. 2008. "Defining the Group: Latino Identity and Political Participation." *American Politics Research* 36, 1 (January): 33–61.

Mayor's Immigration Study Commission. 2007. *Immigration: Legal and Illegal, Local Perspective—Charlotte, North Carolina* (January). http://www.charmeck.org/Departments/Mayor/ImmigrationStudy/Home.htm.

Mazzolari, Francisca. 2005. "Determinants of Naturalization: The Role of Dual Citizenship Laws." Working Paper 117 (April). La Jolla, CA: Center for Comparative Immigration Studies, University of California, San Diego.

McCain, John. 2008. "John McCain's Acceptance Speech." http://www.npr.org/templates/story/story.php?storyId=94302894.

McClain, Paula D., Monique L. Lyle, Niambi M. Carter, Victoria M. DeFrancesco Soto, Gerald F. Lackey, Kendra Davenport Cotton, Shayla C. Nunnally, Thomas J. Scotto, Jeffrey D. Grynaviski, and J. Alan Kendrick. 2007. "Black Americans and Latino Immigrants in a Southern City: Friendly Neighbors or Economic Competitors?" *Du Bois Review* 4, 1: 97–117.

McWhirter, Cameron, and Mary Lou Pickel. 2009. "Tough Illegal Immigration Law Ignored." *Atlanta Journal-Constitution*, January 25.

McWilliams, Carey. 1968. *North from Mexico: The Spanish-Speaking People of the United States*. New York: Greenwood Press.

Menjívar, Cecilia. 2000. *Fragmented Ties: Salvadoran Immigrant Networks in America*. Berkeley: University of California Press.

MercoPress. 2008. "Mercosur Blasts EU Immigrants' 'Return Directive.'" June 21. http://www.mercopress.com/vernoticia.do?id=13769&formato=HTML.

Mindlin, Alex. 2007. "A Homeland Beckons," *New York Times*, November 11.

Mitchell, Christopher. 1992. "Introduction: Immigration and U.S. Foreign Policy toward the Caribbean, Central America, and Mexico." In Christopher Mitchell (ed.). *Western Hemisphere Immigration and United States Foreign Policy*. University Park: The Pennsylvania State University Press, 1–30.

Mohl, Raymond. 2005. "Globalization, Latinization, and the Nuevo New South." In James C. Cobb and William Stueck (eds.). *Globalization and the American South*. Athens: The University of Georgia Press, 66–99.

Mohl, Raymond A. 2002. "Latinization in the Heart of Dixie: Hispanics in Late-Twentieth-Century Alabama." *Alabama Review* 55, 4 (October): 243–274.

Mohr, Holbrook. 2008. "Immigration Raid Is Largest in U.S. History." *Seattle Times*, August 27.

Moloney, Anastasia. 2004. "Displaced in Colombia." *NACLA Report on the Americas* 38, 2 (September/October): 9–12.

Moreno, Sylvia. 2007. "Immigration Raid Leaves Texas Town a Skeleton." *Washington Post*, February 9.

Morin, Richard, and Dale Russakoff. 2005. "Social Security Problems Not a Crisis, Most Say." *Washington Post*, February 10.

Morrill, Jim. 2005. "3 Want Services Tied to Legal Status." *Charlotte Observer*, November 29.

Mulkern, Anne C. 2007. "Senators Propose Changes After Swift Raids." *Denver Post*, January 23.

Myers, Dowell. 2008. *Old Promises and New Blood: How Immigration Reform Can Help America Prosper in the Face of Baby Boom Retirement*. The Reform Institute, Reform Brief, November 24. http://www.reforminstitute.org/uploads/publications/Old_Promises_New_Blood_Final_11-21-08.pdf.

National Conference of State Legislatures. 2008. "2007 Enacted State Legislation Related to Immigrants and Immigration." January 31. http://www.ncsl.org/programs/immig/2007immigrationfinal.htm.

National Conference of State Legislatures. 2006. "2006 State Legislation Related to Immigration: Enacted and Vetoed." October 31. http://www.ncsl.org/programs/immig/6ImmigEnactedLegis3.htm.

National Drug Intelligence Center. 2008. *Atlanta High Intensity Drug Trafficking Area Drug Market Analysis*, June. http://www.usdoj.gov/ndic/pubs27/27485/dtos.htm#start.

Navarro Fierro, Carlos, Isabel Morales, and Maria Gratschew. 2007. "External Voting: A Comparative Overview." In *Voting from Abroad: The International IDEA Handbook*. Stockholm: International Institute for Democracy and Electoral Assistance, 11–39.

Nazario, Sonia. 2007. *Enrique's Journey*. New York: Random House.

Nelson, Eugene. 1975. *Bracero*. Los Angeles: Peace Press.

Nevins, Joseph. 2002. *Operation Gatekeeper: The Rise of the "Illegal Alien" and the Making of the U.S.-Mexico Boundary*. New York: Routledge.

News & Observer. "Opportunity Lost." Editorial, August 16.

Obama, Barack. 2008. "Fighting for Comprehensive Immigration Reform." http://www.barackobama.com/pdf/issues/ImmigrationFactSheet.pdf.

Office of Management and Budget. 2007. "Department of Homeland Security." http://www.whitehouse.gov/omb/rewrite/budget/fy2007/dhs.html.

Okie, Susan. 2007. "Immigrants and Health Care—At the Intersection of Two Broken Systems." *New England Journal of Medicine* 357 (August): 525–529.

Organización Internacional para las Migraciones. 2004. "Fifth South American Congress on Migration, La Paz, Bolivia, 25 and 26 November 2004." http://www.oimconosur.org/docs/pdf/302.pdf.

Organization of American States. 2008. "Insulza Rejects European Measures Against Immigrants." Press Release, June 19. http://www.oas.org/OASpage/press_releases/press_release.asp?sCodigo=E-243/08.

Orner, Peter (ed.). 2008. *Underground America: Narratives of Undocumented Lives*. San Francisco: McSweeney's Books.

Özden, Çağlar. 2005. "Brain Drain in Latin America." Expert Group Meeting on International Migration and Development in Latin America and the Caribbean, November 30–December 2. http://www.un.org/esa/population/meetings/IttMigLAC/P10_WB-DECRG.pdf.

Padilla, Beatriz, and João Peixoto. 2007. "Latin American Immigration to Southern Europe." Migration Policy Institute (June). http://www.migrationinformation.net/Feature/display.cfm?id=609.

Paerregaard, Karsten. 2002. "Power Recycled: Persistence and Transformation in Peruvian Transnationalism." In Ton Salman and Annelies Zommers (eds.). *The Andean Exodus: Transnational Migration from Bolivia, Ecuador and Peru*. Amsterdam: Centre for Latin American Research and Documentation, 1–28.

Pantoja, Adrian. 2006. "Against the Tide? Core American Values and Attitudes Toward U.S. Immigration Policy in the Mid-1990s." *Journal of Ethnic and Migration Studies* 32, 3 (April): 515–531.

Pantoja, Adrian D. 2005. "Transnational Ties and Immigrant Political Incorporation: The Case of Dominicans in Washington Heights, New York." *International Migration* 43, 4: 123–144.

Papademetriou, Demetrios G., and Aaron Terrazas. 2009. *Immigrants and the Current Economic Crisis: Research Evidence, Policy Challenges, and Implications*. Migration Policy Institute (January). http://www.migrationpolicy.org/pubs/lmi_recessionJan09.pdf.

Passel, Jeffrey S. 2006. *The Size and Characteristics of the Unauthorized Migrant Population in the U.S., Estimates Based on the March 2005 Current Population Survey*. Washington, DC: Pew Hispanic Center.

Passel, J. S., and D. V. Cohn. 2008. *Trends in Unauthorized Immigration: Undocumented Inflow Now Trails Legal Inflow*. Washington, DC: Pew Hispanic Center.

Paul, Ron. 2006. "A North American United Nations?" http://www.house.gov/paul/tst/tst2006/tst082806.htm.

PBS NewsHour. 2000. "The Elian Gonzalez Case: An Online NewsHour Focus." http://www.pbs.org/newshour/bb/law/elian/.

Pear, Robert. 2007. "Failure of Senate Immigration Bill Can Be Lesson for Congress, Experts Say," *New York Times*, June 30.

Pellegrino, Adela. 2001. "Trends in Latin American Skilled Migration: 'Brain Drain' or 'Brain Exchange'?" *International Migration* 39, 5: 111–132.

Penhaul, Karl. 2001. "The Lure of a Better Life." *U.S. News and World Report*, January 8: 28.

Pérez, Enzo, and Corey Dade. 2007. "An Immigration Raid Aids Blacks—For a Time." *Wall Street Journal*, January 17.

Perez, Lorenzo. 2008. "Johnston Sheriff Apologizes." *News & Observer*, September 8.

Perry, Marc J., and Jason P. Schachter. 2003. *Migration of Natives and the Foreign Born: 1995–2000*. United States Census Bureau, Census 2000 Special Report, August. http://www.census.gov/prod/2003pubs/censr-11.pdf.

Pew Hispanic Center. 2008. "Hispanics in the 2008 Election: North Carolina," Fact Sheet, February 20. http://pewhispanic.org/files/factsheets/vote2008/NorthCarolina.pdf.

Pew Hispanic Center. 2006a. "Estimates of the Unauthorized Migrant Population for States based on the March 2005 CPS," Fact Sheet, April 26. http://pewhispanic.org/files/factsheets/17.pdf.

Pew Hispanic Center. 2006b. "Hispanic Attitudes Toward Learning English," Fact Sheet, June 7. http://pewhispanic.org/files/factsheets/20.pdf.

Pew Hispanic Center. 2006c. "The Labor Force Status of Short-Term Unauthorized Workers," Fact Sheet, April 13. http://pewhispanic.org/files/factsheets/16.pdf.

Pew Hispanic Center. 2006d. "The State of American Public Opinion on Immigration in Spring 2006: A Review of Major Surveys," Fact Sheet, May 17. http://pewhispanic.org/files/factsheets/18.pdf.

Pham, Huyen. 2005. "The Inherent Flaws in the Inherent Authority Position: Why Inviting Local Enforcement of Immigration Laws Violates the Constitution." *Florida State University Law Review* 31: 965–1003.

Pickel, Mary Lou. 2008. "Various Immigration Bills Still Alive in Legislature." *Atlanta Journal-Constitution*, March 11.

Plato. 1960 [360 B.C.]. *The Laws*. Translated by A. E. Taylor. London: J.M. Dent and Sons, Ltd.

Political Database of the Americas. 2004. Mexican Constitution. Edmund A. Walsh School of Foreign Service, Center for Latin American Studies, Georgetown University. http://pdba.georgetown.edu/Constitutions/Mexico/mexico2004.html.

Portes, Alejandro, and Rubén Rumbaut. 2006. *Immigrant America: A Portrait*, 3rd ed. Berkeley: University of California Press.

Preston, Julia. 2007. "Short on Labor, Farmers in U.S. Shift to Mexico." *New York Times*, September 5.

Preston, Julia, and Marjorie Connelly. 2007. "Immigration Bill Provisions Gain Wide Support in Poll," *New York Times*, May 25.

Proffitt, Thurber Dennis. 1994. *Tijuana: The History of a Mexican Metropolis*. San Diego: San Diego State University Press.

Purdum, Todd S. 2007. "Prisoner of Conscience." *Vanity Fair*, February.

Quintero, Fernando. 2007. "Impact of Swift Raid Still Being Felt." *Rocky Mountain News*, May 12.

Ramakrishnan, S. Karthick, and Thomas J. Espenshade. 2001. "Immigrant Incorporation and Political Participation in the United States." *International Migration Review* 35, 3: 870–909.

Ramírez, Eddy. 2008. "Should College Enroll Illegal Immigrants?" *U.S. News and World Report*, August 7.

Rasmussen Reports. 2007. "Arkansas Toplines: Survey of Likely Voters, December 3." http://www.rasmussenreports.com/public_content/politics/election_20082/state_toplines/arkansas/arkansas_toplines_december_3_2007.

Reagan, Ronald. 1989. *Public Papers of the President of the United States, Ronald Reagan, Book II—June 28 to December 31, 1986*. Washington, DC: United States Government Printing Office.

Recacoechea, Juan de. 2007. *American Visa*. Translated by Adrian Althoff. New York: Akashic Books.

Regional Conference on Migration. 2010. http://www.rcmvs.org.

Renshon, Stanley A. 2001. "Dual Citizenship + Multiple Loyalties = One America?" In Stanley Renshon (ed.). *Political Leadership, National Identity, and the Dilemmas of Diversity*. Washington, DC: Georgetown University Press, 232–261.

Republican National Committee 2008. "2008 Republican Platform." Quoted in Debrah J. Saunders, "GOP Platform Targets Sanctuary Cities." *San Francisco Chronicle*, September 1. http://articles.sfgate.com/2008-09-01/opinion/17157800_1_city-s-sanctuary-policy-john-mccain-comprehensive-immigration-reform.

Restrepo de Acosta, Nydia. 2007. "Colombia: Representation of Emigrants in the Congress." In *Voting from Abroad: The International IDEA Handbook*. Stockholm: International Institute for Democracy and Electoral Assistance, 78–82.

Reuter, Peter. 2004. "The Political Economy of Drug Smuggling." In Menno Vellinga (ed.). *The Political Economy of the Drug Industry: Latin America and the International System*. Gainesville: University Press of Florida, 127–147.

Richmond-Times Dispatch. 2008. "46 Tied to Gangs are Arrested, U.S. Says." June 30.

Ring, Wilson. 2009. "Farms in Vermont Value, and Protect, Illegal Immigrants." *San Diego Union-Tribune*. May 17.

Rios-Neto, Eduardo L. G. 2005. *Managing Migration: The Brazilian Case*. Belo Horizonte, Brazil: UFMG/Cedeplar.

Rosenblum, Marc. 2004. "Moving Beyond the Policy of No Policy: Emigration from Mexico and Central America." *Latin American Politics & Society* 46, 4 (Winter): 91–125.

Rumbaut, Rubén, and Walter Ewing. 2007. *Criminality and the Paradox of Assimilation: Incarceration Rates among Native and Foreign-Born Men*. Immigration Policy Center Special Report (Spring). http://immigration.server263.com/images/File/specialreport/Imm%20Criminality%20(IPC).pdf.

Ruzich, Joseph. 2009. "Struggling Illegal Immigrants Yearn for Reform," *Chicago Tribune*, February 26.

Rytina, Nancy, and Selena Caldera. 2008. *Naturalizations in the United States: 2007*. Department of Homeland Security, Annual Flow Report (July).

Sacchetti, Maria. 2008. "El Salvador Officials Urge Émigrés to Invest," *Boston Globe*, July 14.

Saenz, Roselio, JanieFiloteo, and Aurelia Lorena Murga. 2007. "Are Mexicans in the United States a Threat to the American Way of Life?" *Du Bois Review* 4: 375–393.

Santiago Times. 2005. "Chile Ex-Pat Community Totals Nearly One Million." August 18.

Saravia, Nancy Gore, and Juan Francisco Miranda. 2004. "Plumbing the Brain Drain." *Bulletin of the World Health Organization* 82 (August): 608–615.

Sassen, Saskia. 2001. *The Global City: New York, London, Tokyo*. Princeton, NJ: Princeton University Press.

Schuck, Peter H. 2007. "The Disconnect between Public Attitudes and Policy Outcomes in Immigration." In Carol M. Swain (ed.). *Debating Immigration*. New York: Cambridge University Press, 17–31.

Schulman, Mark, and Tara Regan. 2006. "Poll Analysis: Large Majority Favors 'Guest Workers.'" *Time*, March 26.

Schumer, Charles E. 2009. U.S. Senate, Committee on the Judiciary, Testimony, April 30. http://judiciary.senate.gov/hearings/testimony.cfm?id=3793&wit_id=86.

Schwartz, Jeremey. 2008. "Returning Migrants Remaking Mexico Through Politics." *Seattle Times*, June 28.

Schwartzman, Kathleen C. 2008. "Lettuce, Segmented Labor Markets, and the Immigration Discourse." *Journal of Black Studies* 39, 1 (September): 129–156.

Seattle Times. "Immigrants Consider Going Home for Work." November 9.

Secure American and Orderly Immigration Act. 2005. http://frwebgate.access.gpo.gov/cgi-bin/getdoc.cgi?dbname=109_cong_bills&docid=f:s1033is.txt.pdf.

Seghetti, Lisa M., Stephen R. Viña, and Karma Ester. 2006. *Enforcing Immigration Law: The Role of State and Local Law Enforcement*. Congressional Research Service, CRS Report for Congress, RL32270 (January 27).

Sejersen, Tanja Bronsted. 2008. "'I Vow to Thee My Countries'—The Expansion of Dual Citizenship in the 21st Century." *International Migration Review* 42, 3: 523–549.

Sessions, Jeff. 2007. "Immigration Reform," Text from the Congressional Record. Congressional Chronical, June 7. http://www.c-spanarchives.org/congress/?q=node/77531&appid=595526751.

Shannon, Thomas. 2008. "Central America and the Mérida Initiative." Statement Before the House Committee on Foreign Affairs Subcommittee on the Western Hemisphere, Washington, DC, May 8. Reproduced in *DISAM Journal* 30, 3 (September): 48–51. www.disam.dsca.mil/pubs/Vol%2030_3/Shannon.pdf.

Shear, Michael D. 2007. "Immigration Stance is Costly for McCain." *Washington Post*, June 28.

Shepard-Durni, Suzana. 2008. "Mexico's Other Border: Issues Affecting Mexico's Dividing Line with Guatemala." Council on Hemispheric Affairs Report, September 12.

Simon, Julian. 1999. *The Economic Consequences of Immigration*, 2nd ed. Ann Arbor: University of Michigan Press.

Sims, Bob. 2008. "The Recommendations: Immigration Committee Reports to Legislature," *Birmingham News*, February 12. http://blog.al.com/bn/2008/02/the_recommendations_immigratio.html.

Sklair, Leslie. 1989. *Assembling for Development: The Maquila Industry in Mexico and the United States*. Boston: Unwin Hyman.

Smith, Daniel Scott. 1999. "Population and Political Ethics: Thomas Jefferson's Demography of Generations." *William and Mary Quarterly* 56, 3 (July): 591–612.

Smith, Heather Anne, and Owen J. Furuseth. 2004. "Housing, Hispanics and Transitioning Geographies in Charlotte, North Carolina." *Southeastern Geographer* 44, 2: 216–235.

Smith, Michael Peter, and Matt Bakker. 2008. *Citizenship Across Borders: The Political Transnationalism of El Migrante*. Ithaca, NY: Cornell University Press.

Smith, Robert Courtney. 2006. *Mexican New York: Transnational Lives of New Immigrants*. Berkeley: University of California Press.

Smith, Robert C. 2003. "Migrant Membership as an Instituted Process: Transnationalization, the State and the Extra-Territorial Conduct of Mexican Politics." *International Migration Review* 37, 2: 297–343.

Snipp, C. Mathew. 1989. *American Indians: The First of this Land*. New York: Russell Sage Foundation.

Solis, Dianne. 2007. "Meatpackers File Lawsuit over Immigration Raids." *Dallas Morning News*, September 12.

Somerville, Will, Jamie Durana, and Aaron Mateo Terrazas. 2008. "Hometown Associations: An Untapped Resource for Immigrant Integration?" *Insight* (July). http://www.migrationpolicy.org/pubs/Insight-HTAs-July08.pdf.

Soraghan, Mike. 2008. "House Dems Grapple With Their Rebels." *The Hill*, March 18. http://thehill.com/leading-the-news/house-dems-grapple-with-their-rebels-2008–03–18.html.

Staton, Jeffrey K., Robert A. Jackson, and Damarys Canache. 2007. "Dual Nationality among Latinos: What Are the Implications for Political Connectedness?" *Journal of Politics* 69, 2: 470–482.

Stephens, Challen. 2008. "City's Hispanic Students Climb." *Huntsville Times*, July 20.

Stevenson, Mark. 2007. "Mexico Deports Thousands of Central American Stranded after U.S. Rail Line Closes." *San Diego Union-Tribune*, August 15.

Stock, Erin. 2008. "Ailing Economy Hits Immigrants Hard." *Birmingham News*, December 11.

St. Onge, Peter, Franco Ordoñez, Kerry Hall, and Ames Alexander. 2008. "An Epidemic of Pain." *Charlotte Observer*, September 30.

Storrs, K. Larry. 2006. "Mexico-United States Dialogue on Migration and Border Issues, 2001–2006." Congressional Research Service, CRS Report for Congress, RL32735 (January 20).

Studstill, John D., and Laura Nieto-Studstill. 2001. "Hospitality and Hostility: Latin Immigrants in Southern Georgia." In Arthur D. Murphy, Colleen Blanchard, and Jennifer A. Hill (eds.). *Latino Workers in the Contemporary South*. Athens: The University of Georgia Press, 68–81.

Stycos, J. Mayone. 1971. *Ideology, Faith, and Family Planning in Latin America: Studies in Public and Private Opinion on Fertility Control*. New York: McGraw-Hill.

Sullivan, Teresa A. 2000. "A Demographic Portrait." In Pastora San Juan Cafferty and David W. Engstrom (eds.). *Hispanics in the United States: An Agenda for the Twenty-First Century*. New Brunswick, NJ: Transaction Publishers, 1–29.

Suro, Roberto. 1998. *Strangers among Us: How Latino Immigration Is Transforming America*. New York: Alfred Knopf.

Suro, Robert, and Gabriel Escobar. 2006. "2006 National Survey of Latinos: The Immigration Debate." Survey, July 13. http://pewhispanic.org/files/reports/68.pdf.

Sutton, Paul D., and T. J. Mathews. 2006. *Birth and Fertility Rates for States by Hispanic Origin Subgroups: United States, 1990 and 2000*. National Center for Health Statistics, *Vital and Health Statistics* 21, 57.

Swarns, Rachel L. 2006. "In Georgia, Immigrants Unsettle Old Sense of Place." *New York Times*, August 4.

Sweet, Lynn. 2009. "Congressional Hispanics Poised to Meet with Obama." *Chicago Sun-Times*, March 17.

Tancredo, Tom. 2006. *In Mortal Danger: The Battle for America's Border and Security*. Nashville, TN: Cumberland House Publishing.

Taylor, Paul, and Richard Fry. 2007. *Hispanics and the 2008 Election: A Swing Vote?* Washington, DC: Pew Hispanic Center, December.

Teitelbaum, Michael S. 2008. "Demographic Analyses of International Migration." In Carolina B. Brettell and James F. Hollifield (eds.). *Migration Theory: Talking Across Disciplines*, 2nd ed. New York: Routledge, 51–62.

Thibodeau, Patrick. 2008. "New Push in Congress for H-1B Visas," *New York Times*, June 6.

Thompson, Ginger. 2005. "Mexico's Migrants Profit from Dollars Sent Home." *New York Times*, February 23.

Thompson, Ginger. 2004. "Jerez Journal: Mexico's 'Tomato King' Seeks a New Title." *New York Times*, June 6.

Tobar, Héctor. 2006. "Border Plan Seen as U.S. Conceit." *Los Angeles Times*, February 26.

United Nations Population Division. 2009. "World Population Prospects: The 2008 Revision." http://esa.un.org/unpp/.

United States Census Bureau. 2009. American Community Survey. http://fact finder.census.gov.

United States Department of Homeland Security. 2008a. "Testimony of Secretary Michael Chertoff before the Senate Committee on the Judiciary on Oversight of the Department of Homeland Security," April 2. http://www.dhs.gov/xnews/testimony/testimony_1207231284950.shtm.

United States Department of Homeland Security. 2008b. "Yearbook of Immigration Statistics 2008." http://www.dhs.gov/ximgtn/statistics/.

United States Department of Homeland Security. 2007. "Yearbook of Immigration Statistics: 2007." http://www.dhs.gov/ximgtn/statistics/publications/YrBk07Na.shtm.

United States Department of Homeland Security. 2006. "Yearbook of Immigration Statistics: 2006." http://www.dhs.gov/ximgtn/statistics/publications/yearbook.shtm.

United States Department of Justice. 2007. *Report of the Attorney General to the Congress of the United States on the Administration of the Foreign Agents Registration Act of 1938, as Amended for the Six Months Ending June 30, 2007*. http://www.usdoj.gov/criminal/fara/reports/June30-2007.pdf.

United States Department of Labor. n.d. "Foreign Labor Certification: New H-2A Notices." http://www.foreignlaborcert.doleta.gov/h-2a.cfm.

United States Department of State. n.d. "Dual Nationality." http://travel.state.gov/travel/cis_pa_tw/cis/cis_1753.html.

United States Department of State. 2007. "United States Chairs Regional Conference on Migration." Media Note, April 25. http://www.state.gov/r/pa/prs/ps/2007/apr/83753.htm.

United States Department of State. 1964. *Foreign Relations of the United States: Johnson Administration 1964–1968*, Vol. XXXI, South and Central America: Mexico. http://www.state.gov/r/pa/ho/frus/johnsonlb/xxxi/36313.htm.

United States General Accounting Office. 2004. *Undocumented Aliens: Questions Persist about Their Impact on Hospitals' Uncompensated Care Costs*. Report GAO-04-472 (May).

United States House of Representatives. 2005a. "Dual Citizenship, Birthright Citizenship, and the Meaning of Sovereignty." Hearing Before the Subcommittee on Immigration, Border Security, and Claims of the Committee on the Judiciary. One Hundred Ninth Congress, First Session. September 29, 2005. Serial No. 109–63.

United States House of Representatives. 2005b. "The 287(g) Program: Ensuring the Integrity of America's Border Security System Through Federal-State Partnerships." Hearing Before the Subcommittee on Management, Integration, and Oversight of the Committee on Homeland Security. One Hundred Ninth Congress, First Session, July 27, 2005. Serial No. 10–36.

United States Immigration and Customs Enforcement. 2008. "Delegation of Immigration Authority, Section 287(g), Immigration and Naturalization Act," August 18. http://www.ice.gov/partners/287g/Section287_g.htm.

United States Social Security Administration. 2008. *Justification of Estimates for Appropriation Committees, Fiscal Year 2009*. February 4. http://www.ssa.gov/budget/2009cjapp.pdf.

University of North Carolina at Charlotte Urban Institute. 2006. *Mecklenburg County Latino Community Needs Assessment* (June). http://www.ui.uncc.edu/docs/DocumentArchives/LACNAP_Report_Final7-11-06.pdf.

Urdal, Henrik. 2006. "A Clash of Generations? Youth Bulges and Political Violence." *International Studies Quarterly* 50, 3 (September): 607–629.

Urrea, Luis Alberto. 2005. *The Devil's Highway*. New York: Little, Brown, and Company.

USA Today. 2007. "Ambassador: Ambassador to Lobby Hard for Immigration Reform." February 20.

USA Today/Gallop. 2008. September 5–7. http://www.pollingreport.com/prioriti.htm.

Vaca, Nicolás C. 2004. *The Presumed Alliance: The Unspoken Conflict Between Latinos and Blacks and What It Means for America*. New York: HarperCollins.

Valenzuela Jr., Abel. 2007. "Immigrant Day Laborers: Myths and Realities." *NACLA Report on the Americas* (May/June): 25–29.

Verduzco Igartúa, Gustavo. 1995. "La migración mexicana a Estados Unidos: Recuento de un proceso histórico." *Estudios Sociológicos* 13, 39: 573–594.

Waldinger, Roger. 2008. "Between 'Here' and 'There': Immigrant Cross-Border Activities and Loyalties." *International Migration Review* 42, 1 (Spring): 3–29.

Wallerstein, Immanuel. 1974. *The Modern World System*. New York: Academic Press.

Walsh, Casey. 2000. *Demobilizing the Revolution: Migration, Repatriation, and Colonization in Mexico, 1911–1940*. The Center for Comparative Immigration Studies, University of California, San Diego, Working Paper 26 (November).

Warren, R., and J. Passel. 1987. "A Count of the Uncountable: Estimates of Undocumented Aliens Counted in the 1980 United States Census." *Demography* 24, 3: 375–384.

Washington Post. 2007. "Pr. William Passes Resolution Targeting Illegal Immigration." July 11.

Watts, Julie Renée. 2002. *Immigration Policy and the Challenge of Globalization: Unions and Employers in Unlikely Alliance*. Ithaca, NY: Cornell University Press.

Weekly Compilation of Presidential Documents. 2002. "The President's news conference with President Francisco Flores Perez of El Salvador in San Salvador, El Salvador—President George W. Bush—Transcript," March 24, 505–509. http://www.gpoaccess.gov/wcomp/v38no13.html.

Weeks, Gregory B. 2008. *U. S. and Latin American Relations*. New York: Longman.

Weeks, Gregory B., John R. Weeks, and Amy J. Weeks. 2006–2007. "Latino Immigration in the U.S. South: 'Carolatinos' and Public Policy in Charlotte, North Carolina." *Latino/a Research Review* 6, 1–2: 50–71.

Weeks, John R. 2008. *Population: An Introduction to Concepts and Issues*, 10th ed. Belmont, CA: Wadsworth Thomson Learning.

Weeks, John R., Piotr Jankowski, and Justin Stoler. 2009. "Who's Knocking at the Door? New Data on Undocumented Immigrants to the United States." Unpublished manuscript.

Weeks, J. R., R. G. Rumbaut, and N. Ojeda. 1999. "Reproductive Outcomes among Mexico-Born Women in San Diego and Tijuana: Testing the Migration Selectivity Hypothesis." *Journal of Immigrant Health* 1, 2: 77–90.

Weill, Susan, and Laura Castañeda. 2004. "'Empathetic Rejectionism' and Inter-Ethnic Agenda Setting: Coverage of Latinos by the Black Press in the American South." *Journalism Studies* 5, 4: 537–550.

Westoff, Charles. 2007. "Immigration and Future Population Change in America." In Carol M. Swain (ed.). *Debating Immigration*. New York: Cambridge University Press, 165–172.

Wides-Munoz, Laura. 2008. "Mexico Quietly Helps Emigrants to US Learn Spanish." Associated Press, September 24.

Wiener, Myron, and Michael S. Teitelbaum. 2001. *Political Demography, Demographic Engineering*. New York: Berghan Books.

Wiest, Jason. 2007. "State Legislature Discusses Illegal Immigration." *Arkansas News Bureau*, August 14.

Wilson, Kenneth J., and Alejandro Portes. 1980. "Immigrant Enclaves: An Analysis of the Labor Market Experience of Cubans in Miami." *American Journal of Sociology* 86, 2: 259–319.

Winders, Jamie. 2007. "Bringing Back the (B)order: Post 9/11 Politics of Immigration, Borders, and Belonging in the Contemporary US South." *Antipode* 39, 5: 920–942.

Woodward, Douglas P. 2006. "The New Face of South Carolina's Labor Force." *Business and Economic Review* (July-September). http://www.allbusiness.com/specialty-businesses/minority-owned-businesses/4098534-1.html.

Woodward, Ralph Lee. 1999. *Central America: A Nation Divided.* Oxford: Oxford University Press.

Wright, Thomas C., and Rody Oñate Zúñiga. 2007. "Chilean Political Exile." *Latin American Perspectives* 34, 4 (July): 31–49.

Index